W9-CIB-333

The Practitioner Inquiry Series

Marilyn Cochran-Smith and Susan L. Lytle, *SERIES EDITORS*

ADVISORY BOARD: Rebecca Barr, Judy Buchanan, Robert Fecho,
Susan Florio-Ruane, Sarah Freedman, Karen Gallas, Andrew Gitlin,
Dixie Goswami, Peter Grimmett, Gloria Ladson-Billings, Roberta Logan,
Sarah Michaels, Susan Noffke, Marsha Pincus, Marty Rutherford,
Lynne Strieb, Carol Tateishi, Polly Ulichny, Diane Waff, Ken Zeichner

TEACHING, MULTIMEDIA, AND MATHEMATICS
Investigations of Real Practice

MAGDALENE LAMPERT
DEBORAH LOEWENBERG BALL

Teachers College, Columbia University
New York and London

Published by Teachers College Press, 1234 Amsterdam Avenue, New York, NY 10027

Copyright © 1998 by Teachers College, Columbia University

All rights reserved. No part of this publication may be reproduced or transmitted in any form or by any means, electronic or mechanical, including photocopy, or any information storage and retrieval system, without permission from the publisher.

Library of Congress Cataloging-in-Publication Data

Lampert, Magdalene.
    Teaching, multimedia, and mathematics : investigations of real
practice / Magdalene Lampert, Deborah Loewenberg Ball.
        p.   cm. — (The practitioner inquiry series)
    Includes bibliographical references and index.
    ISBN 0-8077-3758-5 (cloth). — ISBN 0-8077-3757-7 (pbk.)
    1. Mathematics—Study and teaching (Elementary)   2. Interactive
multimedia.   3. Mathematics teachers—Training of.   I. Ball,
Deborah.   II. Title.   III. Series.
QA135.5.L25   1998
372.7—dc21   98-17105

ISBN 0-8077-3757-7 (paper)
ISBN 0-8077-3758-5 (cloth)

Printed on acid-free paper

Manufactured in the United States of America

05   04   03   02   01   00   99   98   8   7   6   5   4   3   2   1

Contents

Preface

Since 1980, we (Magdalene Lampert and Deborah Ball) have been designing a new role for ourselves, one that combines teaching mathematics in a
public school classroom on a daily basis with doing teacher education and
research on teaching. This new role is not meant to be simply an amalgam
of each of these three jobs. It is an opportunity to rethink, fundamentally,
what it might mean to do *teaching* in a way that could provide a setting for
teacher education and research, what it might mean to do *teacher education*
in a manner that is deeply rooted in teaching practice and the scholarly
study of pedagogy, and what it might mean to do *research* that would examine teaching from the point of view of practice and make that point of
view available in settings where teacher education occurs. The intent of
all of this work is to make it possible to study teaching by investigating
practice directly, whether the studies are done by newcomers to the profession or established academic scholars.

In 1989, we received a grant from the National Science Foundation
(NSF) to develop an approach to teacher education that would be rooted
in the study of practice. One component of the work was for us to study in
depth the kind of mathematics teaching and learning practices envisioned
by the current reforms: We argued that we needed to *understand* more about
the kind of teaching we were trying to do as we considered how to teach it
to others. Drawing on video, graphic, and textual records of a year's worth
of mathematics lessons in our two elementary classrooms, we did research
on curriculum and instruction, children's learning, and the culture of the
classroom across the school year. We also did research on the process of
using multimedia records of practice to understand teaching.

Multimedia computing technologies newly available in the 1980s made
it possible to document thoroughly in many media what occurred during
lessons and make a comprehensive collection of these materials available
to others. We used video, audio, and text tools to capture information about
what occurred in our two mathematics classrooms during the 1989–90
school year and to catalog that information in ways that would support
the investigation of teaching and learning. With the members of our research group on the Mathematics and Teaching Through Hypermedia

(M.A.T.H.) Project, we experimented with how new technologies and tools could support our efforts to use this study of teaching practice as a context for teacher education.

This book is our attempt to communicate what we learned. First, we situate our work in the context of teacher education and its endemic challenges. Shifting from the dominant epistemology of training or knowledge application, we propose the idea of "investigation" as a medium of learning to teach and we explore what it might mean to "investigate" the practices of teaching. Second, we describe how opportunities to investigate teaching might be designed and used in teacher education. Finally, we examine closely what beginning teachers might do when given the opportunity to do such investigations using multimedia and computing tools. We recognize that neither the pedagogies nor the technologies we write about here are new. Pedagogies involving investigation have been used for teacher education in this country for at least a century. The pioneering work of Lucy Sprague Mitchell in the 1920s is perhaps the best example. The multimedia technologies that we experimented with in 1989 are no longer new. They have been replaced by even newer hardware and software and have become commonplace in schools, homes, and workplaces. Nevertheless, we believe there is an interesting story to tell in bringing together these strands of work in a mainstream teacher education setting.

We begin in the first two chapters with stories about ourselves, each telling of the—quite different—sets of personal experiences we had had with teaching and teacher education that led us to the idea of investigation as a pedagogy for teacher education. Through this account of the genesis of our ideas about teaching and learning to teach, these first two chapters begin to develop the idea of investigation as a method of learning about practice and why we have been exploring it. Investigation in any field allows simultaneously for appreciating extant knowledge of the field and constructing new frameworks. Investigating a relationship or a phenomenon or an issue is a different way to think about coming to know something: It may result in more knowledge or new understandings, but is not merely a search for the right answer to a question or the correct solution to a problem. Multiple investigations might be carried out on a single phenomenon, topic, or question, and will not necessarily result in a definitive statement about what is right or true in all circumstances. Knowledge matters in such work, but so do methods of knowing. They matter especially to the capacity to figure out new things in particular situations, or when confronted with something unprecedented. They matter also to the capacity to appraise others' claims and theories.

The pedagogy of investigation is at the heart of current efforts to improve schools. Whether students are studying temperature or democracy or poetry or probability, they are to learn from investigating practice, that is, from working on problems, talking with others about potential solutions, building on their own ways of thinking about concepts, and engaging with significant disciplinary ideas. In this book we explore what these ideas about pedagogy might mean for the way we teach prospective teachers about *teaching*. In teacher education, the investigators would be prospective teachers. The teaching that we depict in this book portrays how children learn mathematics by investigating mathematical ideas and methods: identifying equivalence, finding patterns, representing part-whole relationships. In learning teaching, prospective teachers would investigate pedagogical ideas and methods: establishing classroom culture, defining the teacher's role, examining children's thinking, appraising learning activities, analyzing mathematics content, and even considering the instructional implications of "what it means to know something."

K–12 students investigate mathematics and other subjects by working on and thinking about the problems of practice. Classroom teachers have used new technologies for making available in schools a wide range of such problems and the tools for reflecting on strategies used to solve them. This book explores the potential of using new technologies in similar ways to transform opportunities for learning *teaching*. We explore how these new technologies can be deployed to support the construction of usable knowledge for teaching, describing and appraising what we have learned about how to create opportunities for constructing knowledge about teaching and learning in teacher education.

In Chapter 3, we turn to situating our work within the enduring arguments about teacher education and learning to teach. Chapter 4 describes the collection of records of practice that we assembled. In Chapter 5, we illustrate the multimedia environment in which these records can be accessed and used to investigate teaching and learning and the pedagogy of teacher education we have designed around this environment.

We report on what we have seen happen when prospective teachers investigate teaching, beginning in Chapter 6 with an overview of the character of a large number of investigations and case studies of a few projects, and continuing in Chapter 7 with an example of work by one of our preservice students. Chapter 8 concludes with questions and challenges raised by this work. The book concludes with an essay by David Cohen, in which he analyzes where this work fits in the history and politics of efforts to bring experience with "real" teaching into teacher preparation and speculates on where the work might lead.

In Chapters 1, 2, and 3, as we examine the foundations of this project and this book, we acknowledge the many people who were central to our learning. In this preface we would like especially to acknowledge a few key people without whom this project would not have happened. First we thank Thom Dye and Sylvia Rundquist, the teachers at Spartan Village School in East Lansing, Michigan, who generously allowed us to share their classrooms and their students over several years (see Ball, D. L. & S. Rundquist, 1993). Our work with each of them provided us with unparalleled opportunities to stay connected with teaching and the challenges of daily practice. Their interest, confidence, support, and intellectual and practical company were seminal professional and personal experiences for each of us. Jessie Fry, Spartan Village School principal in the years we taught there, enabled and supported our work in the school. Other teachers and staff, as well as the students and their parents, were also welcoming and supportive. We thank our former dean, Judy Lanier, and our former department chair, Henrietta Barnes, for having a vision of the relationship between schools and universities inspirational of fundamental redesign of teacher education. Working in the company of talented and wise colleagues in teacher education at Michigan State, especially Dan Chazan, Susan Donnelly, Helen Featherstone, Jay Featherstone, Susan Florio-Ruane, Glenda Lappan, Bill McDiarmid, Jeremy Price, Janine Remillard, Dirck Roosevelt, Cheryl Rosaen, Kathy Roth, and Suzanne Wilson, was a rare privilege. We learned many different things from these colleagues. They were pivotal to our being able to work over many years on ways to integrate teaching, teacher education, and research. Next, we thank Leticia Altamirano, Merrie Blunk, Warren Buckleitner, Carol Crumbaugh, Erin Eberz, Mike Goldenberg, Stephanie Grant-Joyner, Pam Hayes, Alice Horton Merz, Angus Mairs, Steve Mattson, Jim Merz, Christie Nowak, Margery Osborne, Don Peurach, James Reineke, Peggy Rittenhouse, Mark Sartor, Angia Sperfslage, and Peri Weingrad, all staff members on the M.A.T.H. project, for their intellectual, practical, technical, and organizational assistance between 1989 and 1996. We also wish to acknowledge the invaluable assistance of Merrie Blunk, Mark Hoover, and Jennifer Lewis with the final stages of manuscript preparation. Three additional members of the M.A.T.H. Project staff deserve special mention: Mark Rosenberg, who helped us to imagine from the beginning what was possible (and some things that were impossible); Ruth Heaton, whose careful attention to questions about teacher learning kept us focused on the concrete particulars of the challenges of practice; and Kara Suzuka, whose boundless imagination, energy, and enthusiasm fueled the project's work and supported her learning to become the principal designer of our first hypermedia environment.

Last, but certainly not least, we thank our spouses, our funders and our universities for their belief in and generous support of this work. David Cohen has been a continuing influence on our thinking. He read and re-read drafts of our earliest attempts to convince others that we had something worth funding and he engaged the core ideas of our work in the context of his own. At several key points, he helped us navigate institutional and organizational mazes and advised us on strategy. In addition, as Maggie's husband, he has been sympathetic and caring, ever patient with her many technology-induced rants. Richard Ball, a wise and experienced middle school teacher, supported us with his appreciation for a different approach to teacher education, and relentless reminders of the complexities of practice for which beginning teachers must prepare. Keeping the busy Ball household going at some of the intense points of this project was no less complex: He often did more than his share and always with generous grace and skill. The NSF provided major support for the collection of the records of practice, their cataloging, and their incorporation into an electronic learning environment for preservice teachers, as well as funds for sharing our ideas with other teacher educators from around the nation. The Spencer Foundation provided support for Lampert and several graduate students to analyze the records of practice and understand their potential. Apple Computers provided the hardware for our first multimedia workstation at a point where we needed it to convince ourselves to continue. Our institutions, Michigan State University and the University of Michigan, provided significant additional resources and institutional support. We are grateful for all these colleagues and sources of learning and support, without which this project never could have happened.

CHAPTER I

Where Did These Ideas Come From?

Lampert's Story

In 1973, I taught my first teacher education course. It was entitled "Zero, One, and Multiplicity." It was a preservice master's level course for students intending to become elementary school teachers. Looking back on it now, the title seems grandiose, a bit obscure, and mathematically pretentious. Still more pretentious-seeming is the last item in a list I made in my journal, at that time, of the things I wanted those intending teachers to learn.

> To count is to have some control over the
> multiplicity
> by reducing its diversity
> (the implications of 1 + 1 + 1 + 1 . . .)

Why did I imagine that such a profound notion had a place in an elementary math methods course? Was I suffering from late adolescent hubris? Lingering 1960s romanticism? Examining, in hindsight, what I might have had in mind may help to explain not only why I designed *that* course the way I did, but what I brought with me to the M.A.T.H. Project.

LEARNING ABOUT KNOWING MATHEMATICS

Early in my academic career, I made some observations about knowledge that have stayed with me.

1. Mathematics is a way of knowing that gives us a particular perspective on experience. It evolves out of people thinking and talking together and building on one another's ideas.
2. Persons are knowers and makers of meaning, and language and symbols are both tools and products in that process.

Because of the particular situations in which I learned to teach, these two observations became related to a third.

3. Studying learners and studying the stuff of teaching (i.e., what is to be taught and learned) are an integral part of the work of teaching.

The first observation was gleaned from my undergraduate education in the late 1960s. I majored in mathematics at a small liberal arts college. But it was not simply getting a strong mathematics education that influenced my thinking about the nature of knowledge. As part of the required program for all students at that college, I also studied philosophy and intellectual history. I chose to do a senior thesis in the philosophy of mathematics and began to listen in on the centuries-long argument about what it means to know that a mathematical statement is true. I read several histories of mathematics and investigated the relationship between the development of mathematical knowledge and the kinds of problems that mathematicians were trying to solve. I focused my studies on the view of mathematical truth expounded by a group of mathematical scholars who referred to themselves as "intuitionists." Intuitionism was established as a school of thought in the 1930s when argument about the nature of mathematical truth was rampant. Intuitionists countered the absolutism of the formalists and the logicists with the notion that mathematics is what is known by persons and it is invented out of their ideas about quantity and shape. The famous Dutch mathematician L. E. J. Brouwer promulgated the idea of "constructivist proof." I wrote a few such proofs in my thesis, setting them alongside their more conventional formal counterparts.

Perhaps the most significant thing I learned from this work is that there are at least three different ways of thinking about why a mathematical statement is true, all reasoned and warranted. I observed that what it means to know something is a question that twentieth-century scholars can and do argue about. Having prepared myself to see mathematics—the most "certain" of subjects—in this light, I was disposed to wonder about how assertions might be warranted in other domains as well.

The academic domain of mathematical epistemology and its esoteric disputes seem far from the realm of schools and teaching and learning. At the time I was studying them, I had no plans to be an educator. But now, looking back, I recognize in those disputes the foundations of my ability to entertain many of the ideas that are central to contemporary educational reform. We live in a society where it is now fashionable to question academic authorities as the source of right answers, and where formal logic is regarded as only one among many tools for creating and applying information. From the perspective of mathematics, I began to recognize that slightly different assumptions could lead to radically different conclusions, and to appreciate that the choice of one set of assumptions over another was a human decision made in a moral, social, and political context. Appreciating the relatively simple case of non-Euclidean geometries, for example, wherein we must conclude that under appropriate conditions parallel lines *can* meet (as they do at the North and South Poles), meant that I had to acknowledge early in my life that sound reasoning *and* multiple truths could exist in the same scholarly universe.

LEARNING ABOUT CHILDREN'S WAYS OF THINKING

The second idea listed above—about persons as makers of meaning—seems equally esoteric on the face of it. In a rather unusual course on the psychology of learning, which I took in 1973, I was introduced to phenomenological observation and description as a research method. At the time, I was engaged in preparing to be an elementary school teacher, and Piaget was winning the battle against Skinner in courses on learning theory. Writing about a few children and how they thought about questions like where the sun goes at night or what is inside the human body, Piaget and his colleagues made even more real to me the idea that people base their actions on very different assumptions about what is "true." I observed that it was not only academic mathematicians who had different perspectives to bring to bear on their arguments about what was true and what was real. Ordinary children differed in how they thought about truth and reality too!

Heinz Werner's *Comparative Psychology of Mental Development* was one of the texts we read in that course. It was full of observations of "the Scupin boy," who, for example, at the age of 8 years, 7 months, "counts sixteen things that were given him for Christmas, but leaves out the new overcoat, gloves, and shoes. To his mother's protest he replies, 'Pah! Those are just things you need. I'll just count them as one, and then I'll have seventeen things.'"[1] Both the boy and his mother make sense, each from a different point of view. They are both doing mathematics; in fact, they are doing what might be called "set theoretics."

I read Werner with Pat Carini, who had been his student at Clark University, and together we waded through Merleau-Ponty, Cassierer, and Barfield as she thoughtfully translated their theories into a way of thinking about studying and teaching children: methods of research and teaching that respected each person's attempts to understand and impose meaning on experience. Carini taught me in the context of the teacher education and child development research program at the Prospect School in North Bennington, Vermont. She had started the Prospect School in 1967 with two psychologists: her husband, Louis Carini, and Joan Blake.[2] Like other educational reformers of the 1960s and 1970s, the founders of Prospect drew on ideas about curriculum and pedagogy that were being enacted in British Infant Schools and earlier had been a part of the Progressive Movement in the U.S.[3] In these schools, teachers organized instruction around the idea that children think differently from adults, and teachers need to observe and listen to children's attempts to investigate ideas through play as a basis for figuring out how to teach them. I was familiar with this idea from reading Dewey, but at Prospect I saw that it could be used to understand and design schooling. By watching children in such a school, I saw that they could represent their ideas with paint and clay and blocks and talk, and that they had lots to do and say even before they "learned" what the teacher was there to teach. By watching and working with the teachers who also watched and taught the same children, I saw how curriculum materials and instructional methods could be tailored to engage particular groups of learners.

LEARNING ABOUT THINKING AND DOING IN TEACHING

The teacher education program at the Prospect School was school-based. That is an organizational statement, but it also says a lot about the kind of community in which I formulated my ideas about what learning is, what teaching is, and how both interact with subject matter.[4] Teacher education courses were taught by teachers and scholars who themselves were engaged in the study of children and curriculum. We read learning theory, developmental psychology, science, mathematics, literature, history, and philosophy. In this setting, I could be adventurous both as a scholar and as a teacher, even though I myself had attended traditional schools. I not only read Werner and learned that children look at the world differently at different ages, but I had interactions with *actual* children that confirmed this. On the playground one day, for example, Willie, an imaginative 6-year-old, came up to me—the teacher-in-charge—and said, "We've been playing in the woods, and there are monsters in there!" Thinking I was being responsive, I said, "I'd be scared if I were you." He responded, flatly, "But you're not playing." The assumptions on which Willie based his sense of reality were not simple. In that context, Merleau-Ponty was not an obscure phenomenologist, but a helpful guide, warning me to watch and listen and describe action and interaction as carefully as possible to gain insight into the persons whom I was to teach.

When I was learning to be an elementary school teacher, I worked in the midst of a professional community who saw scholarship and teaching as two sides of the same activity. And I knew the people I worked with were not idiosyncratic isolates. Although Prospect was a small, independent school in rural Vermont, it was connected to larger public movements in American educational reform. My introduction to a different kind of teaching and teacher education was further situated in the context of two larger institutions that gave legitimacy to this approach: the Antioch Graduate School and the state of Vermont. Prospect was a satellite campus of Antioch, licensed as such to educate and certify teachers in Vermont. Antioch, founded by Horace Mann, is a long-standing experiment in progressive higher education, in which the program deeply integrates work and study, theory and practice. At the time, it included, in addition to the New England site, a graduate program in urban education where students worked with curriculum developers and school leaders in Philadelphia, and a law school focused on issues of social reform in Washington, DC. Besides being associated with Antioch, Prospect was also an official site for teacher development in the state of Vermont, which, with North Dakota and New York, had decided at the time to reform its entire school system around "open education."[5] The first director of Prospect was Marion Taylor, who was also chair of the Vermont State Board of Education when the "Vermont Design for Education" was developed. Harvey Scribner, then Vermont's commissioner of education, went on to become chancellor for the New York City schools, taking with him many of the ideas that were nurtured at Prospect.

I began to teach teachers in 1973 when I was hired by Antioch New England. In that year, Antioch New England was transforming itself from a small group of educational and political activists who met in a farmhouse in Putney, Vermont, to a state-licensed institution in New Hampshire. At the New England site, Antioch's mission was to educate teachers, counselors, and school administrators for public schools. Being a teacher educator was a form of political and educational activism for me, and the Antioch setting supported my development in that role. Among Antioch faculty, the roles of practitioner and scholar were blurred, and students were expected to do much of their academic work in the form of "projects." Three other Prospect School teacher education program alumni, Tina Staller, David Sobel, and Mary Kongsgaard, also were hired by Antioch in 1973. We learned to be teacher educators at the same time as we were starting a school for 4- through 7-year-old children. We designed the school to function as a place for faculty and students and children to work together on developing curriculum and pedagogy and for local public school teachers to come to observe and try out new ideas.

While on the Antioch faculty, I began doctoral work at Harvard Graduate School of Education. While I completed my doctorate, I kept with me the Antioch idea of integrating work and study, thinking and doing, even though this was not part of the Harvard culture.[6] When I next worked as a teacher educator, I used my own mathematics classroom as a study site for myself and the novice and experienced teachers I worked with in the Lesley College/Buckingham, Browne and Nichols Teacher Education Collaborative in Cambridge, Massachusetts. I had many more teacher education students in this setting than I had had at Antioch, and both their backgrounds and their career intentions were more diverse. But it was still a private, perhaps even precious, situation.[7]

As a teacher and teacher educator at Buckingham, Browne and Nichols (BB&N) and Lesley, I became more focused on mathematics as the "stuff" of teaching and learning. My position there was "curriculum coordinator" and teacher of fourth-, fifth-, and sixth-grade mathematics. In that position, I had the opportunity to bring together my project-based ideas about developmentally appropriate instruction with my interest in mathematics—and to be in on some of the earliest and most creative thinking about how to use computers in education. In my fifth-grade classroom and my teacher education courses, I piloted *The Voyage of the Mimi*, a multimedia, interdisciplinary collection of materials and technologies for engaging students in mathematical and scientific problems.[8] I wrote about my work with *Mimi*, and this put me in touch with the cognitive psychologists and mathematics educators who were at the forefront of the reform movement in the mid-1980s.[9]

At BB&N, I entered a professional culture of teaching colleagues who had been uniformly well educated and continued to be active in the creation and use of professional knowledge. At each grade level, teachers worked as a team to review curriculum resources and develop programs of instruction, and our conversations about what and how to teach were grounded in considerations of the important ideas in history, literature, biology, and the like. We also worked in these teams assessing students' portfolios and developing interventions for problem situations. The atmosphere at BB&N, like the culture of teaching at Prospect, was one of serious collaborative study of both the "stuff" to be taught and learned and the learners in our care. Both the schedule and the structure of professional incentives supported this culture of inquiry, and teacher education was a responsibility assumed by everyone on the faculty. The school had a cadre of "assistants" each year, master's degree candidates from nearby Lesley College, assigned full time as apprentices in each classroom. They took some of their courses at Lesley and some at BB&N, taught by the primary grades faculty. So everyone at the school made his or her teaching "public," open to analysis with a colleague who was teaching the same group of children. Across the school, teachers were encouraged to pursue their own intellectual interests in relation to curriculum development projects, and thoughtful practitioners were rewarded with summer travel grants to support this work. Every week, there was time in the schedule for teachers and assistant teachers to meet around curricular topics or grade levels or special problems, and once a year the entire faculty read the same agreed-upon professional book in preparation for a day's worth of collaborative analysis of our programs and practice. Thinking and doing at BB&N were seamless—we talked about ideas and children and curriculum in the same sentences, in the lunchroom and at teacher meetings, with parents and administrators.

LEARNING ABOUT MAINSTREAM TEACHER EDUCATION

In 1984, I accepted a faculty position at Michigan State University, wondering if such a culture of inquiry focused on teaching and learning could be established in a much more ordinary setting. My trajectory and the trajectory of the mainstream American educational reform movement came together at Michigan State. At a time when national leaders in teacher education were beginning to argue for closer connections with both the schools and the disciplines, I was hired specifically to be a teacher who was also a scholar and a teacher educator.[10] That a cohesion among these roles was possible, even desirable, became a mainstream idea with the publication of the first Holmes Committee Report and the institutionalization of "professional development schools." Ann Lieberman and Lynn Miller[11] laud the creation of such schools in the 1990s for "building a culture of support for teachers' continuous inquiry into practice" and said they were characterized by

- norms of colleagueship, openness, and trust
- opportunities and time for disciplined inquiry
- teacher learning of content in context
- reconstruction of leadership roles
- networks, collaborations, and coalitions

I had learned and taught teaching in such schools. Prospect School in the 1970s certainly had all of these features, for both beginning and experienced teachers, at the school and in the network of public schools where teachers cooperated in their program. Buckingham, Browne & Nichols, with its connection to Lesley College, had a long history of taking responsibility for the professional development of new and experienced teachers.

In order to carry out the multiple roles of teacher, teacher educator, and researcher on teaching in the context of a large state university, I taught mathematics for an hour a day at Spartan Village School, a public school near campus. In concert with the national efforts to make subject matter preparation a central concern of teacher education, my own studies of teaching and learning began to center on the particular problems in mathematics education that came to light in this setting—namely, the gap between knowing mathematics as a discipline and as a way of understanding practical problems, and knowing mathematics as a school subject. Prior to this, I had not worked in settings where the gap was so noticeably wide.

As a teacher educator in a large state university, I became curious about just how unusual my own education for teaching might have been: What was going on in mainstream teacher education programs in the 1960s and 1970s when I was learning mathematics in a liberal arts college and then studying child development at the Prospect School? What I did not know then, but do know now, is that from the beginning of the twentieth century, educational scholarship and teacher education had been moving further and further apart in mainstream institutions. The contrast to my own experience was radical. Beginning in the 1950s the normal schools were absorbed into state colleges and a two-tiered faculty developed: one to do research and another to train teachers. Laboratory schools, once at the "cutting edge" of pedagogy and teacher education, became less and less adventurous and more and more like other private schools after World War II, or they closed. In their book, *Ed School*, Geraldine Clifford and James Guthrie (1988) observe that during that period,[12] teacher education programs in schools of education in colleges and universities were chronically underfunded, and as a result, "teachers [were] being taught how to teach by being lectured to about teaching, often in large classes" and placed "for observation and practice teaching in local public schools whose practices often contradicted the pedagogical and curricular principles being enunciated in the university, and under the supervision of teachers often untrained and unrewarded for these duties"(p. 183). At the same time, substantial resources in schools of education increasingly were devoted to research in "applied social science." Students were prepared for careers as scholars at the expense of the "vocational" teacher and school counselor training programs. Education professionals sought to increase their intellectual standing by radically distancing themselves from the low status of the "schoolteacher." Not only were scholarship and teaching not considered to be two sides of the same activity, but they were aggressively in contention for scarce resources.

I mention all of this educational history here because it puts my own professional trajectory in a different light and explicates what I brought with me to my work at Michigan State University and the M.A.T.H. Project. From the perspective of the larger history of American education, the sort of reform of teacher education advocated in the Holmes Report—teacher education that begins in the investigation of pedagogy and subject matter—seems like yet another change in direction on the roller coaster of reform. But from the perspective of my personal experience, the ride has been a smooth one, and it could be interpreted as a ride along the crest. In the 1970s, I experienced a kind of teacher education and worked as the kind of teacher that the 1990s reform documents aimed to produce. My effort has been to move the kind of teaching and teacher education that occurred in precious few pockets of practice in the 1970s further and further into the mainstream. The M.A.T.H. Project was a major part of that effort. But I am ahead of myself. Next, we turn to Deborah Ball, with whom this project was conceived and carried out.

CHAPTER 2

Where Did These Ideas Come From?

BALL'S STORY

What is quite striking about my story and Magdalene Lampert's is how different they are: We developed in dramatically different contexts, and through significantly different experiences. Whereas Magdalene studied mathematics and philosophy at a small private liberal arts college, I majored in French at a large midwestern state university. True, philosophy was embedded in the curriculum of the French major: We read Diderot, Rousseau, Voltaire, La Mettrie, and, of course, Camus and Sartre. But although we studied Descartes, we did not spend time contemplating truth in mathematics. While Magdalene was learning to teach surrounded by teachers deeply engaged in progressive ideas, where professional conversation was the norm, I was completing a field-centered elementary teacher education program. We were out in schools a great deal of the time. The teachers in whose classrooms I was placed were amazingly willing to hand the reins to this 20-year-old without much talk about what we were supposed to be doing or why. But it was not so amazing after all: Learning to teach, they believed firmly, was a function of practice and experience. Learning to practice was another matter. With only curriculum guides and the advice of my neighbors, I was on my own to sift through all that was happening. We did not construct portfolios, or talk about particular children. Overall, my education was at the heart of the mainstream; Magdalene's, at the heart of progressive, alternative, private settings. Yet, despite all these differences, Magdalene and I shared a remarkable overlap of interests, orientation, and ideas. How did this happen?

The roots of my work on the M.A.T.H. Project can be traced deep into my history as a teacher. One important root had to do with my stance toward teaching as intellectual work. A second grew from my work as a teacher-leader and my tentative steps into ways of situating professional development for others in artifacts from my practice. A third emerged from the first two: an intense curiosity about teachers as learners. Out of my years as a teacher developed a set of ideas about the practice of teaching and about what was entailed in developing it. These are experiences and ideas on which I have taken scant opportunity to reflect. But asking, "What did each of us bring to our work together on the M.A.T.H. Project?"—a question that we routinely ask about others as learners—has provided an occasion to consider explicitly how this undertaking was connected to my history as a teacher, teacher educator, and scholar.

LEARNING TO LEARN TO TEACH

The story I will tell begins with my first year of teaching in 1975, fresh from majoring in French and elementary education at Michigan State University. The elementary education program was unusual: At a time when most programs were turned toward elaborate skills-oriented, "competency-based" professional education, this program was heavily field-based and emphasized firsthand experience as a site for learning.[1] Although we had assignments from our courses, which were quite directed and skills-oriented, we also were expected to try things out in our classrooms, examine what happened, and revise what we were doing. The strong message I took from this program was that teaching required experimentation, adaptation, and critical reflection. I am not sure if this was the message of the program, or if this is what I took from it, given how much time we spent in schools teaching, and talking with the "consultants" who visited us in our classrooms.

After a full year of student teaching, we were placed as "interns" with full teaching responsibilities and the guidance of an experienced teacher who functioned as an "intern consultant" to four or five interns. The consultant assigned to me was near the end of her 40-year career and focused her efforts for the most part on gently socializing us into the occupation. She instructed me on classroom management, dress, and handwriting. I tolerated her rather maternal interventions and engaged more closely with the building principal, Jessie Fry, a strong, intellectually incisive African-American woman whom I admired deeply. Jessie and I held somewhat different views of good teaching—she more focused on structure and order than I—but we formed a strong bond that was to last for years, well beyond my early teaching. She inspected my lesson plan book and commented on elements of my plans; she observed me teach and left brief written notes on my desk. Meticulous and demanding, Jessie influenced the development of standards I held for my work. She expected me to know about individual students, and she expected me to be able to explain and justify what and how I was teaching. Professional reasoning was paramount in my meetings with her.

That first year of teaching I had an extraordinary and significantly formative teaching assignment: four sections of elementary school science (two third-grade classes, one fourth-grade, and one fifth-grade) and one section of language arts in a departmentalized elementary school. I was handed three grade levels' worth of Science Curriculum Improvement Study (SCIS) materials[2]; Mindy Emerson, a colleague in the building who was well acquainted with the materials, helped orient me. I could not have been less prepared for this assignment. In college, as a French major, minoring in English, I had not studied any science other than the requirements for my teaching certificate. Even in high school, I had followed my passions and specialized in foreign languages of all kinds and taken no science other than a year of biology in which the two teachers seemed endlessly engaged in debates about creation and evolution. Out of sheer necessity, my teaching became an investigation into science and how to engage children in learning science.[3]

It was no small coincidence that the materials out of which I was constructing my teaching used an investigative design for children's learning. The lessons were designed to set the children to exploring, experimenting, and discussing what they saw. Synthesis lessons were about "invention" of key ideas such as environmental factors, habitat, interaction of systems, and energy transfer. Methods of inquiry were also focal, such as investigating, recording, and being intentionally systematic. The teacher was to guide discussions gently. In contrast to my formal teacher education coursework, which had stressed "diagnosis" as a mode of listening to and interpreting children, the SCIS curriculum guided me to engage children in talk and writing. I encountered their hypotheses and explanations, their theories and facts. I learned that they had many fascinating ideas, that they were busy thinking and making sense of the phenomena we were exploring. Because the SCIS curriculum was structured around big ideas in science—interaction and systems, communities, life cycles, motion—I also learned science myself. Even though I could not have articulated it, I also glimpsed the value of organizing content around some framework of important, generative structures of the domain.[4]

My own lack of pedagogical or content resources left me reliant on the curriculum materials.[5] My efforts to engage children in scientific investigation intertwined the learning of my students with my own learning as a teacher. Since I knew so little about science or how to teach it, I had no alternative but to design my lessons drawing heavily from the curriculum materials and to work with my students on those lessons. I read the teachers' guides closely and tried to follow the suggestions. But because the materials were designed to engage students in scientific activity, we often were quickly into a question or a puzzle for which the guide could be little help. Afterwards, it was natural to stand back to see what I and they had done, where we had veered off unproductively, where I had made a fortuitous move, where we needed to head. The iterative process of design, experimentation, and analysis was etched into my work during these first 2 years, mostly as a matter of survival. Quite likely the guidance I received from the curriculum materials oriented me strongly in this way, with its heavy emphasis on guiding students to explore, conjecture, design, experiment, analyze, and invent. I am not sure I even knew the term *pedagogy* at this point in my career, but I was beginning to understand how important it was to be deliberate about the ways in which I engaged learners with curriculum materials.[6]

That my teaching assignment was in a departmentalized "team" structure also meant that I shared the same 100 students with three other teachers: Ron Meloche, who taught math to all four classes; Mindy Emerson— the teacher who had guided me in the scis curriculum—who taught social studies; and Shirley Quimby, who taught reading. While three of us were relatively new teachers (Shirley Quimby had been teaching over 30 years), I was the only first-year teacher in the group. The four of us met regularly to discuss the children in the team and how they were doing in different areas. We talked about what we were teaching and shared ideas. We did not always see eye to eye and we had some provocative and useful disagreements about philosophy, pedagogy, and interpretation. Between my meetings with Jessie Fry, the principal, and my team colleagues, I was initiated into a professional discourse about practice.

The next few years of teaching moved me into other classroom assignments: second grade for 2 years, a multi-primary-grade team that I was able to design and construct with a wonderfully talented teacher, Meredith McLellan, for two more, then fifth grade. Like most elementary teachers, I was now teaching all subjects. Many—often more than a third—of our students spoke English as a second language and there were challenges embedded in figuring out how to help them learn to read and write well. I experimented, adapted, and analyzed the results of my efforts. It was intellectually challenging and interesting. Somehow I had managed not to discover that most people, including many teachers, did not consider teaching intellectual work. Approaching it as a process of inquiry and examination in and from practice, I found a steady stream of complex practical challenges as I tried to engage students in ideas.

During the early years, I focused particularly on science, reading, and language arts. Science was central because of that first teaching assignment and my engagement with the scis curriculum. Reading and language arts were central both because these were areas of emphasis and strength for me personally, and also because all the messages I heard were about the primacy of these areas. Jessie Fry's questions to me were always about how students were reading, and students' progress in school was measured in relation to their reading achievement. We had a reading consultant who was a fountain of ideas, and faculty meetings were often about the reading program. As a faculty, we discussed books, grouping, methods of teaching, and even particular students.

LEARNING ABOUT TEACHING AND MATHEMATICS

About 6 years later, teaching fifth grade, I confronted mathematics as a teaching and learning problem for the first time. My teaching of mathematics during the early years probably could be described best as reasonably effective direct instruction. I explained procedures and concepts to my primary-grade students—addition and subtraction of multidigit numbers, measurement, even and odd numbers, shapes, word problems. But things were different than when I was teaching younger children. Despite my good intentions and careful step-by-step explanations, long division and complex work with fractions loomed as a large impenetrable curricular wall for many of my fifth graders. My students would go home on Friday able to solve a long division problem and on Monday no longer seem to remember how to begin. No one seemed to be able to explain what we were doing, despite my efforts to model and explain the procedures I so desperately sought to teach them. When I graded papers, students got many problems wrong. Merely re-explaining and then asking them to correct their work repeatedly proved futile. All the imagination and cleverness in the world was not helping my students grasp the material. Studying their errors did not help me know how to help them understand or perform differently. I was at a loss. For the first time, neither my own resources nor those of my colleagues were adequate to help me figure out what to try. Just talking with others did not get me leverage on my struggles. They produced suggestions too much like what we were all already doing, or other suggestions that did not seem to me likely to address the problems I was seeing.

I asked around and soon was fortuitously introduced to the Comprehensive School Mathematics Program (CSMP) curriculum by Perry Lanier, a professor at Michigan State University, where I was enrolled in a master's program.[7] Profiting from his wise experience and from conversations with him, I began experimenting with the curriculum in my classroom, and the next year, teaching first grade, I used the materials as the primary mathematics curriculum. The material was structured in a completely unfamiliar way, and the central mathematical ideas were big ones, as in

SCIS: structure of number, functions and their composition, classification. A few powerful representational tools, all pictorial, were provided and their use encouraged.

Adherence to the CSMP curriculum developers' plans produced a classroom full of talk about mathematics. I was astonished at the serious intellectual work in which my 6-year-olds could engage. Although I did not know that their work was significant mathematically,[8] I began to see connections between the way I had learned to teach science several years earlier and what teaching mathematics might be like. My own and my students' mathematical learning began to grow and expanded into increasingly formal inquiry. CSMP was a critical impetus both for my improvement as a mathematics teacher and my learning as a student of the practice of teaching. My long-term investigation into the improvement of mathematics education had its roots in that year.

As in science, the curriculum materials provided a context for me to learn subject matter. Often this arose as I navigated the problems with my students, for the teacher's guide led me to structure lessons quite unlike any that I had taught in the past. Lessons did not begin with my explanations or consist principally of application and practice. Instead, I was guided to present the students with a puzzle or a problem from the text, and encourage them to explore. After a few minutes, I was to gather them to discuss their solutions. The teacher's guide offered me questions to ask and provided glimpses of what students were likely to say. It was "scripted." The scripts offered me handholds for what I could say and helped me develop new ways of being in the role of teacher. The guide's specific questions helped me find new ways to talk about mathematics with students.

Listening to my students' comments, and trying to understand their solutions, I felt pressed to delve deeply into the mathematical ideas myself. I found I enjoyed this a lot and often was personally quite consumed with a problem or an idea. However, I also began to think that it would make a difference if I knew more mathematics, and so I set out to take some mathematics classes at Michigan State. Over the next few years, beginning with one elementary algebra course, I took the entire calculus sequence, and then number theory. I was fascinated with some of the ideas of calculus. I also remember realizing how these ideas immediately affected what I could see and hear in my first-grade students' ideas, as well as how I read the teacher's guide for the mathematics curriculum. For example, one day I was teaching a lesson on area to my first graders. We were using ½-inch-square graph paper to calculate approximately the area of a set of irregular regions. One of the children had an insight that we should go get some of the "very small graph paper that the fifth graders use" so that we could get closer to the "right numbers" for the shapes' areas. My work in calculus helped me hear this student's idea as an intuition about limits. I never could have heard this in a child's talk before. Appreciating the mathematical potential of her insight, I followed her suggestion, and with the smaller (¼-inch) graph paper, we were able to get closer estimates of the area. The children were gleeful at their greater accuracy. I hoped this experience afforded them a glimpse of increasing approximation to the "true" area.

But it was in number theory that I fell in love with mathematics. For the first time, I glimpsed what it might mean to "do" mathematics, not merely get solutions to standard textbook exercises. I loved the content—divisibility, primes, congruences—and I loved working on proofs. Joseph Adney, then chair of Michigan State's mathematics department, encouraged me and modeled what it might mean to listen to students and help connect them into the formal mathematics that he knew so well. When my ideas or approaches were nonstandard, he did not dismiss them, but appreciated them, and also helped me learn to see things in multiple ways. I found a deep fascination in numbers and their patterns and structure that I had never encountered before. And I felt a kind of intellectual passion similar to my passions for language and text, teaching and learning, inquiry and analysis. I saw how mathematics might entail hunches and intuitions, conjectures and arguments, experiments and reasoning. I began to think explicitly about knowledge—its nature, where it comes from, what it means to "know" different sorts of things. I began to be able to see these issues all around me in my first-grade class.

I entered a doctoral program in education at Michigan State, in pursuit of opportunities to think, read, and reason. Teaching was intellectually challenging and profoundly engaging, but I craved occasions to move in more abstract territories, to connect philosophy and theory with my work in school. I also wanted to continue studying mathematics. I did not have concrete ideas at that point about how this path would intersect with my practice as a teacher, but I was not seeking ways to leave teaching.

LEARNING ABOUT LEARNING TO TEACH
AND TEACHER LEARNING

I continued to work on developing my own teaching—in particular, my mathematics teaching. However, around this time, I spent a year as a "reading helping teacher" in the school district where I had been teaching. This role entailed full-time work helping teachers in two school buildings improve their teaching of reading. I was one of four classroom teachers released to work with colleagues for a year. Underlying this design was the vision that, over a period of many years, a large proportion of the district's teachers would have held this role and would have spent an entire year focusing on reading. This design combined the need for support in reading with an innovative approach to professional development. The district reading coordinator, Carole Dodgson, helped us learn more about the teaching of reading, and we in turn helped teachers in buildings where we worked. I taught lessons to their students while they watched, I helped them assess their students, and we discussed our appraisals of the children's performance and learning. I learned a lot about reading and the teaching of reading; I learned more about the work of working with teachers. I reflected intermittently on how this work was and was not like teaching children.

In the first year of the doctoral program, while studying statistics and probability in my first term of quantitative research methods, an idea flashed into my mind, stimulated in part by my experience as a reading helping teacher. I sought a way to integrate my studies with my practice. I decided to structure a summer school program for local third and fourth graders focused on the same mathematical topics that I'd been studying myself. How might one design ways to engage eight- and nine-year-olds in ideas like sampling, distributions, and inferences to a population? A class such as this could be planned for students across achievement levels, and it seemed appealing to consider how to design the curriculum and pedagogy. I read a little about children's conceptions of probability, but found no research or curriculum development on inferential statistics. I suspected that I could learn a great deal with this design, and it would offer students a summer school option different from most of what typically was available. As I developed the plan for the summer class, I decided to encircle the students' class with a teacher development component for other teachers. The underdeveloped nature of this mathematical and pedagogical territory made working together seem particularly appealing and potentially productive. There was a good pedagogical problem at the heart of the summer school class, and we could try to exploit it as an opportunity for professional learning.

Eighteen third and fourth graders signed up for the class, which met 4 days a week from 9:40 to 11:00. About a dozen teachers participated as well. The teachers came each morning before the children arrived. We would discuss what I was planning for class, which usually was drawn from the analysis we had done the previous day after class. Sometimes we tried out a task I had planned for the students, sometimes we worked directly on the mathematics, sometimes we discussed particular students. With a plan in hand for class, my role was to be a sort of pedagogical daredevil. Whatever we decided to do, I was the one who had to try to make it fly, while the other teachers looked on, observing carefully. We had made ourselves an environment where we could investigate teaching and learning jointly. As we examined what was happening, we had one another's eyes and ears, and we interpreted similar phenomena differently. The teachers and I interviewed children to gain multiple views on what was being taught and worked together both on the design of methods of finding out what children were thinking and on ways to explain or understand it. The teachers looked very thoroughly at children's work and discussed what they could and could not figure out about each child's thinking. Working within a shared context, as we were, was a rare experience. We were looking at the same children, discussing the same teaching, and probing the same mathematics tasks. Our conversations were rich and focused. With the evidence right in front of us, it was possible to question one another's ideas and interpretations. We shared the goal of getting the summer school class to be a good experience for the children, and our discussions were at once ultimately practical (e.g., what should Deborah do tomorrow when she starts off?) and theoretical (e.g., is the notion of a sampling distribution accessible to nine- and ten-year-olds?).

It was a remarkably stimulating experience with learning on so many levels, and yet so much of it inarticulable as a matter of theory or conjecture about teaching and teacher learning. On intuition only had I decided to create an experience that would offer me a way to challenge and develop my own understanding of the content. While I struggled with trying to understand probabilities and to use statistics carefully, I was also challenged with questions about how to teach these mathematical topics. I did not yet know of theories that would suggest that knowing a subject in order to teach it, is different from, and likely more than, knowing it "for oneself."[9] I also did not think explicitly about the value of structuring a common context for experienced teachers to investigate teaching, to examine the same phenomena, and to discuss and disagree about their alternative interpretations. My experience and instincts led me as much as any articulable theory. At Spartan Village School, and in my more recent work in the school district, I had had fruitful informal exchanges with teachers about our common work and it just seemed to make sense to structure an occasion for more of that. Although now when I look back I see the words and ideas of "investigation" all over my lesson plan books and evident in the paths I cut for myself, I doubt these were at the surface of my thinking. I likely could not have articulated my investigative stance toward teaching as a matter of theoretical perspective. And I had no explicit ideas about "curriculum" or "pedagogy" of professional development. But the seeds of this set of ideas clearly were germinating.

Over the next few years, I continued to teach elementary school half time. I often led inservice workshops for teachers, sponsored by the intermediate county district. I learned the format of the 2-hour, after-school workshop session, and I developed a style of conducting these workshops that was consistent with my experimental stance toward teaching, and still responsive to participating teachers' desire for "ideas." But I found this work unsatisfying in terms of contributing to other teachers' learning.

Spurred by my experience as a reading helping teacher, and the experience with the summer school, I inaugurated a role called "mathematics helping teacher" in the school district. On a half-time basis, I was responsible for assisting my colleagues, many with far more years of experience than I, to develop their mathematics teaching. The main context for our work was the CSMP curriculum, which had since been adopted on a district-wide basis, in part because enthusiasm for it had spread among a sizable group of local teachers. In this new role of "math helping teacher," I was responsible for planning and leading half- and whole-day meetings for teachers, and for working in their classrooms to provide individual assistance. I sought to figure out how to use my own intense investigation of mathematics and the teaching and learning of mathematics as the energy and context for this role. I was no expert, after all, and deeply aware of issues of expertise and the ambivalent ways in which authority interfered with professional relationships in teaching. I was also younger than most of my colleagues and sensitive to that fact. I sought to construct a role and a stance, growing from the probability and statistics summer course, for it had seemed successful. It felt like a natural thing to do, for I myself had genuine questions and challenges. But a model of professional development grounded in joint inquiry was not the norm. My colleagues and I were accustomed to sitting through inservice workshops where experts offered us handouts, tips, and seven-step plans, materials and advice. In addition, many teachers were resistant to CSMP. Where was the drill and practice? And what is "composition of functions" anyway and what are arrow roads for?[10]

In my individual work with the teachers, being the pedagogical daredevil was again a comfortable role. Teachers would call me when they came upon lessons they did not understand: composition of functions, negative numbers, mapping. They would ask me to try teaching the lesson so they could watch. But we all knew that my effort also would be an experiment, that I had not necessarily had experience with the particular lesson. I would teach their students while they watched, and then we would discuss and analyze the content, the students, the teaching, and the representations used in the lesson. This "daredevil" way of working played well with my experimental stance toward teaching, offered other teachers that way of approaching their own development, and also helped to mitigate the authority and expertise issues.

As I listened closely to my colleagues' concerns and confusions with CSMP, I began to glimpse a territory of teacher learning that paralleled my universe of elementary teaching. These teachers, like learners everywhere, had ideas and beliefs that shaped their encounters with new ideas. They knew mathematics in particular ways that made it difficult to make sense of what the developers of CSMP had designed. Often the tools became the content, and the mathematical goals were distorted. To the teachers, for example, Cuisenaire rods[11] seemed something to be learned, instead of the ideas about number, computation, and algorithms that could be explored with them. They worried whether students "knew Cuisenaire rods" instead of whether they were becoming more fluent with the ideas that the material could be used to probe.

The teachers thought about learning in particular ways, and about how to tell what students were learning. Tests were important, and getting the right answers was satisfactory evidence that students understood. And as experienced teachers, they had ideas about what helps children to learn mathematics. I was fascinated, realizing that this new territory was one where the teaching and learning of mathematics was the content to be learned, the teachers were the learners, and my challenge was to learn what it could mean to help teachers learn to teach. What was the role in which I found myself as the mathematics helping teacher? How had I been experimenting with it already without having defined the situation as such? And there were curricular questions: What was the terrain—the "content" to be learned? How might one map what is entailed in mathematics teaching, what there is to know and to learn, much as one might map mathematics for children's learning? And pedagogy was crucial: What sorts of experiences and interactions are helpful in teachers' learning? I realized that I had put my head through a ceiling and discovered a new world of teaching and learning. And I saw that I had already been exploring it without realizing it.

I became more aware of my own learning as a teacher and more curious about the experiences, formal and rooted in my practice, that had been important to that learning. And I became intensely interested in what there might be to understand about teachers as learners. At the university, as a research assistant on a longitudinal study of teacher preparation directed by Sharon Feiman-Nemser and Margret Buchmann, I studied two prospective teachers over the course of their 2 years of coursework and field experience, and through their student teaching. From Sharon and Margret, I learned to think conceptually about teacher education and about ideas like experience, theory, practice, knowledge, and knowledge use. I grew aware that, like learners everywhere, prospective teachers' ideas and experiences shape what they take from their work in courses and field placements.

I found myself puzzling at the intersection of questions about teacher preparation and mathematics teaching: What was entailed in learning to teach mathematics? For my dissertation, I conducted a study of prospective teachers, designed to focus both conceptually and empirically on such questions. I asked, "What ideas, understandings, and ways of thinking do prospective teachers bring with them to their formal preparation to teach mathematics?" Pursuing this question required a mapping of the terrain: What was important to learn about what they knew and believed and how they thought? In order to explore assumptions about the role of formal mathematical study in learning to teach and teaching, I chose a sample comprising half prospective elementary teachers and half prospective secondary teachers. The secondary teacher candidates had majored in mathematics, while the elementary teacher candidates had majors in education or psychology and minors in language arts or social studies. This study was an important milestone in my interest in and focus on teacher learning. What I learned deeply impressed me with the need to take teachers seriously as learners.

At the same time, I had become involved with a new large research center at Michigan State, the National Center for Research on Teacher Education, directed by Mary Kennedy. We[12] were ambitiously designing and conducting a comparative study of preservice and inservice teacher education programs, and what the participants of such programs learn. In this study, I played a major role in developing interviews and guides for observing mathematics teaching and talking with program leaders and faculty as well as participants. I learned that my experience as a teacher was a useful resource in mapping what there was to pay attention to about teachers' ideas and practices, as well as in developing accessible and grounded interview tasks. Here was practice guiding research rather than the other way around.

When I completed my degree and started in a faculty position, I was for the first time in 14 years not employed as a classroom teacher. As a new assistant professor, I was challenged to design experiences for prospective elementary teachers that would contribute to their learning to teach mathematics. The mathematics methods course was to become one of my central concerns. What might one try to teach in such a course and how? What were the relative contributions of different kinds of experiences? Of all the things that contributed to the teaching of mathematics, which could be productively learned at the university, in courses?

Although I fell in love with teaching at this level, I also realized that, for my own learning, I would have to continue to teach elementary school. My own classroom was a site for my learning about the practice of mathematics teaching that was as essential to my work with teachers as my study of mathematics was to my teaching of children. I could see that my ongoing work as an elementary teacher was a crucial wellspring of my thinking, a source of insight and questions, of perspective and interpretation. By the time Magdalene and I met, we were both ready to set out into uncharted territories in which teaching and research were fused by their shared foundation in inquiry and uncertainty. The adventures lay ahead.

CHAPTER 3

Teaching and Teacher Education

How Do They Connect? How Might They Connect?

In the 1980s we were both teaching mathematics at the elementary level. We were not piloting curriculum or testing instructional strategies that might be shown to work and then be widely disseminated. We were not proposing to model the application of theory to practice, working out the finer details so that others could copy what we were doing. And yet our work was "experimental" in the Deweyan sense: We were seeking to learn in and from practice in ways that were both deliberate and reflective.[1] We sought to learn from our teaching, to theorize about practice in context.

Our work represented an attempt to construct the kind of teaching and learning widely promoted as "teaching for understanding," which, although widely touted, was difficult for many people—scholars, policy makers, and practitioners alike—to envision in real school classrooms.[2] We were willing to let other people look in on the work we were trying to do. By making it possible for others to watch us teaching and our students learning, we thought we could produce a common experience of classroom events as shared contexts for analytic conversations. From our early forays, we grew increasingly interested in how our teaching might serve as a medium for others' learning. In part because we were both heavily involved in preservice teacher education, and in part because of the acute nature of the problems with teacher preparation, which we take up below, we decided to focus especially on the learning of beginning teachers. Still, although this book focuses on preservice teachers' learning, many of the ideas about teachers' opportunities to learn from records of practice are relevant to the learning of experienced teachers as well.

In bringing our classroom teaching into the arena of formal, university-based teacher education, we were entering a field that for decades had been widely criticized. The weak impact of formal teacher education was recognized both inside and outside the university. In this chapter, we examine features of preservice teacher education that affect inherently its impact on the professional preparation of beginning teachers. Our ideas for a way that teacher education could work differently were formed with an increasing appreciation for its endemic challenges.

TEACHER EDUCATION AND ITS LACK OF IMPACT

The ineffectiveness of formal teacher education is a theme that has surfaced over and over again in the literature, whether from prospective teachers' self-reports, teacher educators' rueful complaints, or researchers' data. What prospective teachers learn in mainstream teacher education often does not seem to "transfer" to the classroom settings in which they find themselves.[3] Teacher educators complain that, in spite of their efforts, all that they do at the university is simply "washed out" by the conservatism of teaching practice.[4] Meanwhile, teachers complain that nothing they learned in their preservice program helped them learn to teach, that all their learning occurred on the job.[5]

Critics note that preservice teacher education is characterized by several recurrent difficulties, among them inadequate time, fragmented and superficial curriculum, and uninspired pedagogy.[6] Prospective teachers' experiences in teacher preparation often resemble their all-too-familiar school experiences, where teachers deliver information and students are expected to absorb it. Rarely do teacher education students have sustained opportunities to engage deeply and practically with alternative approaches to content, teaching, and learning. The teacher preparation curriculum is under fire both for its lack of intellectual challenge and for its lack of connection with practice.[7] Overall, teacher education has been a weak intervention on the powerful images, understandings, beliefs, and ways of thinking that prospective teachers bring with them from their prior experiences as students. In order to design an intervention that might prove more potent, we looked to scholarship in the field to analyze more closely teacher education's lack of impact.

Discontinuities of Experience and Education

One often cited reason for the weak effect of teacher education is the pervasive lack of attention to what prospective teachers bring with them to their professional preparation.[8] Because of their many years of schooling, teacher candidates come with extensive exposure to teachers and the practice of teaching. Sociologist Dan Lortie's analysis of the role of the "apprenticeship of observation" dramatizes the special problems of preparing professionals when they have already spent countless hours observing and absorbing practice.[9] This phenomenon is unique to teaching; prospective doctors, architects, and journalists do not have extended experience watching professionals in their chosen field. While they therefore know less about their intended profession, they also bring fewer preconceptions and habits with them and are more likely to see themselves as engaged in specialized training. In contrast, prospective teachers' unanalyzed experience with teaching has the weight of personal conviction, emotion, and self-evidence.[10] They have watched their teachers over the years and constructed ideas about practice from their own perspectives as students. They have observed what teachers do and are prepared to teach as their teachers taught—to stand at the board, to assign problems, to check homework from the key. They have developed ideas about good teaching, how learning occurs, what is worth knowing, and who can learn.[11] Still, they know little of the deliberations inside their teachers' heads, of the decisions made, of the dilemmas managed. They have not been able to observe their teachers think, figure things out, reason. Despite their long acquaintance with teaching, prospective teachers are quite unfamiliar with core components of practice.

How does teacher education meet prospective teachers who come with all this experience? In the last decade, researchers who have studied teacher education have noted recurrent patterns.[12] On one hand, the curriculum seems to treat teacher education students as though they were blank slates who know nothing about teaching, learning, and schools. These "blank slates" need to be filled with knowledge about how to teach. On the other, the curriculum also can convey an impression that knowledge for teaching comprises little more than common sense and everyday reasoning. For example, beginning preservice teachers are routinely sent out to schools to teach small-group lessons in mathematics or reading prior to any coursework in these areas, unwittingly reinforcing their belief that knowing how to add or to read is sufficient for teaching. Out in schools at the start of their program, they re-enact the teacherly behaviors they remember from being students. Lacking professional standards for judging success, they are likely to feel like teachers and to think that students are learning. Their difficulties often seem to them to be centered on managing students' behavior and orchestrating groups. The more they feel that they can teach using common sense and prior experience, the less likely they are to appreciate the importance of some kind of professional knowledge.

The traditional teacher education curriculum includes a mix of formal knowledge and firsthand experience, theory and practice divided both physically and conceptually. Once they start taking professional courses, prospective teachers encounter generalized theoretical knowledge and methods based on synoptic views of learning and teaching. Novices then are expected to apply these ideas to the particular contexts of their field placements. Their work in classrooms is presumed to provide them with practical aspects of the work best learned in the field, such as running a class discussion, listening to students, reviewing homework, and writing on the board. In their formal studies, the uncertainties of moment-to-moment interpretation and decisions, of dilemmas, of the particulars of context, content, and students, are smoothed. In the field, they are directly confronted with the complexities of working with groups of students, of explaining subject matter ideas, and of managing the complex environment of a classroom. Rarely is theory examined in practice. And little attention is paid to what it means to learn in and from one's practice.

A related problem centers on teachers' opportunities to learn subject matter and ways to help others learn it. Having been through school themselves, teacher education students come with their own understandings of the content they will need to teach. What they have learned from their own studies is uneven and often lacking depth and connection.[13] In teacher education courses, they learn not content but "methods" of teaching, as though pedagogy were somehow merely a medium of pedagogic delivery. Yet, research on teaching and teacher learning has illuminated the ways in which content and pedagogy intertwine. A major contribution to this line of inquiry has been the work of Lee Shulman and his colleagues, whose seminal research on secondary school teachers moved teachers' knowledge of subject matter to center stage in the debates about teaching and its improvement.[14] This group developed a conception of content knowledge combined with understandings of learning and learners, and described it as the kind of knowledge of content that teachers drew on and needed. The concept of "pedagogical content knowledge," or knowledge of the best and most useful representations, of what topics students are likely to be interested in and of the kinds of difficulties students are likely to have with specific academic concepts and procedures draws attention to the special ways in which teachers need to understand content.[15] Teaching children to add fractions sensibly, for instance, would depend on the teacher's own understanding of key ideas about number as well as of what helps children develop their knowledge of fractions.

Institutional and Programmatic Contexts

A second source of problems with teacher preparation is more structural. The ineffectiveness of formal teacher education in challenging what teacher candidates learn from their experience in schools has been noted frequently, and teacher education often has been the target of criticism and reform.[16] But improving teacher education in the institutions where it occurs presents significant problems. In the United States, these institutions appear as a motley landscape of settings, structures, and faculty. This landscape both shapes the problems with teacher education and mitigates against its improvement. What stands out from the landscape is the striking structural variability of teacher education. Compared with teacher preparation in most European countries, teacher education in the United States is basically a nonsystem.[17]

Teachers are prepared in a wide variety of public and private institutions: research universities, large comprehensive universities, 4-year colleges grown from old normal schools, and small independent and religious-affiliated liberal arts colleges. In addition, many 2-year colleges provide substantial portions of the early professional and academic preparation of teachers. In all, almost 1,300 public and private institutions prepare teachers. Sixty-five percent of the institutions that prepare teachers are private, but they prepare only one-fourth of the teachers. About a third of the 1,300 institutions—mostly large public universities—prepare three-fourths of the teachers. This variation is multiplied when one looks at program structure. Some teacher preparation occurs at the undergraduate level as part of either a 4-year bachelor's degree program or a 5-year program; some teacher preparation occurs at the post-B.A. level, as a fifth-year program. There also have always been some programs that constitute alternative routes to certification. Most of these aim to recruit nontraditional students with degrees in other fields.

Moving from institutional settings and program structure to faculty, we note that instructors, too, do not constitute a homogeneous group. A wide variety of people educate teachers, although few of them think of this work as part of their role. Although we tend to think of faculty in schools of education when we speak of "teacher educators," in fact, prospective teachers spend more time in classes taught by faculty in the arts and sciences than by faculty in education departments. This is no small influence on prospective teachers' development. In their subject matter coursework, they develop ideas not only about topics and methods of various fields, but also about how to teach these subjects. Whether or not they so intend, faculty in the disciplines offer images of how to teach their subjects. In the past decade, research on teacher knowledge has raised our awareness of how the ways in which teachers acquire subject matter knowledge plays itself out even in their teaching methods.[18]

While content and pedagogy are intertwined in ways only partially understood, other kinds of knowledge more clearly are taught within schools of education: knowledge of students and theories of learning, for example. But even there, teaching practice is the focus for few education school faculty. More are trained in one of the foundation disciplines (e.g., psychology, sociology, philosophy) and do not think of themselves as "teacher educators" any more than do their counterparts in the arts and sciences.

K–12 teachers also play important roles as teacher educators, teaching prospective teachers who are placed with them as student teachers. Steeped in practice, experienced teachers are repositories of practical wisdom, insight, and skill. What they know and know how to do is essential. However, the skepticism born of experience can be a conservative influence on beginning teachers' work. Teacher preparation must balance the need to ground teacher education in the realities of practice with the agenda to change schools. Experienced teachers may doubt new approaches—wisely or not so wisely. Managing the conservative influence with the need for the practical is a challenge of teacher education.

The overall portrait of "teachers of teachers" and the structures and contexts in which they work is that many people do it, yet few think of themselves in this role, or as having teacher preparation as their central responsibility. Instead, the responsibility is dispersed across many people who have little contact with one another. To coordinate prospective teachers' disciplinary studies with their pedagogical ones so that their knowledge of subject matter had the kind of flexibility and depth needed for teaching, would require substantial learning by all those involved. Yet, K–12 teaching and its critical components are an area of professional expertise for a relatively small fraction of those engaged in teacher preparation. This remarkable diffuseness of the teacher education enterprise presents significant challenges for those who would improve it. As a consequence of both its structures and its instructors, traditional teacher education resides across a major divide from practice, with few incentives or opportunities for change. Universities usually are not connected closely with schools, and many of the faculty who count as "teacher educators" have little or no knowledge of or real concern for practice.

Assumptions About Knowledge

One simple model of learning teaching is that the knowledge *goes in* during teacher education and then *comes out* to be used in classrooms. Theory is dispensed in some preservice courses, practical methods of teaching in others, and success in learning to teach is assumed to depend on applying what has been learned on campus. Such assumptions about knowledge are, however, at odds with knowing in teaching.

Teachers need to know things that one cannot know in advance of any particular encounter. We know this vividly from our own experience as teachers as well as from research on teacher knowledge. From our own work in classrooms, face to face with students, we know how often we are humbled, realizing the gap between particular things we had learned and what we needed to know in the course of moment-to-moment teaching. The knowledge we have does not simply "come out" when we need it.[19] In our scholarly work, we and others have argued that knowing the context in which propositional knowledge was to be used was an essential aspect of doing teaching. Knowing in teaching depends fundamentally on being able to observe in the moment of classroom interaction, interpret the situation, and act "deliberately."[20] It depends on being able to use what one can learn from textbooks, experts, and colleagues as one makes reasoned judgments in the context of action. Acting in a context is a speculative move that is itself a source of new knowledge. Attentive to the consequences of action, teachers need to be prepared to make speedy shifts of direction. When an appreciation for this kind of deliberate action is absent, the connection between knowing and doing is truncated to the "application of theory to practice" or the enactment of learned technical skills.[21] Prospective teachers who view knowledge in this limited way come to their professional education expecting to acquire knowledge that can be directly applied to action; they have little sense for the conflicts and uncertainties that arise in the course of application, and thus little wisdom about the sorts of knowledge that matter in teaching.

When the knowledge acquired from conventionally structured courses does not seem to "work" in some direct way as they try to use it in practice, teacher education students do not look to the context for understanding. Instead, they blame the failure on a conflict between the real world and the world of theory. But this simple dichotomy does not hold up when we consider the relationship between interpretation and action. For a thoughtful actor in a classroom setting (or anywhere else, for that matter) there are many realities, not just one "real world."[22] The multiple possible interpretations of the continuous interactions that characterize classroom work lead to an explosion of contingencies. What one should do next always *depends* on where anyone is in the content, on who is engaged, on what they are engaged in, on how tired or interested the class is, on whether students are "getting it," and so on. Acts of teaching occur in a complex ecological frame whereby the effects of one's actions ripple out into other parts of the immediate social setting as well as into the future. Students have relationships not only with the teacher, but with one another, and an appreciation of how these relationships can change and impact upon students' opportunities to learn is crucial. Practitioners explain to themselves what happens in a particular moment in terms of what has happened and where things might have been going before. The terms in which they think express an appreciation of the ecology of the setting.

Arguments about what knowledge is for teaching and how teachers "think" as they work echoed through a large body of work on teacher cognition in the 1970s and 1980s.[23] These arguments are found also in more general literature on cognition as psychosocial learning theories develop alongside assertions in more traditional psychology.[24] Psychosocial work in the tradition of "activity theory" fits very well with claims that have been made about teachers' knowledge use in practice. For example, in a 1993 paper with Yrjö Engeström, Michael Cole draws on the work of early German and more recent Russian social psychologists to argue that the proper unit of psychological analysis when we are looking at what someone "knows" should be joint socially mediated activity in a cultural context.[25] A "subject" learns an "object" in relation to multiple aspects of the context in which the learner operates. The knowledge that a learner actually can use is part of whole activity systems that include culture, community, tools, and symbols. This view of knowing in relation to learning and context also has developed in the field of cognitive psychology. In grappling with the psychological concept of transfer, for example, James Greeno and his colleagues argue that we cannot simply treat knowledge as being more or less general, without considering the class of situations across which we want knowledge to transfer.[26] The essential relationship between knowledge and its contexts of use means that learning is understood as improved participation in interactive settings.[27] Lauren Resnick calls this improvement "tuning to the affordances" and claims that learning takes place whenever an individual needs to create a new set of actions to fit a specific circumstance. Because learning is what she calls a "tuning process," it does not produce generalizable practice.[28]

If knowledge and context are indeed deeply interdependent, we have further explanation of why professional preparation structured in the form of academic coursework has limited impact on practice. An empirical argument along these lines has been made by Rand Spiro and his colleagues based on an examination of how knowledge taught in traditional medical education is used in diagnostic situations. They constructed a theory they called "cognitive flexibility" to explain the difference between physician candidates who could use knowledge they had been taught and those who had difficulty doing so.[29] Their hypothesis, borne out in several research studies, was that knowledge acquired in the context of the specific and messy details of instances of diagnosis was more likely to be used later in such circumstances than was logically organized material. An essential feature of the situations in which misdiagnosis occurred was the learner's incapacity to consider the specifics of a particular instance of illness and flexibly recombine elements of knowledge to fit the context of knowledge use. Spiro claims that knowledge for medical practice is ill-structured, by which he means that many concepts (interacting contextually) are pertinent in the typical case of knowledge application, and their patterns of combination are inconsistent across cases of the same nominal type.[30]

Teaching shares many features with complex practices such as medical diagnosis. Teachers, like doctors, must flexibly use what they know to develop ideas in particular cases and contexts. Spiro does not claim that academically formulated knowledge is useless in such situations and neither do we. But he does argue that if conceptual knowledge is acquired in such a way as to not make the learner aware that it must be restructured extensively in conditions of use, it likely will not be used. To examine the relevance of these ideas to using knowledge in teaching, consider a teacher who faces a class of 30 students, five of whom have their hands raised to speak. In the situation, this teacher needs to know things she could not know when the school year began, the day before, or even minutes before. Looking for various cues, she must know who is vying to speak. She also must know who has not spoken recently, and it helps to know what different students are thinking, so that she has a sense of who might say what if called on. She might know which children are engaged at the moment, and who is drifting off. She also might seek to have a sense of the dynamics among the students this morning. But students are not all she needs to know. She needs to have a sense of where the class is in their exploration of the problem: How are the concepts under study developing? Are there key ideas that might be highlighted here? Are there any misunderstandings developing? Would a re-diversion of the question help? From moment to moment, the teacher must observe, infer, interpret, and make conjectures. Her conclusions, although tentative, are knowledge claims to herself. The assertions she makes to herself function as knowledge. She knows them the best she can in the moment and must act, treating what she knows as both reasonably reliable and also provisional.

Special Challenges of "This Kind of Teaching"

Teaching is complicated work. The complexities of practice are exacerbated, however, when we consider the kind of teaching that beginning teachers are expected to learn in the context of contemporary reforms. We turn again to the case of mathematics teaching, one arena in which this additional dimension of preparing teachers has been particularly challenging, and the one in which we have focused our work. However, although this book is situated in the context of mathematics teaching, these ideas about learning teaching apply to the teaching of other areas as well. Contemporary ideas about mathematics teaching emphasize the development of students' capacities to reason about and understand mathematics. While skill and performance still matter, mathematical ideas and their connections are also paramount. Teachers are to help students delve more deeply into the underlying meanings of the mathematics, engage their classes in discussions of problems and ideas, reasoning and understanding, rather than merely emphasizing performance. This kind of teaching creates challenges by opening up the classroom discourse as well as the ways in which knowledge is treated and by demanding a finer and more ongoing discernment of students' knowledge.[31] While all teaching requires teachers to work under conditions of uncertainty,[32] this kind of teaching intensifies and extends the uncertainties with which teachers must contend. What this means is that prospective teachers must learn to practice in ambitious ways quite different from those they have seen and experienced. They are not simply learning to move to the other side of the desk, to develop content knowledge and pedagogical skill, problems that are sufficiently daunting. Now teacher candidates and their instructors are facing also the challenge of inventing—across subject areas—what it might mean to "teach for understanding." There is more to learn to know, more to learn to see, hear, and interpret.[33]

Three particular sources of uncertainty and goal conflict stand out as endemic to this kind of teaching: the inherently incomplete nature of knowledge with which teachers must work; the commitment to teach in response to students; and the multiple commitments with which teachers work. These uncertainties have significant consequences for what is involved in learning to teach. Take the following example from first grade as a site for considering sources of uncertainty and goal conflict in this kind of teaching.

A class of first-grade children is studying about polar bears. On this particular day they are working on the question, "How many first-graders does it take to weigh as much as a male polar bear?" A typical male polar bear weighs approximately 1,000 pounds, and the class has been using 50 pounds as a reasonable approximate weight for first-graders. The teacher looks around the class. Some children have begun drawing first-grade children on their papers, complete with shirts, pants, hair ribbons, and caps. They carefully write "50" under each child. Other children have written 50 + 50 = 100 + 50 + 50 = 200 + 50 + 50 = 300, and so on. Still others have drawn stick figures and are adding 50 pounds each time they draw another stick figure.

Pleased by what she sees, the teacher stoops down by one of the children who has written out a series of 50 + 50 = 100. There are 10 pairs of these on Jacob's paper. But when the teacher asks him how many first-graders weigh as much as a polar bear, first he says 50, then 100. Then he says he doesn't know and he spins his pencil on the table. The teacher moves to a pair of girls who were carefully drawing detailed people. Now they are leaning on their arms and talking. "We're tired," one says. "This is too hard." The teacher asks whether they have any predictions of how many first-graders it would take, and immediately they both say 20. "We already figured that out," says one, "but it's boring making the pictures." When the teacher asks how they figured it out, they look at her soberly. "We thought it in our minds," they explain.

Evidence of Learning Is Elusive. A first source of uncertainty in this kind of teaching is the fact that, although its development is central, human understanding is far from a simple visible phenomenon. Who knew what in this example? Jacob, who so apparently skillfully wrote out the addition, was unsure what he had when he was done, and the girls who appeared to be drawing actually already had the question answered. How did they figure it out? And what was going on with Jacob? Did he really not understand what he had done? No matter what kind of research we do in the future—exploring students' knowledge and preconceptions, examining what they know and how—teachers will continue to confront such issues on a daily basis. Teachers can become more skillful at probing and making sense of students' ideas. Yet what teachers know about their students can never be certain or complete.

Responsiveness Requires Close Attention and Relation in Context. A second major source of uncertainty in this kind of teaching stems from the fact that it needs to be designed in response to students. Although much can be predicted and anticipated, teachers must adapt and improvise in the face of what happens as lessons unfold. When Jacob says 50, then 100, and then says he does not know how many first-graders weigh as much as a polar bear, what is he saying? Does he really not know? Is he distracted by something? Is something else on his mind? Does he somehow not really understand what she is asking him? So what makes sense for the teacher to do? Should she ask him more about what he did and why? Or should she help him count the 50s on his paper? Should she ask him to present his solution to the rest of the class and encourage some discussion of his paper? Or should she let him listen to some other solutions and see if he begins to see the connections with what he did? That teachers work with human beings makes their work significantly different from one where practitioners work with materials they can control. No well-formed plan can function to predict and prescribe teaching with certainty. What the learner does and says creates the context for what needs to or can happen next, and for this the teacher must create practice in context.

Practical Commitments Are Both Multiple and Conflicting. A third source of uncertainty in this kind of teaching is a particularly knotty set of dilemmas: competing commitments within which teachers must construct their work. For example, if school learners are to understand a subject, a core commitment is to teach worthwhile content with intellectual integrity. But equally at the core is a commitment to honor students' ideas. When a child presents a novel approach to a problem that is imaginative—and completely nonstandard—what is the right thing for the teacher to do? Learners are bound to reach conclusions that, given what they currently know, are correct. You could say that for the mathematical system in which they are operating, these ideas are true. An example is when children believe that the next number after 2 is 3, or that the smallest number is 0. In the class we described above, the children who wrote: $50 + 50 = 100 + 50 + 50 = 200 + 50 + 50 = 300 + \ldots + 50 = 1,000$ were using an equation format more like a sentence describing an action than a statement about equality. They were describing their thinking in a step-by-step fashion. But $50 + 50$ does not *equal* $100 + 50 + 50$. Yet the first part of this "sentence" does say that. When should teachers be concerned that what students think or say is "wrong" according to more advanced ideas? The first-graders in this example are tackling what is for them a challenging problem and using a variety of mathematical tools and insights to do so. Is it important to be honest to the important mathematical idea of "equation" and to challenge their quite sensible employment? Such are critical judgment calls. Jacob and his classmates are engaged in serious mathematical work, but that does not mean that the mathematics they use and construct will always converge with accepted mathematical thought. The slogans "teaching for understanding" and "mathematics for all" are a lot more complex when viewed up close. Teaching often sits uncomfortably in the cross-talk of several such worthy and yet competing commitments. Wrestling with these in context, on an ongoing basis, is a third source of the endemic uncertainties associated with this kind of teaching.

Special Challenges of Learners of This Teaching

The complexities of this kind of teaching—the matter to be learned—affect and deepen the core challenges of improving teacher preparation. However, as in any question of educational reform, we must ask not only what is it that is to be learned, but who are the learners? What do we know about prospective elementary teachers and what they bring to learning to teach mathematics in ways that respect both mathematics and student thinking? In addition to the more general elements of the "apprenticeship of observation"[34] that we discussed above, prospective teachers often come to formal teacher education with crumpled experiences as mathematics learners. Their prior experiences affect who they are in relation to mathematics and, in turn, learning to be a teacher of mathematics to others. Years of traditional mathematics classes behind them, they conceive of mathematics as "cut and dried," and have difficulty imagining what there might be to understand or discuss. They have never participated in a class where students investigated a mathematical idea or worked on an extended real-world problem, developing mathematical tools in the context of collective work. They may not even think of mathematics as having ideas, let alone able to distinguish a "big idea" from a small one. They have watched their teachers explain mathematical procedures and assign practice, and they cannot envision teachers playing a role more like that which they may have seen an English or a history teacher play, guiding discussion, pressing for diverse interpretations and ideas, inviting comment and dissent.

Moreover, their experiences have done more than shape their images of teaching. Additionally influenced are their mathematical understandings and their confidence in themselves as mathematical knowers. They often come with a view of themselves as being bad at mathematics and unable to learn it. "I'm just not a math person," announced with a smiling shrug, is a frequent remark. And yet, without more developed content knowledge, their capacities to hear and interpret their students' ideas, assess student work, and manage classroom lessons are seriously impaired. Hence, teacher education students come with strong images of traditional mathematics classrooms, and scant idea of or intellectual resources for teaching in ways that might help children make sense of mathematics.[35]

SO WHAT DO TEACHER CANDIDATES NEED TO LEARN IN ORDER TO "KNOW" TEACHING?

Arguments abound about how to remedy this situation. Mathematicians and policy makers argue for more mathematics courses at the undergraduate level. Mathematics educators, many coming out of a tradition of developmental psychology, promote the acquisition of knowledge about how children think about particular mathematical concepts. Policy makers suggest schemes to put in place "mathematics specialists" who would be educated to make up for others' lack of knowledge and provide leadership for this subject. Parents want teachers to know about the kinds of jobs their children might take after graduation so they can tailor instruction toward preparation for future study or work. Curriculum developers believe that more knowledge about how to use better instructional materials is the answer. Each constituency has different ideas about what knowledge should be "put into" teachers in order to prepare them for practice.

Instead of taking a position in the argument about *what* prospective teachers need to know, we would like to enter the fray at another point, asking instead *how* they should know those things. To take this up, we return to what we know about the nature of teaching practice. How does what we know about the nature of practice and the people who must learn it influence our decisions about how teacher candidates need to learn? How might teacher candidates learn about these things? How much can knowledge, and an understanding of what it means to "use" it, be generated outside of the situations of action? How could we design our work in teacher education to give prospective teachers opportunities to develop knowledge as well as an appreciation of what it takes to use it wisely in context? Are there ways we could more deliberately help prospective teachers develop the capacity to know things in the setting? How could we teach them to be cautious about acting on the first meaning they give to a situation? How could we teach them to be cautious without developing the paralysis that an analytic perspective can produce?

Because teaching is underdetermined, teachers, like all other practitioners, are faced with having to make and test conjectures, invent new ideas and approaches, collect and interpret data, and analyze, construct, and challenge arguments in the course of their work. Learning to teach entails learning how to construct and use knowledge in practice. It also entails learning to appreciate the situated nature of knowing in practice. Hence, preservice teacher education must seek to prepare teachers to reason wisely, to develop courses of action in response to particulars, to extend and improvise beyond that which they have acquired or done before. From this perspective, teaching is a field comparable to any other field of knowledge where knowledge is growing and where its practitioners must know how to construct new knowledge.[36] Considering teaching as a field of practice like mathematics or medicine allowed us to explore analyses of knowing in other domains as a resource for the development of this idea.[37] New theories of knowledge see knowing in any field as encompassing theories, concepts, and facts, and also ways of knowing characteristic of the field. Ways of knowing include knowing what counts as evidence, the kinds of questions central to the field, where the uncertainties of knowledge lie, and how to formulate a conjecture or make an argument.[38] Similarly, practitioners must learn the theories, methods, language, questions, perspectives, and standards of their field—learning to be a doctor or an architect or a mathematician means thinking like one.[39] In this view, knowing how to frame problems of practice and solve them is not an exclusively academic undertaking. Thoughtful practitioners learn in and through the work of teaching. Teacher education is therefore better understood as a process of being inducted into a community of practice with its own tools, resources, shared ideas, and debates.

We have not arrived alone at this intersection between what and how teachers need to know. Efforts to reform the initial licensing of new teachers through the Interstate New Teacher Assessment and Support Consortium (INTASC), for example, emphasize beginning teachers' capacities to analyze practice and develop hypotheses about it, also in the company of others. Beginning teachers are expected to assemble portfolios of their work and to describe, justify, and analyze it. As important as what they know is their capacity to reason critically and professionally about their work. Similarly, the development of a National Board for Professional Teaching Standards (NBPTS), designed to certify professional advancement, centers on the role of teachers in developing the knowledge of practice.[40] In its assessment instruments to measure what board-certified teachers need to know and be able to do, the NBPTS includes measurements of teachers' capacity to "think systematically about their practice and learn from experience."[41] The recommendations of the National Commission on Teaching and America's Future reiterate these ideas.

> Successful teacher preparation programs aim to develop a foundation for continual learning about teaching—the capacity to analyze learning and examine the effects of contexts and teaching strategies on students' motivation, interest, and achievement—rather than aiming only to transmit techniques for managing daily classroom activities. This requires building a strong foundation of knowledge about learning, development, motivation, and behavior, including their cognitive, social, and cultural bases. It also requires creating cases and other inquiries that allow students to use this knowledge in applied contexts—to gather information, analyze and learn from their knowledge, and use what they have learned to assess situations and improve instruction.[42]

These reform efforts strive to position teachers in an active role in relation to the knowledge they use in practice.

In the next chapter we move into our own efforts to design a different kind of opportunity for teachers to learn different kinds of things about practice. Taken together, our experience as teachers, our awareness of the ineffectiveness of teacher preparation, our understanding of practice, and our appreciation of prospective teachers as learners helped us see the complex interplay of factors that affect teacher education. How could we draw on these multiple strands of experience and insight to work on this seemingly intractable problem?

CHAPTER 4

From Visions to Reality

Beginning the Mathematics and Teaching through Hypermedia Project

Where were we as we considered the relevance of these problems and debates for the improvement of teacher preparation back in 1989? As teacher educators who were also classroom teachers, we found that our own teaching provided a context for our thinking about learning to do this kind of teaching.[1] We considered the sorts of mathematical understanding that were useful in our teaching. We studied dilemmas that we faced regularly. We examined issues of the teacher's role and of the social complexities of groupwork in classrooms, and we thought about what this meant for teacher education. We both had previous experience in a variety of settings that encouraged us to study our practice.

At the same time, in our teacher education classes, we felt the lack of opportunity to examine teaching in the ways we were doing it in our own classrooms. Something critical was missing. How might teacher candidates learn about these aspects of the work of teaching? What kinds of opportunities were needed? When we and our students talked about real classrooms, students drew examples from their various field placements, or we drew examples from our own classes, some of which some students actually had observed. But these examples provided little of a concrete nature to ground the discussions and no opportunity to disagree or reinterpret. Almost always, only the teller would know the situation, the lesson, the children. Hence, the discussions were centrifugal. They also lacked concreteness because the teacher education students lacked language and tools for representing their experience, and without common referents there were no supports for developing either language or tools.

PREPARATION IN AND FOR PRACTICE

We were attracted to the idea that teacher education could help teachers learn to construct knowledge in the context of practice.[2] But in moving to such an emphasis on teachers becoming more deliberate knowledge-makers, we were aware of the constructivists' risk of making it seem that all knowledge for teaching should be made anew by each teacher. That was not our claim. Just as in learning mathematics, learners deserve to have access to ideas that others already have constructed and worked with. Some of these ideas may be quite unstable and tentative; others serve as tools for further work; some are mainstream and widely accepted and agreed upon. Experiences in teacher education need to be aimed at helping prospective teachers develop both knowledge and means of constructing knowledge.

Turning back to our own classrooms as the site for the study of practice, we designed activities that would make it possible for our teacher education students to investigate teaching in thoughtful and analytic ways, playing multiple theoretical perspectives off particular teaching and learning events. At first, both of us had our teacher education students spend time in our elementary classrooms; several of our colleagues at Michigan State also involved their teacher education students in our classes. This afforded prospective teachers a common context that they could discuss and analyze, as well as access to instances of teaching and learning somewhat different from what they remembered from their own schooling. There were many limitations, however. To begin with, having 30 adults observing in a class at once was more than a little daunting; it was also disruptive. If, in order to remedy these problems, teacher education students came on different days to alleviate the crowding, they had a much weaker common frame of reference since they had seen different lessons. Moreover, even once they were in the room, things went by at a rapid clip. The prospective teachers missed things that children said or did; they could not catch our comments as we walked around the room talking to individuals and small groups. Events moved along ahead of their capacity to see, hear, and make sense. We had been trying to build on earlier work we had done, but realized that when we had been working in smaller, more constrained teacher education settings, we had more control over how our classrooms would function as the learning environment for studying teaching than we could here, in the context of university courses. Unlike in our earlier work, we were unable to arrange for ongoing conversations with observers about our goals and practices. The students had other courses and jobs to go to, and the school we were working in was serving a much larger and more diverse population, requiring complex scheduling for specialist teachers and support staff in addition to regular classroom lessons.

We tried taping our classes and using the videotapes so that the action could be stopped and particular events could be analyzed. Although this slowed the buzzing pace of classroom life, there was still a lot that students of teaching could not see or understand from videotape alone. For example, when they noticed children writing in their mathematics notebooks, they wanted to look closely at what the students were writing. The tape did not allow for zooming in at will on children's written work. When they saw one of us interact with a child in some special way, they wondered what shaped our decisions and how the child made sense of what we had said or done. The tapes did not give them access to our thinking as teachers. Furthermore, prospective teachers would find that they could not really understand what was happening on a given day without being able to see what had happened the day before, or at the beginning of the year, or to know what would happen 3 months later. Some did not know to ask for this kind of information, assuming that what they saw was all there was. And the tapes were not as useful as they needed to be for our colleagues' use. When other instructors used our tapes, they did not have information that they needed to help teacher education students probe beneath the surface to examine what the teacher was thinking or what her aims were.

Whether they visited our classrooms or watched lessons on tape, prospective teachers could observe a kind of practice that challenged their notions about teaching and learning mathematics. But especially because of the kind of teaching we were trying to do, and because of their own limited experience with such teaching, we wished they could have access to more of the complexities of each lesson, to the specific characteristics of each child's work, and to the whole school year. We wanted them to be able to examine how children's thinking developed across the year, to investigate the kinds of tasks that were used, to observe the evolution of the classroom culture. We wanted them to know more about what we and the children were thinking about particular events or ideas. And we wanted them to be able to study these events in a context of collaborative, professional analysis. In short, we wanted them to be able to use our classrooms as sites for inquiry into practice, not just observation.

Teaching Practice as a Text to Be Interpreted

The use of knowledge in practice depends centrally on learning to see, hear, interpret, and design, as well as assess actions in context. This kind of learning occurs in a complex interaction between doing, on the one hand, and talking about the doing, on the other. Studies of learning various kinds of practices view the work as a kind of "text" that the learner can use to study the essential tasks and problems that make up the practice. More and less experienced practitioners can move back and forth across the complex terrain of practice with an eye on particular problems as the focus of their interaction.[3] In this kind of relationship, a beginning teacher would have multiple opportunities to think in grounded ways together with a more experienced teacher. In the case of teacher preparation, prospective teachers would have opportunities to watch, interpret, and discuss teaching and learning together with peers and their instructors. Opportunities for this sort of collaborative investigation of and conversation about practice are not the mode in teacher education. One approach to addressing this problem has been to change the structure of teachers' work so that time and other resources would be available for such activities. Another, complementary rather than different, approach is to change the structures of discourse and knowledge that ground teacher learning.[4] If preservice teachers' opportunities to learn were to be centered in the study of practice, what would it take?

We sought to design an approach to teacher education in which our practice could serve as a common referent for many beginners as they studied teaching in the university, changing at once the content, the discourse, and the setting of teacher preparation. Interestingly for us, scholars who examine the role of language and conversation in learning argue that talk is most effective as an instructional medium when it is organized around a common referent.[5] Young children manipulating and discussing patterns, students talking about texts, a teacher discussing a child's work with the parent—all these provide a medium for grounding the conversation in support of teaching and learning. With a common "text," participants have a shared referent in which differences of meaning or interpretation can be uncovered. When terms are insufficient, the common referent provides a means to ground the conversation and generate mutual understanding.

Such common referents are notably missing in conventional teacher education. Coursework, lacking common access to a referent set of problems of practice, does not provide it. Neither does field work, lacking as it does institutionalized opportunities for joint reflection by experienced and beginning teachers. Teacher education programs have solicited the help of experienced teachers who are willing to work with beginning teachers, but that help traditionally has not been structured as an opportunity to investigate practice with a shared experience of the same teaching and learning.[6] For perhaps none other than practical reasons, the experienced teacher generally does not work in relation to the novice as an *analytic* collaborator; work is shared, but the study of the work is absent. There is little time for observing one another or the class or for investigating what happens as a result of one or another teaching decision. The beginning teacher either copies or improvises without an opportunity to reflect. A more promising mode of collaboration between beginners and experienced practitioners has the beginner working and learning through conversation: by discussing the processes and products of the work.[7] In contrast to more academic studies, this way of learning would retain a close connection to those elements of practice that make the knowledge acquired usable in real situations. In contrast to unsupervised field work where the emphasis is on copying a model, it would provide a structure for deliberation on action.

The Promise of New Technologies

We wanted to design an approach to learning teaching that engaged prospective teachers in the study of practice. We had developed ideas about knowledge and about learning that seemed congruent. And what we had seen of prospective teachers' work with videotape and examples of student work only supported our sense of possibility and promise. We imagined we could begin with artifacts of practice like these and construct an archive of multimedia documents that could serve as a shared referent for the study of practice. As we considered how we could capture sufficiently extensive records of practice, we were simultaneously seeking ways to structure and make available the materials to support this kind of work.

We began to explore how computers could support this approach to teacher education at a time when instructional technology was developing rapidly and educators were beginning to experiment with using computers to engage learners in the investigation of problems. With new technologies, complex problems could be represented in multiple media, and potentially relevant information from a variety of sources could be searched and annotated. The technical capacities of "hypermedia"[8] made it seem possible to overcome some of the limitations we had confronted using video records in our work as teacher educators. Apple Computer was beginning to market Hypercard and produced a booklet for university instructors on how to design and market multimedia course materials.[9] The Intermedia Project at Brown University was designing a hypertext "proof of concept" for using linked information so that undergraduates could investigate problems using multiple sources of textual and graphic information in university courses in literature and biology.[10] At the MIT Media Lab, researchers on classroom teaching and learning were beginning to explore the use of video and computer tools for communicating their findings in a way that maintained the integrity of the records of practice on which those findings were based.[11] These researchers argued that hypermedia could provide multiple perspectives on classroom activity, since records of the learner's work, the teacher's work, the results of that work, and interpretations of it could all be linked and made available to anyone who was interested in seeing what went on. They deliberately rejected the "documentary" genre of videography as representative of a single (the producer's) point of view and chose instead to build systems that would enable users to make their own "documentaries," to be able to view the documentaries of others, and to have the flexibility to remake the story over and over. Teacher educators at Vanderbilt University[12] were using Hypercard to link video vignettes of teaching to learning theories for use in an educational psychology course. The American Federation of Teachers teamed up with developers from Apple to make a Hypercard-based "electronic environment" in which teachers and educational reformers could examine the process of restructuring schools.[13]

We imagined that with Hypercard, we could build a multimedia collection of records of practice from our own classrooms that could be used on commonly available computer workstations to provide a shared text that teacher education students and their instructors would use to investigate teaching and learning. Using newly available tools to collect information on the teaching and learning in our classes, we thought we could document the teaching and learning that occurred across the year from multiple perspectives. We proposed to store, catalog, annotate, and exhibit extensive records of teaching and learning in our classrooms using what were at the time the newest multimedia technologies. We proposed to edit, catalog, and interconnect the material in ways that would make it possible for instructors of university courses to draw on records of real-time teaching, children's and teachers' thinking, and students' work, as a medium for learning to think pedagogically about core problems of practice. Using Hypercard's capacity to relate information in flexible ways, the computer system we wanted to design would allow instructors and their students to stop the action to make hypotheses about what was happening and why, and then to check those hypotheses against the teacher's thinking, the children's work, and other theoretical and practical perspectives on the action. Through this activity, we imagined that prospective teachers would have the novel opportunity to surface the assumptions about teaching that they had from their careers as students and construct knowledge of teaching that was situated in relation to actual episodes of a different kind of practice. They would have opportunities to examine both serious mathematics and children's thinking about it in a context of pedagogical activity.

With the newest video cameras, we could capture clear pictures and reasonably good sound for a small investment and manage to cause minimal disruption in the classroom. We could transfer video to video discs and use computers to get to any point on the disc when we wanted it. With a scanner, we could copy students' work and teachers' plans and translate them into digital form to be stored in a database in computer memory. We imagined software that could call up both video and graphics on demand and enable both to be annotated without danger of destroying the originals. By utilizing the system we would design, we imagined that any

teacher educator could organize a presentation ahead of time around artifacts of practice and then by clicking on buttons display and/or play supporting material (video, audio, graphics, and text) during the lecture/talk.
Also, because of the flexibility of the system, it would be easy for the pre-
senter to link other ideas and examples or pursue questions that came out
of the presentation.

Multiple Journeys Across the Terrain of Teaching

The appeal of new technologies was more than technical. The capacity of
hypermedia to represent multiple perspectives was exciting because of the
conceptual overlaps between what researchers on teaching and other practices had been saying about the acquisition of usable knowledge and the
"hype" surrounding hypermedia. Committed to developing a medium for
teacher education situated in the complexity of practice, we did not want
to design an approach to teacher education that simply displayed models
of "good teaching." We thought this technology could enable us to represent the kind of knowing that we had found to be essential to our own teaching but lacking in teacher education—what Shulman calls "strategic"
modes of knowing in practice.[14] The terms he uses to distinguish strategic
knowledge from other things teachers need to know are strikingly similar
to the rhetoric used by developers of hypermedia technologies. Shulman
observes that propositional knowledge is what is most conventionally
delivered in academic settings to be "applied" in practice. He claims that
case knowledge, with its vivid detail, makes the propositions it illustrates
more memorable, but is still clearly distinguishable from strategic knowledge: knowledge as it is used in actual situations of practice.

> Both propositions and cases share the burden of unilaterality, the deficiency
> of turning the reader or user toward a single, particular rule or practical way
> of seeing. Strategic knowledge comes into play as the teacher confronts par-
> ticular situations or problems, whether theoretical, practical, or moral, where
> principles collide and no simple solution is possible. Strategic knowledge is
> developed when the lessons of single principles contradict one another, or
> the precedents of particular cases are incompatible.[15]

We wanted to use technology to design opportunities for preservice teachers to develop strategic ways of reasoning and knowing in practice. Shulman argues that a pedagogy for teacher education should "involve the
careful confrontation of principles with cases, of general rules with concrete documented events—a dialectic of the general with the particular in
which the limits of the former and the boundaries of the latter are ex-

plored."[16] This was precisely the sort of exploration of the theories and practices of mathematics teaching and learning that hypermedia tools were supposed to make possible. And it was the kind of knowledge that we imagined would support deliberate action in the classroom.

Rand Spiro was drawn to hypermedia for conceptual reasons also. He saw it as a medium that could represent the complexities of strategic practice, with a focus on medical diagnosis. We saw parallels between his argument that cases of "best practice" were not enough to prepare practitioners and our concerns about how providing teacher candidates with good "models" to copy limited their opportunity to think critically about the complexity of pedagogical problems. The metaphor that Spiro and his colleagues used for their hypermedia development work was drawn from Wittgenstein's ideas about knowledge as a terrain to be explored by multiple journeys through it, none of which would capture the terrain in its entirety. This metaphor seemed powerful to us, given what we wanted to represent about teaching. It fit very well with our ideas about "investigation" as a pedagogy of teacher education focused on practice. When Wittgenstein set out to summarize his thoughts about the nature of knowledge into a coherent whole "with a natural order and without breaks," he instead produced *Philosophical Investigations*, a series of remarks representing different journeys across the intellectual terrain that relates meaning, understanding, logic, consciousness, and other things. He says of this work in the introduction:

> After several unsuccessful attempts to weld my results together into such a whole, I realized I should never succeed. . . . My thoughts were soon crippled if I tried to force them on in any single direction against their natural inclination.—And this was, of course, connected to the very nature of the investigation. For this compels us to travel over a wide field of thought criss-crossed in every direction.—The philosophical remarks in this book are, as it were, a number of sketches of landscapes which were made in the course of these long and involved journeyings.[17]

This notion of knowledge as a terrain has persisted in our thinking about teaching and learning as a domain of study. The investigation of practice as a series of different journeys across the terrain of teaching seemed to be a more promising way to represent knowing in teaching than a single coherent representation of "best practice."

Because hypermedia technologies enable access to and tools for navigation of massive quantities of information, they have the capacity to provide rich and unusual experiences, unlike those that are typically possible. Initially we imagined a pedagogy that could give teacher education students an experience that would resemble the experience of observing good mathematics lessons in real classrooms and having multiple opportunities to analyze those lessons with the teacher who taught them and other observers. Quite soon we began to see that what we were designing could afford opportunities not merely imitative of real life, but entirely unimaginable in real space or time. Prospective teachers would be able to explore teaching and learning in real time, but in addition they would be able to relate real-time events to one another in new ways. At a given point, they also could probe the teacher's perspective on the class, or on particular students; similarly, they could investigate students' perspectives. Teacher education students could have access to multiple perspectives on teaching through annotations created by people such as those whose work they read in teacher education courses, school administrators, students, and parents. None of these is possible in real time, whether one is observing or teaching.

As rich with possibilities as it might be, we did not imagine that an electronic learning environment in which prospective teachers and their instructors could study practice would replace learning in the real-world setting of the classroom. In an electronic environment, opportunities to learn the important interpersonal skills that are associated with growing from an adolescent university student into a grown-up teacher would not exist. We had no intention of replacing students' field experience with a "virtual apprenticeship." Instead, we sought to add to their experiences opportunities to approach knowing practice from multiple perspectives.[18] We aimed to create for them the opportunity to get some distance on the events that fly by so quickly when one is in the middle of them, so that they would have additional resources from which to construct their teaching selves. We sought to provide rich documentations of third- and fifth-grade students' work so that the teacher education students could get to know them without the additional burden of building a relationship with them. An electronic learning environment built around records of practice could retain a degree of immediacy and empathy without the pressure of performance.

Our interest in the promise of technology was piqued. We were eager to try out some of these ideas. We made a request to Apple Computer for equipment and software that would enable us to experiment with new technologies. We argued that, given access to a rich collection of documents in multiple media, prospective teachers would be able to form their own hypotheses about teaching and learning and test those hypotheses in the vast collection of information from the two classrooms. The system would enable and encourage exploration and investigation. We wrote:

> In the system we propose to design, teacher education students will
> have the capacity to do research on their own questions. . . . They will
> have access to tools which enable them to move through material
> (audio, video, written transcripts, voice/written annotated notes by the
> instructor or other students, and preplanned tours through the data), to
> construct their own interpretations (which would then be added to the
> existing annotations so that other students could use them as well), and
> to present and defend them. During this process, they would learn to
> revise and review their original thinking based on new information and
> perspectives of others.

We were embarked on an attempt to tinker with the essentials—we would address the problems that have made formal teacher education ineffective, by paying close attention to what intending teachers bring to their professional preparation, changing the resources and the organization of institutional structures in teacher education, and focusing on knowing in context. And we would take advantage of new technologies to do these things within the framework of university teacher education.

In the spring of 1989, we proposed an ambitious undertaking to the NSF. We proposed to develop and study a multimedia, computer-supported learning environment that would make instances of practice available for study by prospective teachers. Our idea was a radical one: We did not aim to record and exhibit lessons to be copied by other teachers. Nor did we intend to illustrate theories of learning using examples of practice. Rather, we said we would document an entire year's worth of teaching and learning by collecting a variety of records that could be studied by ourselves and others. Because we were convinced that extensive records of practice were crucial to the development of a practice-based approach to teacher education, we were prepared to turn the camera on ourselves and our students to produce a "shared text" for the study of teaching and learning. The point was not to study Magdalene Lampert and Deborah Ball, or to study *our* teaching per se. Nor was the point to study the specific children who were in our classes in 1989–90. Instead, our vision was of using our classrooms as sources of primary and concrete material for investigating teaching and learning. We wanted to produce a rich and unique collection of materials that we could use to develop a different approach to teacher education. We hoped prospective teachers would learn how to look at and make sense of what was happening in the classrooms.

Our proposal to NSF sketched a set of ideas raising questions about what is entailed in "learning to teach" in a university classroom. By beginning with instances of practice and organizing the knowledge base around them, we would radically alter the content of that knowledge base. Teacher educators and their students would develop analytic, conceptual, and practical knowledge in relation to actual classroom episodes and samples of children's work. Practice and its analysis would be in the foreground, a different design for the curriculum of learning to teach that had been dominated so long by theory and method. Creating a discourse centered on investigation would mean learning to frame and pursue questions and problems of practice, to seek evidence and to interpret. Emphasizing the situated use and construction of knowledge would be a substantial shift from the traditional discourse of theory-into-practice. Finally, to design a means of grounding analytic work in practice would be to develop a setting for teacher education work different in significant ways from the modal settings of either university classroom or field experience.

Our challenges were many. Two linked sets of problems preoccupied us: First, what would it really entail to document the teaching and learning in two elementary mathematics classes? What would we need to collect? How could we do it? Whom would we need to help us? What problems—conceptual and technical—would we face? Second, what would teacher education students and their instructors do with these materials, and why did we think that would contribute to their learning to teach? How would the materials be accessed? How might instructors use them, and what would they need to know in order to use them? What sorts of assignments or other work would be productive and what would it take to design and use them in teacher education settings? This chapter traces our forays in initial pursuit of our idea, with snapshots of what we did, problems we encountered, decisions we faced, and things we learned as we began to gather the material we needed to realize our vision. Chapter 5 focuses on the environment we developed for use in teacher education and our thinking about the ways in which instructors and their students would make use of it.

THE M.A.T.H. PROJECT TAKES OFF

We were informed that we would be receiving funding from NSF to pursue our vision. We had about a month before the start of the school year to hire a staff, decide what records to collect and what tools to use to collect them, and develop a plan for the year. We hired Mark Rosenberg to fill a position we called "project manager"—a luxury, from some perspectives, as many research and development projects of this scope are managed by the principal investigators. However, since the project we had proposed centered on us being in the classroom teaching mathematics every day for the first year, and being videotaped on most of those days, we argued for and acquired the funding to hire Mark. But Mark was more than a manager. He had several skills that were essential to doing the project and, more important, he had a better sense than we did of where we might be going with interactive multimedia technology.

Mark had just returned to Michigan State from a summer internship at Apple Computer, where he worked on development projects in the Advanced Technologies Group and the Multimedia Lab. He ignited our imagination with videotaped examples of demonstration multimedia projects he had brought from Apple. It seemed as if computers could enable us to have videos and other artifacts of practice right at hand and refer to them interactively with our audience! We began to envision all kinds of possibilities for linking information about the teaching and learning in our classrooms, which we would collect in multiple media using Hypercard "buttons" and "stacks" and referring to that information interactively with groups of teachers and researchers.

We hired six graduate students to work with us as both record collectors and co-researchers on teaching. The duality of their role was important. As researchers and prospective teacher educators, they wanted to learn about the kind of teaching that we were trying to do. So they would not only manage the observation, video- and audiotaping, interviewing, photocopying, and filing, but they would participate with us in the collaborative study of teaching mathematics "for understanding." Under this umbrella of common purposes, we sought diversity in the team we were assembling. Some members brought experience with elementary school teaching; others, experience with teacher education. Some brought backgrounds in learning psychology. And some brought strong backgrounds in the study of mathematics. Three graduate students (Margery Osborne, Jim Reineke, and Kara Suzuka) were assigned to the "Ball team" and three (Ruth Heaton, Nan Jackson, and Virginia Keen) to the "Lampert team." We began our teamwork by devising interviews that would be administered to the third- and fifth-grade students in the first few weeks of school in order to assess their mathematical skills, knowledge, and dispositions, and their more general feelings toward themselves and toward school. From the first day of school, all three members of each team were in the classrooms with Lampert and Ball during their mathematics lessons. They shared the experience as observers and recorders of the teaching and learning that went on every day. During that year of documentation, we simultaneously collected and assembled an electronic archive of multimedia documents that mapped a year's practice of mathematics teaching and learning in two classrooms.

Collecting the Multimedia Materials

What kinds of records would be needed to communicate the complexity of the practices of teaching and learning? We made three major decisions at the outset: to collect records for the whole year in two classrooms, to use our own classes, and to collect records of teaching and learning as well as interpretations of events produced in near-time to the events themselves.

Based on our perspectives as teachers, teacher educators, and scholars, we reasoned that the school year (rather than isolated lessons or short series of topically related lessons) was the appropriate unit of study for examining the kind of teaching and learning we were doing. In traditional teaching there is an atomistic structure to curriculum and instruction whereby single topics are associated with single lessons. In portraying this kind of teaching, events can be reliably associated with topics, and topics distinguished from one another. In contrast, in the kind of teaching we were trying to do, the mathematical topics were multiply connected over time as curriculum was built in the course of instruction that tried to be responsive to students' mathematical ideas. Also, the kinds of interactions that underlay the type of work on mathematics that occurred in these classrooms (conjecturing, argument, disagreement) were dependent on the establishment of long-term relationships between teacher and students and among students themselves—risk taking, trust, predictable habits of challenge, and comradeship. Finally, we wanted to collect records across the year as a whole because it would make record collecting a regular part of the classroom routine. Neither students nor teacher would be able to produce an unsustainable "performance" for the camera or make unusual preparations to produce a special piece of work.

We chose to tape our own classrooms because we were willing to be recorded day after day, to have our students' work scrutinized, and to keep careful records of our own plans and reflections. Although we were not "typical teachers," we knew it would be difficult to get any other teacher to let a video camera into the classroom every day. At the same time, we were committed to the idea that teaching practice could not be captured in a few "model" lessons, and we were willing to have documentation occur no matter what was happening in the room. Even with this level of record collecting, we wondered whether we could do enough: Would it be adequate to make records of every lesson across the year? We understood teaching and learning as seamless activities that occurred in the continuous stream of our experience and interactions. We knew we were teaching, for example, when, in the car on the way to school, we reflected on what would be happening that day. Should we keep records of those musings? One does not start teaching when the morning bell rings or stop learning when it is time for recess. Students did homework, sometimes alone, sometimes with parents, or friends, or tutors. What of records of those interactions? The events we would call "teaching" and "learning" do not have neat boundaries around them. Although they are interactive, they do not occur only when teacher and students are face to face. Any particular event is connected in multiple and complex ways to the events that preceded it. By making ourselves the subjects of the investigation of teaching, we could keep these complexities on the table as the records of practice were assembled.

With our commitment to a year-long unit of analysis as the foundation, we would have to choose to collect a limited set of records. That was clear. But how would we choose? We could have decided on a few coherent "story lines" at the outset, like "the development of students' capacities to represent their ideas in multiple formats" or "the establishment of a classroom culture that supports mathematical discourse" or "the teacher's and students' roles in determining lesson content," and collected the records we would need to tell that story. But we knew that many such "stories" could be told about any class over a year, and we wanted a collection that would make it possible to assemble numerous stories after the fact. Rather than imposing coherence from our own point of view, we wanted to have a set of materials that users could try to make sense of, bringing their own assumptions into play along with annotations by multiple participants and commentators. With this goal in mind, we made our decisions about the structure of the collection as a whole and about what should be collected on any given day and periodically throughout the year. We were guided throughout by the idea of producing "multiple representations" of the phenomena under study.

The idea that what we were producing would be a record of practice played itself out in two ways: multiple *records* of events and multiple *interpretations* of events.[19] For making records, we wanted to use tools that would enhance our capacities to perceive and remember what was happening and produce multiple images of events for others to look at and listen to. Such a multiplicity of images would enable post hoc triangulation and description. We also wanted to collect multiple interpretations of the events as they were occurring, created by "participant observers" of different sorts. So we collected written notes and interviews from the third- and fifth-grade students, the teachers of other subjects in each classroom, and ourselves. We also wanted the perspectives of outsiders to the events. It seemed important to have interpretations of what was happening from a variety of visitors who would see only one or two classes, as well as from a consistent small set of observers who would see every lesson. We assumed that even with similar protocols and training, observers with a strong mathematical background would take note of some aspects of the phenomena, and those with a focus on children's learning would notice others. We predicted that experienced teachers and teacher educators would find still different elements of the teaching and learning worthy of attention.

Our plan included three categories of records: those produced as a matter of course in everyday teaching and learning, those collected specifically for this project, and annotations on events and documents. We take these up in turn.

Ordinary Artifacts of Practice. In this category are the records that we routinely would keep for the purposes of planning and reflecting on our teaching and student assessment. These include daily teaching journals and student classwork, tests, and homework, as well as reports to students and their parents on students' work. These artifacts serve both as records of what occurred and as representations of what one *does* in the course of doing the kind of teaching and learning we wanted to study.

As teachers, we had been keeping journals as a matter of course for more than 10 years. Except for the convention that we would write something every day, we did not standardize our entries. We both had developed the habit of writing reflections for an hour for each hour of teaching time and variously included notes on lesson preparation and evaluation, including long- and short-term plans, observations on individual students, design of mathematical problems for each class session, and comments on general pedagogical problems. We did not alter this practice during 1989–90, or make any changes to the form of our journal entries. We reasoned that those who wanted to study the teaching and learning that went on in our classrooms should have access to these notes in order to get (some) insight into the teacher's thoughts, perspectives, reactions, and plans. Teacher thinking is a central component of teaching practice. Teacher reasoning is complex and often does not take the form of "lesson plans" as they are taught in teacher education courses. As we wrote in our journals across the year, in bound notebooks, with pens, our writing and drawing were transferred to electronic text and graphics so that it would be possible to do "word searches" on the text to find information about particular students, issues, and problems.[20]

We also had developed, as a regular part of our practice, routines for students to record their work on mathematics in and out of the classroom in a bound notebook. At the fifth-grade level, students wrote down the "Problem of the Day," recorded their experiments with aspects of the problem, stated their conjecture about a solution, and composed a reasoned argument for why their solution "made sense." This material was available for the teacher to look at while students were working individually and in small groups. Students also used their notebooks to illustrate ideas they were trying to explain to other students. In addition to being a running record of what students did during math class besides thinking and talking, the notebooks document something about the "content" of the lessons for each student. Because of the way lessons were structured, students differed in their experiences of and interpretations of the curriculum, so it would not have been enough simply to record each day's assignment. For any particular day, we wanted a record of what mathematics students were working on. The notebook as a whole could demonstrate the continuity and coherence of each student's experience. We differed in how we used these notebooks as teachers, but we both examined students' work and we both used what we learned from those notebooks. After the notebooks had been photocopied, page numbers were added to each page and they were filed by date and student. We also photographed the notebooks on occasion to record the feel of the whole.

Records Collected for this Project. Structured field notes[21] on every lesson were written during class by observers, describing mathematical content, pedagogical representations, problems that arose from the perspective of the students, activities of five focal students in each class, incidents of potential interest to teacher educators and teacher preparation students, and overall agenda. These standardized field notes would provide a complex index of lessons that would make possible searches of various kinds. We rotated the preparation of notes among graduate students with mathematical background, teaching experience, and teacher education experience, to vary the perspective of the notes and avoid a singular focus.

We supplemented these notes with video and audio documentation of the same events. The same graduate students who wrote the field notes rotated through periods of taping. Although their videography skills were not at a professional level, they brought school-sensitive tact, knowledge, and insight to the task, which technical assistants would have lacked. We began taping each day as students came in the door from recess and continued taping for a few minutes after each lesson was over so as to avoid judgment about what constituted a "complete" class period. We wanted to portray the fact that teaching and learning go on outside the conventional lesson boundaries imposed by bells or teachers' announcements. Students often do or say things as they come into the room, or as they are packing up their books, that are highly connected to what goes on during a lesson. In both classrooms, the formal lesson period had roughly three parts, a short beginning segment in which the teacher communicated the problem of the day, about half an hour during which students worked in groups of four to six on the problem, and another half hour of teacher-led discussion of some aspect of the mathematics in the problem. Considering possible types of shooting and editing, we chose neither conventional documentary procedures in which we would collect shots that varied greatly in scope and piece them together in an order different from the original sequence in which they were shot, nor the opposite extreme of "locking on" the camera to one perspective and letting it run for the duration of the lesson. Instead, we filmed long "takes" with the camera zooming in and out and the camera person moving around focusing on salient details. This allowed us to acquire a continuous record of events while at the same time doing some situated interpretation.[22]

During all the time we taped, there were many different kinds of activities going on simultaneously. When watching earlier tapes we had made, viewers often asked, "What is the teacher doing when . . . ?" or "What is the rest of the class doing while . . . ?" Although realistically we could not capture everything viewers might want to see, we decided to have two cameras running simultaneously at all times, one that would follow the teacher and one that would "roam," off the tripod, during small-group time and film the whole class from the tripod during large-group time. While keeping the camera on the tripod was less distracting for students, we knew we wanted close-ups of student work while it was in production as well as documentation of students' talk and body language as they tried to communicate their mathematical ideas to their peers. We decided each day which children to focus the cameras on, to vary who was being recorded and take advantage of the variety of activity available to record. Much of the time, the cameras captured several small groups seriatim as they worked on the problem. The fifth-grade class was large and the classroom in which it met was small, which sometimes made it difficult to get good sound quality. During a portion of the year, one small group each day met in an anteroom within view of the teacher and part of the class so that their conversation could be recorded more clearly. We decided to follow some small groups continuously for a whole period or even for a week because the work done by small groups of children often has a narrative that extends beyond a given class period.

We began taping on the first day and taped until the last day of school. We audiotaped all lessons in order to generate a complete record of whole-group interchanges. We videotaped most lessons with two cameras. We also decided to audiotape conversation in a different small group than the one that was being videotaped, to expand the regions of the classroom that were recorded. The daily audiotapes made it easier to produce "first pass" transcripts of each lesson. These transcripts then would be "enhanced" by a member of the research team who could recognize individual students' speech patterns because he or she had done extensive observations in the classroom. We anticipated that transcripts would be invaluable to users unfamiliar with the classroom and its discourse, even if the sound on the videotapes was of good technical quality.

Multimedia Annotations on Lessons. In addition to records of the events that transpired during lessons, we wanted to include interpretations of those events in the multimedia database that would be available to teacher candidates and their instructors. By making multiple perspectives on each event available, we hoped to model this kind of thinking for users. Table 4.1 lists what we planned to include and why. Our intentions outstripped our resources, and we actually did not collect all of these annotations in 1989–90. We have, however, continued to add annotations of various sorts to the records of practice over the past 7 years.[23]

CATALOGING, ACCESSING, AND LINKING MULTIMEDIA RECORDS OF PRACTICE: NEW CHALLENGES

As we collected all of these records, we simultaneously had to figure out how to file them, and how we filed them had implications for how teacher educators eventually could use them. At this point, we found ourselves bumping up against the ever-changing boundary between what we could imagine and what was real in the world of new technologies. The dream of hypermedia developers in the 1980s was that large and diverse collections of information such as the one we set out to amass could be stored electronically, accessed instantaneously, cataloged and cross-referenced in multiple ways for multiple users, and—most important of all—linked. And the developers made it easy to imagine that users without extensive knowledge of computer programming could create such systems. Flexible electronic cataloging and linking, in our collection of records of practice, for example, would mean that a teacher educator could prepare to engage students in an investigation of classroom culture by choosing some relevant video clips, attaching them to the reflections the teacher wrote on those moments in the lesson, writing some commentary about ideas in the sociology of small groups that were related to what was happening, putting this all together with children's work to make it possible for novices to investigate how ideas traveled from one part of the room to another, and making everything accessible at a few mouse clicks for printing or projection. Then both the instructor and the students could record their reflections on these materials—questions, commentaries, interpretations, and the like—for real-time and nonsynchronous collaborative analyses. This activity would produce the sort of multiple journeys across the same terrain

TABLE 4.1. Multimedia List

DECISIONS ABOUT WHAT TO COLLECT	WHY WE COLLECTED IT		
	Technical	Audience	Teaching
Videotaped Interviews With Observers (mathematicians, sociologists, anthropologists, psychologists, teacher educators)	to invite outsiders to view tape and to comment on the lessons or interviews observed. to invite outsiders to class and to comment on the lessons observed		to help users broaden their perspectives in looking at and interpreting teaching and learning	interpretations and analysis of teaching and learning must be made from a variety of perspectives
NCTM Curriculum Standards And Teaching Standards	to create Hypercard stacks with statements of the NCTM standards about curriculum and teaching	to make it possible to access and create links with the NCTM standards	to help users make connections with and interpret reform statements and visions	
State And School District Curriculum Guidelines	to create Hypercard stacks with lists of state and district goals and objectives for mathematics	to make it possible to access and create links with state and district objectives	to help users analyze the language and spirit of curricular requirements as teachers receive them	
District Report Cards And State And Commercial Standardized Tests	examples of report cards required by the school district examples of tests administered to students in mathematics		to help users examine the kinds of benchmarks to which teachers are held responsible	
Videotaped Interviews With Parents	to invite parents to talk alone and in small groups with other parents, reflecting on their own experiences with mathematics and their hopes, and wishes for their children		to make it possible to pursue questions about what parents' reactions are to this teaching	parents' own feelings about mathematics are often anxious; some parents have high expectations for their students' mathematical achievement
Audio Taped Commentary And Analysis By Practicing Teachers And Teacher Education Students	comments by teachers on lessons observed comments by teachers on their own views of mathematics teaching		to help users access the opinions and insights of other experienced and beginning teachers	

that we imagined could represent the study of teaching from the perspective of practice. The ease with which this could be accomplished would mean that such linked collections could be created anew for each class and revised if they did not spark the kind of thinking the instructor had anticipated. New links could be made on the fly and different materials readied for use in response to novices' inquiries and the teacher educator's contextual assessment of their understanding. And, of course, different teacher educators, and even their students, could collect, rearrange, and comment on the records of practice differently in the process of investigating teaching.

In the past 7 years, we have learned more than we ever wanted to know about what it would take to do what we envisioned. Most fundamentally, we learned that what we were able to imagine far outstripped the multimedia hardware and software available at the time to consumers in the educational marketplace. We chronicle the decisions we made to cope with this realization as a backdrop for introducing the electronic learning environment we began to pilot in teacher education courses in 1990.

Collecting and Cataloging Pre-Digital Records

In order for us to use the computer in the way we had imagined, all of the records we collected would need either to be in digital form or to be electronically coded so that the computer could find them. In 1989–90, we did not have access to tools that would make it possible for us to collect records of teaching and learning in digital form. We produced hi-8 videotapes, audio recordings, and still photographs. Black ink on white paper was used for all material that was to be photocopied and later scanned. The only records we could produce digitally from the start were the observation notes and the transcripts. We gambled on the fact that the tools for digitizing the rest of what we were collecting would become cheaper and more widely available in the near term, making the idea of computer storage and software-driven access to materials in multiple media realistic. We began to experiment with scanners and audio and video compression technologies, and we put some of the information like seating charts and problems of the day into graphic form.

Our first attempt to file materials in printed and film form was based on the simple notion of attaching records to a particular *day* or to a particular *student* without cross-referencing. Our decision to put things in only one place was a simple resource issue: The clerical time and effort available to us was already overtaxed with just getting things collected, copied, and labeled. What we could easily file electronically, such as word processed transcripts or observation notes and students' work that had been scanned, was filed using the Macintosh Finder. Here again, we had only enough capacity to put records in one place and we could establish no links between records.[24] As we carried out this filing process, we added crucial pieces of information to the classroom records—students' names and dates. This information was the first step in making the kinds of links we imagined. But we were not able at first to establish electronic relationships among the records.

Learning About Software

We had set out on our quest to collect a rich set of records with visions for an approach to studying these records inspired by demonstrations of Apple's new Hypercard software on reasonably simple and affordable multimedia workstations. What we wound up with was a multifaceted archive produced using various computer applications, which very quickly had outdistanced Hypercard's capacity for making the kinds of relationships among the records that were part of the design we envisioned for using the records in teacher education. The programming required within Hypercard to make dynamic links between, for example, the seating chart for a given day and the work of the students sitting in a particular group or between the lines of a transcript and a segment of videotape, would have entailed several highly competent technicians working full time.[25] Running such programs and storing the volume of data we collected would require hardware far beyond the level of the personal computers ordinarily available in college classrooms and laboratories. When a set of multimedia records is digitized and stored on a computer in a database, they can be rearranged over and over again with no cost in time or technical effort because of the built-in capacities of database systems. Commentaries can be easily added, sorted, and linked without changing the original records. In contrast, using Hypercard with a limited technical staff, we were able only to "hard-wire" links between items in the collection by creating buttons and scripts for buttons. This severely constrained the quantity of material we could work with.

When we collected the records of practice, relational database software that would make a system of even simple cross-referencing available was growing and changing quickly, but at the time we needed it, there was nothing available for use on standard personal computer hardware that could accommodate the sort of multimedia data we had collected in the way we wanted to access it. In a relational database, objects are broken down into table structures, which then can be queried in complex ways to find different parts of the data. Typically, relational databases have been built that deal well with numbers, times, and simple text. Only recently have databases been able to deal in a dynamic way with complicated data such as text with a complex format and multimedia; most databases provide the limited ability to store such complex data as an indistinct unit that can only be saved and retrieved, but not searched or manipulated. The ability of several simultaneous users to store, access, and manipulate data of the type we collected is still on the leading edge of computer science research. Making a user interface that clearly communicates what is there and how to get to it, complicates the problem even further.[26] Even today, with currently available software, we would not be able to do all of these things using the level of computer workstations that we could reasonably expect to provide teacher education students and their instructors.[27]

As we began to recognize these limitations to the hardware and software we had to work with, we set out to design the best approximation of our original vision with the resources at hand, which were, indeed, considerable. We chose to work in Hypercard, even though the linking process was tedious, because it was relatively easy, with a small technical staff, to construct a robust working environment that would be simple for multiple users to operate. We transferred a small subset of the nonvideo data into Hypercard stacks and a small subset of the video data onto videodiscs and made catalogs to access them by date and student, as we had in our other filing systems. We would not be able to have instructors and students make "live" and flexible links between elements of the collection, but we designed tools for finding teacher and student notebook entries according to date and problem of the day, finding video clips by linking them with transcripts, and searching most of these records using keywords. Using the developing graphics capacities of Microsoft Word, screen-level, cut-and-paste software called Capture, and Apple's Quicktime Movie software, we established a system of multimedia "scrapbooks" into which users could paste text, graphic, and video excerpts from the records they had looked at and copied, and comment on them. The scrapbooks could be saved on a server and annotated by other users. We called all of these tools and resources, together with the hardware needed to use them, the "Student Learning Environment."

Technology Meets Pedagogy in Teacher Education

Although it was easy to get sidetracked, both by the "magic" of the technology and the new problems it presented, we recognized that collecting and cataloging the records of practice and designing an environment in which teacher education instructors and their students could use these records was only the first step. In order to make the use of the records educative for college students who sought to study teaching, we needed

to consider *how* the records of practice should be used if they were to provide opportunities for the kind of learning we considered to be important.
The records of practice had to be arranged in relation to tasks that were
designed with particular pedagogical purposes in mind and their use had
to be guided by a teacher educator in ways that would support the construction of knowledge for practice. In addition, we needed to figure out
how we could get teacher educators to use records of practice as a tool for
investigating teaching. There were other models around for using such
materials that did not fit our purposes. We did not see the records of our
practice as illustrative of a particular research finding such that they could
be used to illustrate a theoretical proposition about learning or teaching.
Nor did we see what we were producing as a rhetorically more powerful
"proof" that a particular way of teaching was the right way.

   In the following chapters, we illustrate the kinds of records we collected
and describe the computer environment we created to make them accessible. We analyze the pedagogy we designed in relation to a set of tasks
for teacher education students in the context of an extended example of
student work in a course using the multimedia environment. We end with
a survey of the sorts of work that teacher education instructors and students have done with the records of practice and a summary analysis of
the opportunities these records present for constructing an understanding
of knowledge in and for teaching.

CHAPTER 5

Composing Materials and Curriculum Making

It is September 18, a few days into the new school year. The children in Deborah Ball's third-grade class are working on a problem that she has written on the chalkboard at the beginning of their daily math lesson:

> I have pennies, nickels, and dimes in my pocket.
> If I pull three coins out, what amount of money could I have?

Looking at the videotape of the lesson and the seating chart, we can see that the children are seated at "tables" made up of groups of three, four, or five desks and chairs. The desks and chairs are arranged around the room so that the students face one another.

The class begins with the teacher asking a student to read the problem from the board. She asks how it is linked to a previous problem on which the class has worked. Together with another student, she generates one solution to the problem and writes it on the board. She asks another student to reason through that solution and then assigns the class to work for a few minutes and come up with "different combinations." Most of the time she is talking, the teacher stands in front of a chalkboard which covers one entire wall of the classroom and that looks like it might be the "front" of the room. Otherwise, she walks slowly around the room, pausing periodically near one group or another.

Ball: Can I ask somebody to read the problem on the board? Daniel, could you read it?
Daniel: I have pennies . . . nickels . . . and dimes . . . in . . . my pocket. If . . . I . . . pull three . . . coins . . . out, what . . . amount of money (*pause*) . . . would?
Ball: Put a C. Could.
Daniel: —could I have.
Ball: What problem is this similar to? (*pause*) Chris?
Chris: The one with the coins.

Ball: What number of coins did we work with last week?

Chris: Um, two.

Ball: Two coins. (*pause*) Can somebody give *one* example of an amount of money that you could have? Sean?

Sean: Like you, like, you could have, um . . .

Ball: Could you speak up just a little, I'm not sure that Betsy can hear you.

Sean: You could have like, five—you could like, pull out one of each of them and you could like, you could get, um, 16.

Ball: Okay, one penny, one nickel, and one dime. Is that three coins?

Sean: Uh huh.

Ball: And he says that's 16 cents all together. What do other people think about that? (*pause*) Mei?

Mei: I agree with him.

Ball: How would you get 16 cents?

Mei: Um, one dime would be 10 cents, a nickel, a nickel, 10 cent—wait, a dime is 10 cents and then a nickel is 5 cents and it's 15 cents and if it's a penny it will be 16 cents.

Ball: Okay. I would like you to work on this for a few minutes, and see what different combinations you can figure out and use the money if you want to help you. And then after a little bit we will stop and talk about it together. First I would like you to work on it a little bit alone and see what you can come up with by yourself. Make sure you have the whole problem copied. And then write down whatever you need to write down in your notebook to help you remember what you're figuring out.

We can see on the videotape that the children have actual coins on their desks—pennies, nickels, and dimes. The camera zooms in on one girl working and we can see the notebook in which she is working: a bound quadrille-ruled composition book. Many of the students are sliding coins around on their desks and writing in their notebooks. Some are talking quietly with others at their tables.

After about 12 minutes the teacher asks the class how many solutions they think they will find. Students offer speculations. From time to time, the teacher asks the children if they can hear and reminds them to listen to one another. After a few minutes she asks the students to think about how they might know whether they had found all the possible solutions. Two students venture guesses.

Ball: I have a question to ask. Does anybody have a prediction of how many solutions they think they will find for this problem?

Riba: I'm not that—

Ball: Sean?

Sean: How 'bout around 10.

Ball: Excuse me just a second. Ofala and Mei, can you hear Sean?

Mei: Yeah.

Sean: Around 10.

Ball: Around 10. Is there a reason why you predicted 10?

Sean: Because um, I'm not sure. I'm not . . .

Ball: Any, any different predictions? Mei?

Mei: Nine.

Ball: Anybody else? Mark?

Mark: I've found nine.

Ball: You came up with nine already? Mark has already found nine. How are you going to know when you have all the solutions? (*pause*) Any ideas? How would you know if you had found them all? Lucy?

Lucy: You would start um . . .

Ball: Excuse me just a second, Tembe and Devin, and Harooun, right now Lucy is talking and I would like you to be able to hear her.

Lucy: You would start doing the ones that you've already done over.

Ball: Devin, could you hear Lucy?

Devin: Yes.

Ball: What did she say?

Devin: (*shakes head*)

Ball: Excuse me? Can you say it one more time? I'm sorry. Devin, listen to Lucy, okay? Speak a little louder.

Lucy: Okay. Um, you would start—you would use the, the same ones over again.

Ball: You would use the same ones over again? Anyone have any other ideas of how you would know if you had gotten them all? Is there any other way to tell? (*pause*) Sheena?

Sheena: When we confer with somebody and if they have the same answers as you. If they don't, then you don't have all the answers and you need to write it down, then you'd know you have all them.

Ball: I have a small concern right now. I would like everybody to put their coins down and their pens down. I would like everybody to put their *coins* down and their *pens* down for a moment. One of the things that's very important is that if one person in the class is talking other people need to listen, because people are saying things that can help you think about the problems. Sheena said some interesting things, and so did Lucy, but lots of people were not listening to them. I know it's because you're finding more solutions yourself. But, one of the things that I would really like you to, to see you doing is to listen—to be listening really hard when someone else has an idea, because it might help you with your thinking. I'm sure a lot of people didn't hear Sheena. And I had to ask Lucy to say what she said three times. Stop for a moment now, and listen hard to Sheena and see what you think about what she is saying. Could you say it one more time?

Sheena: Well, when you think you're done, confer with somebody else at your table and if they have the same ones as you do then . . . then, you have all of them and if they don't, then you have to write down the ones they have and they have to write the ones you have.

Ball: So Lucy and Sheena gave us two different ideas. Lucy said when you start repeating yourself in the ideas you come up with, you think you probably have them all. Sheena said—Sheena added something to it. Sheena said when you think you have them all, you can confer with somebody else at your table and see if they found any that you haven't found. Are there any other ways to know if you have all the answers? Mark?

Mark: It's not about the answers.

Ball: So, it's—another comment?

Mark: Yeah.

Ball: What?

Mark: Um, I think it's 10 because I just came up with one more.

Ball: Okay, wow, Mark just came up with one more. He's up to 10 possible answers. Take a few more minutes to work on it and then I would like to spend a few minutes talking about what you've come up with.

At this point, the children return to working on the problem individually and in their small groups. After about 4 minutes, Ball calls them together again. She asks them to share their solutions and asks students to comment on how they think other students arrived at their solutions. At the end of the class, she makes some remarks about the students' listening and the ways in which they were making sense of the problem.

Ball: Let's stop for a moment. Put your coins down. I can tell when people have stopped with the coins, because the coins make a lot of noise. Put the coins down and put the pens down for a moment. You're going to want your pen though, because while we have—while we discuss the problem, if somebody brings up an answer you didn't find, you might like to record it in your notebook. We have one answer recorded on the board, one solution. Who'd like to share another solution they came up with? Harooun?

Harooun: 12.

Ball: Okay, 12 cents. Could somebody tell how Harooun got 12 cents? What coins did Harooun use to get 12 cents? Who thinks they know? Daniel?

Daniel: Um (*pause*) Harooun used dime um, and two pennies.

Ball: What do other people think about what Daniel said? Daniel said he thinks Harooun used two pennies and one dime. What do other people think about that? Lisa?

Lisa: I agree.

Ball: Can you prove that that's right?

Lisa: Yeah, because it's three, three coins.

Ball: Three coins. How can you prove that that's 12 cents?

Lisa: Because . . . 10 and 2 is 12 and that's three coins.

Ball: Any comments? Lucy?

Lucy: I agree with that.

Ball: Anybody disagree with it? (*pause*) Okay, another solution? Another possible way to do this problem? No, I just asked you. Somebody different? Betsy?

Betsy: I got 7 cents.

Ball: Who thinks they know how Betsy got 7 cents? Tembe?

Tembe: A nickel and two pennies.

Ball: Cassandra? What do you think about what Tembe said?

Cassandra: I agree with him.

Ball: Can you prove that, that's 7 cents?

Cassandra: Yeah. Because um, a nickel and two pennies is—a nickel is 5 cents and two pennies will add to 7 cents.

Ball: Comments from anybody else? Anybody disagree with this? Okay, do we have another solution? How about Ofala, do you have something different in your notebook? (*pause*)

Ofala: 30 cents.

Ball: How much?

Ofala: 30.

Ball: Ofala, do you want to tell us how you got it or should we ask if other people can figure it out?

Ofala: Three dimes.

Ball: Okay, three dimes. Jeannie, what do you think about what Ofala said?

Jeannie: I think she's right.

Ball: Why do you think she's right?

Jeannie: Because . . . 10 plus 10 is 20 and plus another 10 is 30.

Ball: Any comments from anybody else? Daniel?

Daniel: 25.

Ball: Oh, you're already giving another one?

Daniel: Uh huh.

Ball: Did you agree with Jeannie?

Daniel: Um, yeah.

Ball: Okay, what is your solution?

Daniel: 15.

Ball: 15. Who thinks they know how Daniel got 15 cents? Lisa?

Lisa: Um, three nickels.

Ball: Sean, what do you think about that?

Sean: (*pause*) I'm not sure.

Ball: Why are you not sure? (*pause*) What are you figuring out?

Sean: Oh.

Ball: Sean, how much is one nickel?

Sean: Uh, 5 cents. And two nickels are 10 cents and three nickels are 15.

Ball: So—Do you agree with this then or disagree?

Sean: Um, agree.

Ball: We're going to stop. I would like everyone to look over this way for a moment. When we start math tomorrow, we're going to continue with this problem a little bit longer. I have a question to ask before we stop and a comment to make. I'll make my comment first and then ask my question. My comment was, I thought people did a better job just now listening to each other's solutions and giving each other time. Did you notice that when somebody was figuring something out people weren't going *uh, uh, uh* (*raises hand eagerly*) or interrupting, people were listening and thinking about whether it made sense. Did you notice that? And did you also notice that people were explaining why it made sense. Like people would say, it's 30 cents because—Jeannie said because 10 plus 10 is 20 and 10 more is 30. Was that a good explanation? It was a good explanation because it helped us understand why that answer made sense.

What we have "seen" here are excerpts from a mathematics lesson in the third-grade class. What we could imagine seeing on the tape has been supplemented by the seating chart for that day, a copy of the problem the students were working on, and a transcript. Using these as we watched, we could associate names and locations in the room with speakers and "hear" more clearly. We could watch the elements of the problem be taken up by the students, and we could trace the teacher's role in the ongoing evolution of the problem.

STUDYING THE RECORDS OF PRACTICE

We turn next to look in on a class of preservice teacher education students who have just watched this piece of videotape in the second week of their mathematics methods course. The tape has provided a "common text" for the class and the instructor to look at together as they begin their study of teaching. That it is a common text affords the instructor the opportunity to learn how the teacher education students are thinking. The instructor asks, "So what thoughts or questions do you have about what you have seen here? I would like you to get into your work groups and discuss what stood out to you in the segment we watched. What questions does it raise for you? What do you think is going on? What do you want to know more about?"

Teacher Education Students' Reactions

As we walk around the room, we overhear snatches of the prospective teachers' conversations.

> Is it a good idea to give the kids actual money? In my school, someone would probably be tempted to steal it.
> Yeah, but it's a good idea to make problems real world so that the work is meaningful.
> They use a pretty sophisticated vocabulary—we don't even talk like that in some of my college classes. Is this typical?
> I wonder if this is a gifted class. Most third graders can't talk like this.
> The teacher doesn't say much—she doesn't do anything to reinforce the kids who are getting it right. And she doesn't tell them when things are wrong. I would think it would be frustrating for them not to get any feedback from her.
> Yes, but you know I was always afraid of being wrong in math class. I bet these kids feel a lot more comfortable.

> But how will they know whether they are getting it?
> This is a neat problem!
> I am trying to figure out the answer. Is eight right?
> I wonder whether the other teachers in this school also do this.
> How does the teacher decide whom to call on?
> The teacher does a lot of probing of kids' thinking. Whenever I had teachers who did that, it usually meant that the answers were wrong. That doesn't seem to be what she is doing, because, look, these answers are all right.

I would think that it would be confusing to work on a problem that has so many different answers. Can third graders really handle that? Don't they get confused?

The teacher seems to take a lot of time away from math telling them to listen to one another, not to interrupt, and so on. I think if she would put them in small groups and not be trying to have a whole-group lesson, they would be more engaged. A lot of kids simply aren't able to attend in this setting. My cooperating teacher would never stand for that. She would have consequences for students who weren't paying attention.

It seems like they spend a lot of time going over and over the same thing. I used to hate when teachers did that. It seems like they are beating the question to death. It's not that complicated a problem.

I remember in math classes that everything went by me so fast. I think I would have liked being able to work on something for some time like this. Maybe I would have been good at math if I could have gotten to do this.

Yes, but don't they need to get through everything they are supposed to learn in third grade? How can they do that if they work so long on one simple problem at a time? She can't do this every day.

How Might We Understand These Reactions?

As we have observed, prospective teachers come to the study of teaching and learning already knowing a lot about the object of their study. The teacher education students in this discussion interpret what they see on the tape by relating it to something that they know. They understand what is going on in Ball's classroom on September 18. It is not something new or unfamiliar.

When they watch the teacher, they remember how they felt when they gave answers in class. They remember how much they valued praise and feared error. Assuming the need to get through the textbook, they worry about covering the curriculum and being prepared for tests and the next grade. Their own preferences and experiences shape their impressions of the interest and appropriateness of the classwork. Their ideas about young children are rooted in their experiences as baby-sitters, camp counselors, teacher aides, and older siblings. Overall, they tend to assert more and ask less, for they think they already know a lot. They believe that what they need to learn is what to *do*, not what to see or hear.

What we see is that prospective teachers know about teaching from having watched it happening around them in school since they were in kindergarten. Teacher education adds to this prior experience. They spend time in classrooms, something they tend to think is the most valuable part of their professional program, and yet their field experiences often do little more than reinforce what they already know from their own experience as students. In classes they learn about Piaget and motivation, about co-operative learning and reinforcement, about set induction and checking for understanding. They read about gender and socialization, about child development and theories of reading instruction. They develop professional language.

Still, although theoretical knowledge pokes through their interpretations, most of the typical comments in reaction to the videotape above reflect teacher candidates' "case knowledge." Organized in terms of specific instances or cases that one has been a part of, read, or heard about, this case knowledge enables them to see instances on the video as similar to other classroom events. For example, the teacher education student who said, "I would think it would be frustrating for them not to get any feedback from her," may have been connecting what she saw Ball do on the tape with an experience she had or a classroom in which she watched. For her, this event was a case of the teacher doing something that would frustrate rather than facilitate learning, and based on her experience she felt that she knew what would happen in such cases. The prospective teacher who worried how the curriculum could be covered was probably relying on her own experiences with classes and textbooks, remembering chapters and ideas that were rushed through just before tests or the end of the year.

Shaping Reactions into Investigations

In Chapter 3, we explored the nature of teaching as a practice and what that implies for teacher education. We argued that, because teaching is uncertain and complex work, teachers are faced with having to construct knowledge as they work. They must make and test conjectures, invent new ideas and approaches, collect and interpret data, and analyze, construct, and challenge assertions. This view of teaching led us to claim that learning to teach entails learning how to construct and use knowledge in practice. It also entails learning to appreciate the situated nature of knowing in practice. Preservice teacher education, therefore, must seek to prepare teachers to reason wisely, to develop responses and courses of action in response to particulars, to extend and improvise beyond that which they have acquired or done before.

Given that, what do the prospective teachers who reacted to the records of teaching and learning from Ball's class on September 18 need to learn in order for them to develop these pedagogical ways of knowing? Their comments in response to the concreteness of the videotape help us as teacher educators to understand more of their current thinking. We notice that they tend to rely most on theoretical constructs (such as "reinforcement") or unmediated firsthand case knowledge. They have acquired these in the two conventional components of teacher education, college courses and classroom field experiences; they also rely significantly on their prior experience as students. They tend, however, to lack interpretive and contextual knowledge, often speaking with more conclusiveness than is warranted by the information available to them. The teacher education students who viewed the videotape of Ball's class asserted what they saw to be happening in the class, taking the video to be a representation of "real-world" events. But agreeing on what is happening in a classroom is not a simple matter. Neither is it merely academic analysis. How the teacher interprets what is happening becomes part of her actions. If she decides she is facing a case of frustration, she will act accordingly. If she thinks what she sees is a case of engagement, she may take a different next step. In teaching, thought and action are intimately intertwined. Hence, in order to act responsibly as a teacher, one must ask two kinds of questions: What evidence do I have that the students are indeed "frustrated" and "overwhelmed"? What evidence do I have that they are engaged? And what other interpretations could I imagine placing on the evidence available to me?

Missing from the teacher education students' statements of what was happening on the tape was a curiosity about the context in which the viewed segment of the lesson occurred. They do not even raise any questions about the context, suggesting that this is not a salient feature in their thinking about what is entailed in understanding a piece of teaching. Yet knowledge of context plays a crucial role in careful interpretation and thoughtful action. For example, that half the children were not native English speakers and that four of them were new to the school are important to understanding what is happening on the tape. Knowing that students had worked on a similar problem the day before is another important piece of contextual information. What the teacher education students need to develop is an increased capacity for judging what and when action is appropriate in a given time and place—they are not simply missing knowledge of the context of this particular lesson. What they are missing is an appreciation for context as an aspect of pedagogical knowledge. Lacking such contextual knowledge, they do not seem to notice how important this lack is. They also are missing an appreciation for the underdetermined and interpretive nature of knowing. They speak with certainty, not tentativeness.

In the following sections of this chapter, we describe the multimedia environment we designed to support prospective teachers' investigation of teaching with an eye toward helping them develop capacities related to interpretive and contextual aspects of knowing in teaching.[1] (The rationale for this approach and the history of our work with new technologies are found in Chapters 1 through 4.) In addition to describing the sort of materials and tools we developed for this environment, we also discuss a framework for what is entailed in creating educative experiences with them.

EXPANDING THE COMMON TEXT

The multimedia environment we developed has three components:

1. a subset of all of the records of practice we collected in the form of electronic graphic and print documents and videodiscs
2. notebooks in which collections and annotations can be stored and displayed
3. tools for finding particular records, copying and collecting them, and attaching annotations to them

These components are assembled in computer hardware and software workstations for use by teacher education students in preservice courses and lab settings. Although the multimedia environment does not represent the full-blown hypermedia system we imagined, it was a start on building something that could work reliably in programmatic settings, thus making it possible for us to learn about the potential of such technologies for supporting a new pedagogy of teacher education as the technologies themselves were developing rapidly.

Records

Over the course of 5 years of development, three sets of records have been included in the multimedia environment: "Beginnings," which represents teaching and learning in Ball's classroom in September; "Fractions," a set from Ball's classroom in April through June of the same academic year, and "Time/Speed/Distance," a collection of records from a unit in Lampert's classroom in October and November. These time periods were not selected by chance. We chose them for several reasons. Including the first few weeks of the year seemed important because people often want to know what the children and the class were like at the beginning of the year, and we thought that much good work could be structured for teacher education students around what we called "Beginnings." The records from the spring of third grade offered the complementary opportunity to explore the end of the year and to ask about and pursue comparisons between the beginning and the end of the year. How did particular children change across the year? How did the class discussions evolve? What did the children seem to be learning? Was the teacher's role different at different points? In addition, this period was when the third grade was studying fractions, a mathematical topic we thought particularly fruitful for prospective teachers to consider. The unit we took from Lampert's classroom was selected because it represented a period when the classroom was already established, and the kinds of problems and mathematical content that students were working on offered viewers a substantial opportunity to focus on mathematics and mathematical representations and connections. The fifth graders' written work was rich and complex, and we thought it provided access to student work in ways that could be very useful. The content of this unit also made it possible to compare third-grade and fifth-grade work with rational numbers.

Each of these sets of records includes the full teacher's journal from the period and all of the students' work (daily classwork, homework, and quizzes); video catalogs of excerpts from lessons and of interviews with teacher and students; and transcripts of the video. A point-and-click menu gives the user access to these records of practice, as well as to his or her own notebook, to the text of the National Council of Teachers of Mathematics Curriculum Standards and Professional Teaching Standards ("other materials"), and to notes taken in the class in which the user is enrolled (see Figure 5.1).

The multimedia environment menu window provides a way to access the different kinds of records of teaching and learning that are available. Except for the video, all of the data is filed in Hypercard stacks. There are also stacks that provide a catalog of the video available on videodiscs. Each dataset gives the user access to a unique set of children's portfolios and video transcripts. After choosing which dataset to explore, the arrow buttons ⊡ can be used to

- Create a new user notebook or open an existing user notebook.
- Open the teacher's journal.
- Open the children's portfolios that are available for the dataset selected.
- Open the video transcripts that are available for the dataset selected. The user can get information about what is on each videodisc from the video catalogs.
- Open the video catalogs that are available from the dataset selected.
- Open other materials that are independent of the dataset selected. The user will find the Curriculum Standards and the Professional Teaching Standards here.
- Open class notes from the course in which the user is enrolled.

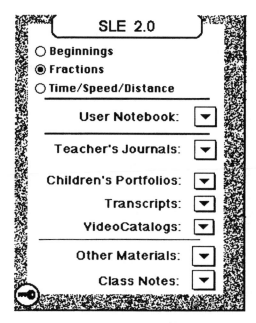

FIGURE 5.1. User entry to the multimedia environment.

Each type of material is cataloged to make particular items accessible. Children's work and teacher journal pages are indexed by class date and the mathematics problem of the day. Video segments are accessible through a video catalog, an index that provides an abbreviated table of contents for each videodisc, with times and brief descriptions of classroom activity.

In selecting videos to include in the multimedia environment from all those we had collected, we strove to maintain the class sequences as much as possible, cutting out things only when we needed to due to limits of storage media and resources. We decided to use videodiscs because of the speed and accuracy of access that they afforded as compared with videotape, and we chose videodisc over digitized video because of the large storage requirements of digitized video at the time.[2] It was crucial to us that the video be as clear and easy to view as we could possibly make it; this seemed important for the kind of close analysis and careful viewing that we wanted to support.

For similar reasons of maintaining clarity, the children's work was scanned electronically at full size, which at the time required 21" computer monitors in order to view the pages well. Although this raised the cost and made our materials less "transportable" from one computer setup to another, it seemed important for teacher education students to be able to see the children's work as clearly as possible. The teachers' journals were typed rather than scanned. (The scans of the original handwritten journals were very difficult to read.) Typing made it possible to do word searches on the text the teacher had written.

We decided to include transcripts of the video that was available on the videodiscs. The transcripts were a resource that could be studied closely, used to assist viewers in listening as they watched the video, and used for word searches and navigating the video. Although one might argue that beginning teachers need to learn to listen through children's mumbled statements, soft voices, overlapping talk, nonverbal communication, and emergent language, we wanted to make available a resource that could support such learning. In the multimedia environment, they could have a support unavailable in real time.

Notebooks

Users of the multimedia environment keep track of their investigations in notebooks. Individual and group notebooks can be created and saved for later revision, presentation, or review by the instructor. These collection and thinking "spaces" were modeled—in both appearance and function—after the notebooks that the children keep in Lampert's and Ball's elementary classes. The user notebooks are intended to be a record of the user's multiple "journeys" across the terrain of teaching, complete with artifacts collected along the way. Each week, the current version of the notebook is saved as a record of the students' work up to that point, but since these are electronic documents, they can be edited and revised easily to reflect repeated journeys over the same territory.

The electronic notebook first appears as a blank cover on which the user can type his or her name and add graphic embellishments. (An example of a completed student notebook is included in Appendix A.) Using a common word processing program, users type in their notes and record their thinking about the student work, teacher journal pages, and video of lessons that they study. Copies of all three forms of records can be pasted into the notebook and annotated with the graphics tools that are in the word processing program.

In the elementary classrooms and in the multimedia environment, the notebooks serve as a place for teacher education students, as they work individually and in small groups, to prepare for the whole-class discussions. In these whole-group discussions, ideas and meanings are shared and negotiated, arguments are made, and evidence is given. Students try to convince one another of particular ideas or conclusions, drawing on the work they have done in their own notebooks.

Tools

Two types of tools are available in the multimedia environment: navigation tools that make it possible to get at the records, and construction tools that enable users to cut and paste from the records into their notebooks. To select a particular item, users first identify the type of record they wish to see (e.g., teacher journal, video catalog) and then select the particular date, child, or entry. The system quickly brings up the identified record (see Figure 5.2).

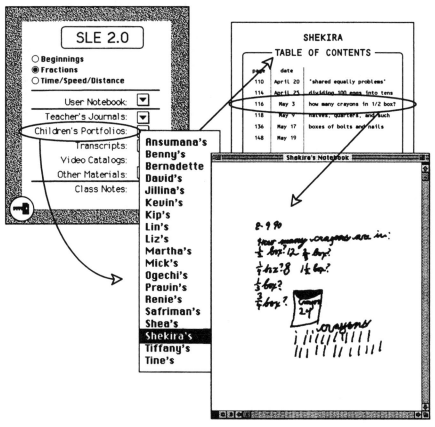

FIGURE 5.2. Examples of different types of records.

Within text records (e.g., teacher's journal, transcripts), users also can search further within the record to find particular dates, names, or topics. Such information is literally available on the surface of the records; no interpretation is needed to look for every instance of a particular girl speaking during a specific day. We made a deliberate choice not to design a means to search for interpretive categories of information. For example, we might have chosen to make it possible for users to search for all instances of children offering incorrect answers in whole-group discussions, arguments, or the teacher providing information. To do this, we would have had to code the records ourselves, using our own definitions of "incorrect answers," "arguments," or "teacher telling." We thought that this sort of interpretation was central to learning to teach and so we did not want to do this for prospective teachers. We wanted instead for instructors to design means for their students to develop this interpretive capacity in the context of their work in the multimedia environment.

Construction tools, such as Capture[sw] software and various features of Word, allow users to select, copy, and paste specific excerpts from the children's notebooks, the teachers' journals, and the lesson transcripts into their own notebooks. In addition, there are tools for annotating the information pasted in one's notebook, as well as tools for drawing and writing. Users also are able to copy, paste, and comment on bits of classroom video.[3]

Multimedia Workstations

Each workstation includes a powerful computer allowing it to run many programs simultaneously and to support the integrated viewing of text, graphics, and video. A software package is installed on each machine including Hypercard, Word, and Capture[sw]. Each machine is equipped with a 17" high resolution monitor for displaying both computer and video output, and a 20" monitor for displaying actual-size teacher and student notebooks. Video input comes from a videodisc player and a videotape player at each station. A speaker and several sets of headphones are available for listening to audio. The classrooms in which teacher education students meet and work with this environment contain nine linked workstations and a "lead workstation" with slightly higher-end equipment from which presentations can be made to the whole class. All workstations are connected to a file server where student notebooks are stored.

The multimedia classroom also includes a seminar area, with dual projectors and a keyboard that can display and control any computer in the room. The projection wall uses a special wallpaper that can be used as a whiteboard as well as a projection surface. This makes it possible for students to display something easily from their own work for the entire class.

FROM A MULTIMEDIA ENVIRONMENT
TO CURRICULUM AND PEDAGOGY

Although it was certainly a challenge, gathering and organizing records of practice and designing tools for accessing, navigating, and manipulating them was only the beginning of our work in designing a new pedagogy of teacher education. Next we faced the problem of figuring out how to use these materials to support prospective teachers' learning. One step in solving this problem was to develop tasks that could create *opportunities for learning*. Another was to develop an interactive role for the instructor such that these opportunities for learning were in fact *educative*. The composition of pedagogy necessarily involves both anticipatory design of materials and tasks, and the interactive development of the curriculum in action.

An example from the teaching of elementary school mathematics may help to clarify why we could not simply produce materials—in this case, a multimedia environment in which intending teachers could examine records of practice. In mathematics teaching, many advocate the use of manipulatives and other materials to help children learn mathematical ideas. Designers of these materials have given careful attention to representing fundamental mathematics. Teachers bring well-conceived materials like base ten blocks, fraction bars, and multilink pieces into their classrooms. Some offer them to students as a transitional support to the "real thing"—that is, manipulating symbolic expressions rather than blocks— while others teach as though touching the materials automatically gives meaning to the ideas.[4] Some recognize that the materials themselves do not inherently carry the content to learners, and they develop problems and tasks designed to focus children's attention on the key ideas. Yet even when they are given well-designed tasks to do, children do not necessarily see the mathematics that their teachers want them to see.[5] They often draw conclusions quite different from those aligned with the conventional mathematics their teachers expect them to learn.[6] Without careful attention to what students are to learn and to how the teacher is to mediate between particular learners and these learning goals, manipulatives alone will not help students learn important mathematical ideas. In other contexts, investigating materials without an orienting task, and without a teacher to mediate the sense that learners are making, is similarly problematic. In no field is learning reliably produced by simply putting learners in contact with materials. The same pedagogical challenges arise in using primary sources in the study of history, for instance, or in using literary texts in the study of language or in observing physical phenomena in the study of science. In these subjects, too, designing a pedagogy also

must include purposeful attention to tasks and to what it takes for students
to be productively engaged in the materials.[7] This includes attention to the
teacher's role and to the nature of classroom discourse.

The same challenges face teacher educators who use records of practice such as those in the multimedia environment to help prospective teachers learn. Curricular thinking in teacher education must consider fundamental purposes: What is it about practice—about teaching and learning,
about children and their mathematics, about classrooms—that we want
teacher education students to learn from their studies in the multimedia
environment? What kinds of tasks can we design in these materials that
can provide a medium for that learning to occur? What is the role of the
teacher educator in helping teacher education students learn things from
those tasks using these materials?

Designing Curriculum

The records of practice in the multimedia environment provide teacher
education students with opportunities to examine views of teaching, learning, classrooms, children, and mathematics, that they may never encounter otherwise. The tools in the environment offer them the capacity to access and manipulate records that make it possible to consider questions
impossible in real life. For instance, prospective teachers, watching a class
discussion taking place in September, often wonder whether the students
will ever progress beyond solving the three coin problem if they continue
to work so intensively on one problem. They wonder about particular children and they wonder about the class as a whole. When they see the children later in the year, they wonder: How did the teacher teach them to do
what they are doing? These are excellent questions, important from a host
of perspectives. But only with records of practice can they be pursued directly. In a field placement, a prospective teacher would be limited to asking the classroom teacher to explain what and how learning occurred
across the year. The prospective teacher's opportunity to pursue this
issue would depend on the depth and detail of the teacher's recollections,
and even then would be accessible only by listening to the teacher's interpretations. This is very different from what is possible for prospective
teachers to do in the environment where they can instantly locate and
view a video to compare a lesson in September with one in May. They
can read the teacher's journal to see if she makes mention of a particular
matter at either time. They can compare students' work at these two points
in time. Even if prospective teachers spend all year in a field placement
and therefore are able to see the classroom evolve, they do not have the
capacity to juxtapose simultaneously images and information from both

points in time, as they can in the environment, and to discipline their investigation of these questions.

Still, the mere availability of these sorts of records constitutes no more than the opportunity to examine some question about the development of the classroom. An opportunity to examine questions such as the multimedia environment provides does not in itself yield a pedagogy for helping prospective teachers frame and pursue appropriate questions. It is not an opportunity to *learn teaching* unless the questions intending teachers pursue take them in the direction of the big ideas in teaching. They may not be able to develop a fruitful question. An example of a less useful question is one that is framed with so many foundational assumptions that it is difficult to pursue. For example, prospective teachers sometimes ask, "Does this classroom work equally well for the fast and slow kids?" This question assumes that some students are "slow" and others "fast." Without some help in reframing or designing a pursuit for this question, a prospective teacher quickly will run aground or simply will reinforce her assumptions that some students are slow and others are not. Just as in any inquiry, what is learned is fundamentally shaped by the initiating question and the capacity to identify and work with and against one's entering assumptions—to be surprised by the evidence.[8]

In Chapter 3 we posited that a central aim of teacher education is to put beginning teachers in a position where they have the capacity to knit the resources of theory with those of practice as they explore "big ideas" in knowing teaching. Just as place value and functions are big ideas in knowing mathematics, discourse, curriculum, the teacher's role, and classroom culture are all big ideas in knowing teaching. Ideas such as these can afford a power to know, perform, make connections, and learn, as a function of their central conceptual role in practice. As with the idea of place value in mathematics, the importance of these ideas to the practitioner lies in their power to identify and manage problems in the domain. Just as there are many ways to "know" a mathematical idea like place value, some of which are more powerful in practice than others, there are many ways to know about an idea like the teacher's role. Our challenge was to design a pedagogy that would enable teacher education students to know such ideas in a way that would be powerful for them in practice.

Rather than seeing theory as determining practice, or seeing practice as developing wholly from firsthand experience, the challenge is for beginning teachers to develop both knowledge about teaching and teaching itself. The work in the multimedia environment has the potential to be different from most consideration of theory and yet can be designed to be an opportunity for developing theoretical knowledge and ways of knowing. The work also has the potential to be different from field experience and yet can be designed to be an opportunity to develop practical knowledge and ways of knowing. Most important, and perhaps most challenging, the work can be designed to intertwine the investigation of practice with the examination and development of theory in ways that integrate rather than fracture their relations.

In the next two chapters we examine two scenarios for curriculum development work in the context of a new pedagogy of teacher education that seeks to engage learners at the intersection of theory and practice. In Chapter 6, we examine one approach more rooted in response to learners, and in Chapter 7, another more rooted in anticipatory design. The first puts the instructor in the role of following students' explorations and, equipped with a sense of big ideas and important domains for learning, responding to and directing students' work in the environment. In this mode, the development of curriculum occurs largely interactively, guided by the instructor's internal map of the big ideas and processes in learning teaching. We examine a collection of students' work produced from this curricular path. The second approach to using multimedia records of practice, which we take up in Chapter 7, emphasizes the design of tasks aimed at focusing teacher education students' work in particular directions.

Making Experience Educative in Learning to Teach

Even with a question that provides an opportunity to learn teaching, prospective teachers may not be sure to what elements they should attend.[9] Bringing what they know to look at questions about a classroom means that they are inevitably limited by what they have been able to learn as students. These limits affect both the questions they know to ask and the means they have for pursuing their questions. Prospective teachers would likely be able to notice that the class looks and behaves differently in September than it does in April, but probably would not have useful ways of seeing and probing such differences. For instance, they might notice that children speak more in the spring than they do in the fall, but might not know how to notice specific features of what the teacher is saying and doing and the relation between that and what the students say. They might not know that it would be productive to probe the different kinds of questions or tempo or tones of voice used by the teacher. Inexperienced with theoretical and analytic issues related to discourse and norms, prospective teachers looking at tape may learn little more than they already know to see or to think about. Such interaction with these materials would be unlikely to be educative toward the purpose of learning to teach, for it would not contribute to prospective teachers' increasing capacity to learn in and from their experience, reinforcing instead what they already know. Just as manipulating multilink cubes or wooden blocks does not inevitably develop young children's concepts of place value or multiplication, merely viewing videotape will not inevitably develop prospective teachers' conceptions of classroom norms and environment. The context of the opportunity—multimedia records of practice—must be coupled with fruitful means of interacting with that context in order for the experience to be educative.[10] How learning to teach can be educatively situated in practice is the question that underlies most fundamentally the design work of using the multimedia environment in teacher education. Shaping a role for the instructor that will move prospective teachers from their initial responses to the teaching under study toward a fruitful line of inquiry, is central to this design work.[11] In the next section we discuss the investigation project, an assignment we developed and used in the courses we and our colleagues taught. The investigation project represents the first phase of our thinking about the interactive construction of curriculum in teacher education; in Chapter 6, we examine how teacher education students' work on this assignment developed and what we learned from looking closely at the assignment and at the evolution of students' projects.

THE INVESTIGATION PROJECT

The rationale for the investigation project (an example of this assignment can be found in Appendix B) was articulated to the students on the written assignment sheet:

> We believe that learning how to ask and pursue questions is central to being a good teacher and to learning how to continue learning on your own—from your own practice as a teacher. This project is designed to help you learn to do that, as well as to give you an opportunity to define and pursue an issue of interest to you. For this project you will plan and carry out an inquiry related to some issue of teaching and learning mathematics, using the materials in the environment as the context and medium for your investigation. To do this, you will first frame and define a question and focus for your investigation. Then you will use the multimedia environment to create a collection of evidence or information related to your question. You will analyze what you are finding, formulate a tentative conjecture about an answer to your question or about your topic, and support it with the evidence you have been able to uncover. Then you will organize your collection, arranging and annotating it to show your tentative analysis and findings. You will make a short presentation in class based on your investigation. Specifics about each part of the project are explained below.

Project Design

The parts of the project were:

- Identify and articulate a starting point for your investigation.
- Create a collection of items or evidence as you pursue your question.
- Make a presentation of some of your examples, including commentary on what you think they show related to your question or focus.
- Write an analysis of what your collection suggests about your original question (put in your notebook).
- Appraise your work on this project (put in your notebook).

What inspired the development of this task? What ideas—about practice, teacher education students as learners, and means of engaging teacher education students in learning teaching—undergirded its structure and design?

Considering Inquiry as Content. The investigation assignment did not have a particular a priori substantive focus. What was to be investigated was deliberately left open. It was designed instead to focus on the processes of pedagogical inquiry. Because learning to teach involves learning to inquire into teaching and learning, to frame and pursue questions, gather and interpret evidence, analyze information, and reformulate issues, this assignment sought to create an opportunity for prospective teachers to identify an area of concern or interest, develop a strategy for pursuing it, collect and interpret information, and reach a new understanding of the original inquiry. Still, depending on what particular teacher education students decided they wanted to investigate, much of the task remained to be designed.

Considering Prospective Teachers as Learners. Since this project was designed to focus on processes of knowing in teaching, we considered what we knew about prospective teachers' approaches to knowing. We knew that they have many questions. We knew that they also make many assumptions that are not well founded. We imagined that this assignment would provide us with ways of surfacing and responding to teacher education students' ideas, and of helping them pursue the ideas and learn with and from their investigations. We expected that they would be glad for the opportunity to pursue something that they had been puzzling about. Some of these puzzles, we assumed, would grow out of the particulars of Ball's third-grade teaching or Lampert's fifth-grade class. But some might emanate from some more general idea, interest, or curiosity. Finally, we knew that they were not likely to have thought a lot about where to look for evidence of different kinds regarding questions of teaching and learning, and that this assignment would put them explicitly in the position of seeking and using appropriate evidence. An example of this might be their common concern for whether children are engaged. They often base their claims on whether children are talking in class, not appreciating the complexity of defining and determining "engagement."

Considering Learners of Teaching. Designing a way for prospective teachers to shape their questions or concerns into investigations seemed likely to us to be fruitful. The context of investigations would offer us many opportunities to guide the development of their capacities to structure and carry out a reasoned inquiry. We saw advantages in letting them identify their own investigation topics, because they would be engaged in seeking answers, looking for related information, and trying to make sense of evidence, all in pursuit of an issue or question about which they were concerned. Although the identification of a question was left unstructured, we structured the assignment to guide the *process* of investigating. For example, we asked students to identify an interest and then confer with the instructor. This step was crucial because prospective teachers did not always identify investigatable or fruitful topics. Sometimes their questions were not pursuable, for example, wanting to know what happened to children the next year in math class or whether parents helped with homework. The records of practice did not include this kind of information. Sometimes students wanted to know how "low ability" children fared in "this kind of teaching" or what students who were unengaged were learning. These and others like them were potentially good questions, but were loaded with assumptions about "ability," "engagement," and the like. Because questions like this were common, instructors had an important and challenging role to play in helping shape students' work so that prospective teachers might surface and examine their assumptions as well as pursue their questions.

The investigation assignment was designed to guide the process of collecting and making sense of information. It asked students to create a collection of items and evidence pertinent to *their* topics and to work at taking stock of what they were gathering, asking themselves what sense they were making about what they were seeing: "Analyze what you are finding—what sense do you make of what you are seeing and reading? What conjectures are you developing and what new questions are beginning to take shape?" The emphasis was intended to be on inquiry, on asking and re-asking questions, on reformulating and improving hunches and queries.

In order to help this process, we had prospective teachers make presentations to the class before they completed their projects. We hoped that pushing them to talk about their ideas before they were done would encourage them to think about what they might be seeing. Although all versions of the assignment made reference to this stance, one version was particularly explicit about the role of the class presentation.

> You are not completing a finished product. We expect your hunches to be tentative and your examples to be incomplete. Think of the presentation as a chance to try out some of your thinking for your analysis, and to get comments and questions from the rest of the class that can help in completing your project.

Because we knew of prospective teachers' tendency to see matters of practice as cut and dried, and their lack of a sense of the contextualized and interpretive nature of knowing in teaching, we peppered the assignment with words intended to incline them toward a stance of inquiry and conjecture. Conclusions were described as "tentative," "hunches" were promoted, and issues had "conflicting sides." We asked them to articulate the conclusions they had reached "for now." Everything in the tone and specific directions of the assignment was intended to encourage careful speculation rather than definitive answers.

The task was designed to engage prospective teachers in formulating and exploring complex and important questions in the domain of teaching practice and in learning what is entailed in asking and pursuing such questions. In order to provide an opportunity for prospective teachers to focus on issues that mattered to them, we also decided to let them select and define the focus of their inquiry. This decision had important consequences for the work of instructors, for much of what constituted the actual tasks in which individual teacher education students engaged was constructed interactively with students. An alternative might have been to develop two or three fruitful inquiry topics in advance and ask students to select one. In this scenario, instructors would retain in advance more control over the design of the project. As we did it, however, the project tilted away from anticipatory design and leaned heavily on instructors creating the task interactively with students. After examining students' work, we will return to the question of what it takes to make such work educative.

Constructing Curriculum Interactively

Returning to the teacher education class we saw at the beginning of this chapter affords us an opportunity to see the investigation assignment germinate. Consider the responses of teacher education students to Ball's lesson on September 18. How might we develop an educative curriculum given their responses? We begin with some attention to the mathematics in the lesson, engaging teacher education students in the content of the lesson they will watch. Before showing the "records" we looked at above, the instructor does the three coin problem with the teacher education students. At this point, the teacher educator plays the role of a mathematics teacher, and the teacher education students play the role of mathematics learners. This beginning also serves to prepare teacher education students to see and hear in the third-grade classroom.

In posing the same problem to the teacher education students that Ball posed to her third graders, the instructor's educational aim is twofold: One aim is to help prospective teachers enhance their own content knowledge, their own mathematical understanding and insight, problem-solving strategies, and experience with representing and talking about mathematics. Such experiences can help them develop not only mathematical knowledge, but also intellectual confidence and even appreciation and enjoyment. An additional aim, situated in this case, is to develop prospective teachers' mathematical "filters"; such filters for viewing lessons are crucial to "hearing" the children's talk about the same mathematics, "seeing" the teacher's moves as she helps children move around the big ideas, and tracking the classroom discourse. Pursuing these two aims, the instructor seeks to make this opportunity to "be a mathematics learner" in a teacher education class an educative experience for prospective teachers.

After working on the mathematics they will see in the third-grade classroom, the teacher education class views the tape and breaks into small groups to discuss the segment. Their assignment is to comment on what questions it raises for them, what they think is going on, and what they want to know more about. The teacher educator gets a sense of their initial reactions from what she can overhear as she walks around among the groups. The instructor then shifts the discussion to a more public forum, bringing the whole class together, asking for their comments, and writing them on an overhead projector slide for all to see.

From Local to Public Talk. The language for talking about the teaching on the videotape becomes more formal as the teacher education students begin to speak in the public setting of a whole-class discussion led by the instructor rather than in the local register of a small-group conversation with peers. The teacher educator shifts the mode of discourse away from one in which learners are making sense of the teaching on the video in terms of familiar past and currently shared experience. She moves toward a way of talking about teaching in which they might question the assumptions growing out of that experience. When a "comment" made in class discussion is put up on the screen for all to see, it becomes an opportunity for reflection rather than an ephemeral contribution. The role of the instructor here has been to shift what sociolinguists call "the participant framework" in which learning occurs, changing the responsibility of the learners for their own learning. By revoicing the students' comments and making them public, the teacher educator both reformulates the language, orienting it toward inquiry, and gives students a "bigger voice," serving to relay the contribution, originally directed at the instructor, back to the entire group.[12] Students are thus put in a different relationship to one another and in relation to the content under study.

The class ends with teacher education students writing in their journals about which question is of most interest to them and why. The instructor collects the journals in order to glance through their recent writing and also to read their specific comments on this day's initial exploration and discussion. Having access to students' writing offers the instructor an additional representation of their current ideas, interests, and ways of looking at teaching and learning, information useful in planning for class.

From Comments to Questions and Conjectures. In preparation for the next class meeting, the teacher educator takes phrases that appeared on the overhead and transforms them into a list of questions and conjectures. These are made into a handout for the next class meeting. Where students had disagreed with other students in their commentaries on the video excerpt, she formulates "conjectures" and "counterexamples," imposing the semantic character of a logical argument on what otherwise might have been construed as "differences of opinion." The instructor also chooses terms like *reinforcement* and *feedback* from their comments and makes these terms themselves into objects of inquiry. She challenges the students' "shared understanding" of the meanings of these words by examining them in relation to the shared text available as records of practice in the multimedia environment. In so doing, the instructor seeks to scaffold the development of teacher education students' interpretive skills. She also seeks to cultivate a more tentative stance toward knowledge. The word *conjecture* is used deliberately to mirror its use in the children's mathematical lexicon. Likely to be an unfamiliar term, it also represents a view of knowing often less familiar to prospective teachers, who often have had little experience with the formal framing of hypotheses outside the contexts of their high school science classes. The instructor wants both to make this stance more familiar—the framing of a well-founded hunch—and to use the term as a name for a more tentative kind of knowing. Just as it offers elementary children who first encounter it a label for a speculative kind of mathematical knowledge, the word *conjecture* suggests that the viewer might want to look again and again at the situation—something that is not possible in live classroom observations. It also can serve to deflect students away from the search for the "correct" interpretation, since there can be many different conjectures.

We list some examples here of questions, conjectures, and counterexamples included on a handout that was developed for a mathematics methods class. Compare them with the overheard snatches of conversation that happened right after the students looked at the tape of September 18 (on pages 67–68). In translating first from a local to a more public form of discourse in the class and then from records of spoken phases to questions and conjectures, the teacher educator is constructing the tasks that will guide investigation in the multimedia environment. She is working to structure opportunities for prospective teachers to learn, based on their current interests and understandings. In this approach to making the multimedia records into curriculum, the instructor is working to develop opportunities to learn in response to what she can ascertain about her learners—the prospective teachers—against a map she holds of what is both important and possible to learn in this environment. She takes their collection of assertions, questions, and speculations, and organizes them into a more coherent list. Not unlike the teacher's role in developing common knowledge in and from classroom mathematics discussion,[13] the instructor's role here is to create some common paths of inquiry that will help students move in productive ways in their explorations of pedagogical "big ideas." For example, she notices that there are many questions about the children's language. This, she thinks, is an important element of a classroom in which discussion is so central as a site for learning, and so she organizes and slightly rewrites their observations and questions, as follows:

Question: How do the children gain this vocabulary (especially when it seems that the teacher isn't talking very much)?
Question: How do the children learn to use these words?
Question: What has gone on in the past that has led to this kind of atmosphere where the kids do so much discussing and Deborah so little?
Vocabulary noted:
"confer"
"solution"
"agree"/"disagree"
"prediction"

She notices also that many of the prospective teachers are concerned with the teacher's lack of what they variously call "feedback" or "reinforcement."

The instructor sees this concern as related to a developing conception of the teacher's role, of teacher–student relations, and also of knowledge about young children. She creates a second category. This time, she decides to take what are many rather definite statements and represent them in conjectural terms for the first time. In order to develop prospective teachers' ways of thinking with such conjectures, she structures other observations that they make as potential "counterexamples" for the conjectures. Here again she is using a mathematical structure for knowledge to develop pedagogical ways of knowing.

Conjecture: There is really *no feedback* given to kids (e.g., "good answer," "that's correct," "nice idea," etc.), only redirection (i.e., the question is redirected to someone else).

Counterexample: There *is reinforcement* given to the children—for example, there are occasions when Deborah checks to see if everyone heard what someone said; this communicates that the students' opinions have value and is a form of reinforcement.

Counterexample: There *is reinforcement* given to the children—for example, there are occasions when Deborah describes an explanation as being "good" or an idea as being "interesting."

Immediately after these arguments, she adds a question based on theirs, designed to help them scrutinize their terms.

Question: Are *reinforcement* and *feedback* the same? Are they related? If so, how? If not, how are they different?

Next, she develops a few more of their ideas into conjectures and collects them together with the overarching interest in "feedback."

Conjecture: Maybe Deborah just goes on when an answer is right but stops to ask questions—to probe more—if it is not right. When Deborah moves on, this might be a form of reinforcement—a way students can know if they were right or not.

Conjecture: Giving less feedback (e.g., "good job," "that's correct," "that's incomplete," etc.) puts more responsibility on the students to prove and disprove right/wrong answers. It is every students' responsibility to be aware of why each problem is right or wrong.

Conjecture: Making sense of something is reward in itself for students.

Conjecture: Giving inadequate feedback, not asking just the right questions and not guiding students in the right way, can be a disservice to students. It can become too frustrating and overwhelming.

She ends by including a question worded just as it was raised by one of the groups.

Question: Don't kids *need* feedback?

What the instructor has done here is to take what was a somewhat informal discussion of what the students saw on the tape and turn it into a series of questions for inquiry. Her transformation of that discussion orients the students' work toward speculation and questioning and away from the statement of foregone conclusions. This move is designed deliberately to challenge what the students assume about "knowing teaching." She is preparing students for looking again at the records of practice in the multimedia environment, this time looking in a way that is more likely to be educative toward the purpose of learning to teach rather than simply reconfirming the way of knowing teaching that they brought with them to the course.

Even though they are phrased by the instructor as questions and conjectures, the responses of prospective teachers to the video excerpt reveal many assumptions about teaching and learning that they bring to learning to teach. For example, their major concern with teacher feedback shows that these students expect the teacher to be the source of validation and authority. In their role as students, they themselves are dependent on praise or correction from teachers, so they assume that this is a necessary part of teaching. By transforming an assertion into a question, the instructor recasts that assumption as something to be investigated: for example, Was it the case that children were receiving no feedback? What kinds of things might count as feedback? To what or whom did the children seem to look to determine whether their ideas and work were good? In the form of questions like this, what the teacher education students called "observations" become hypotheses or "conjectures" that can be tested by looking for illustrative examples or disconfirming instances.

Continuing, the instructor also sees other open questions, not related to the issue of teacher feedback, clear evidence of the prospective teachers' curiosity about this classroom based on their viewing of the September 18 video clips. She lists certain questions, some of which are more pursuable than others. She thinks these questions are important and also wants the prospective teachers to have to encounter problems of how to pursue different kinds of questions.

Question: How does Deborah decide when to probe students further on
      questions and when not to probe?
Question: What would Deborah do if someone gave an answer that was
      wrong (and none of the students caught it)?

Question: What happens when the children disagree? Is there a norm for disagreeing? If so, how was it established?

Question: How does she decide whom to call on? Why does she call on the kids she calls on?

Question: Do students derive a sense of accomplishment from thinking it all out and going up to the board and being the center of focus when they are up at the board (i.e., center of focus in that their ideas are examined by the class)?

Question: Does having many different solutions and approaches to a problem get children stuck? Is it overwhelming?

Question: Are the children engaged in the discussion? Are they bored? Are they restless? Are there kids sitting there not even thinking about the discussion? How can you tell?

The instructor recognizes some signs of subtle analysis in a few of the comments, and she takes one of these and turns it into a conjecture. In it, she has noted how closely the person who raised this issue has followed the classroom discussion, and she wants to encourage others to do the same.

Conjecture: Deborah repeatedly says, "Does anyone *think* they have the right answer?" rather than, "Does anyone *know* the right answer?" This gives more margin for error and makes it less risky to put forth an idea and be wrong.

Working only with the records included at the beginning of this chapter, teacher education students bring assumptions, observations, beliefs, questions, and interpretations to the investigation of this lesson on September 18. Using the resources available in the multimedia environment, the teacher educator can move them out to a wider view, to questions and conjectures to explore in these records of practice that offer them an opportunity to think more broadly about this classroom and teaching of this kind. Students can be challenged to draw on other records in the dataset to refine and revise their knowledge, and they can view the initial set of records repeatedly while considering the assumptions, observations, beliefs, judgments, and curiosities of others—not only those of their classmates, but those of the teacher and the students in the third-grade class, accessible through their notebooks and interviews.

The instructor's role here is to take students' reactions and questions, and transform them into tasks that she hopes will begin to shift students from a focus on definite answers to a focus on inquiry. She takes their definitiveness and reshapes it subtly in the direction of speculation and reasoning from evidence. The conjectures and questions are shaped from students' current interests and ideas, but remade so that their pursuit is likely to yield generative learning.

Beginning an Investigation. What happens once prospective teachers have looked initially at the video, and the instructor has worked with their observations and questions generated from "observations" of the teaching in the video segment to create a list of starting points? From the list of questions and conjectures, the prospective teachers choose a focus for further inquiries in the multimedia environment. They may work on this project individually or in small groups. One group may want to investigate whether children ever disagreed in the first weeks of school and, if so, what happened—what the teacher did, how the children handled it, what came out of it. Another group may want to find out how the children developed the language and norms for discussing mathematics that already seemed to be in use on the tape they saw. They would go back and study the first days of school closely. A third group may be interested in how the teacher handled answers that were wrong, and set out to find examples of this. Overall, in this class, the assignment is to use their questions to initiate an investigation in the multimedia environment.

CONCLUSION

What we have presented here is a scenario for the interactive development of tasks for teacher education students using the multimedia records of practice and the tools available in the electronic environment. In this scenario, the teacher educator creates assignments by reorganizing the reactions that students have to the "text" of an instance of teaching. The tasks that are generated from prospective teachers' initial responses to a piece of teaching are class-customized designs. In Chapter 6, we take the next step in our exploration of constructing a curriculum based on the investigation of teaching: We turn to examine a collection of teacher education students' investigations and analyze what they did and what we learned from looking closely at their work.

CHAPTER 6

An Investigation of Investigations

We engage our third and fifth graders in the investigation of mathematical problems and ideas with the aim of helping them develop mathematics knowledge and ways of reasoning. We have been working on engaging teacher education students in the investigation of pedagogical problems and ideas with similarly fundamental aims. The parallels between our work with elementary students and our work with prospective teachers have been useful. We have asked ourselves: What are the "big ideas" in teaching? What might it mean to "investigate" those ideas? What might be the teacher educator's role in helping students—individually and as a group—do such investigating? Figure 6.1 shows one way to construe the relations among layers of our work: elementary students investigate mathematics, prospective teachers investigate children investigating mathematics, and we investigate prospective teachers investigating children investigating mathematics.

In our investigation of investigation as a pedagogy for teacher education, we have moved back and forth between looking closely at what individual prospective teachers do and examining the larger picture of their work. In this chapter, we offer a broad view of that work, based on analyses of 68 projects conducted by teacher education students in seven sections of mathematics methods at Michigan State University and the University of Michigan.[1] These projects were done for the investigation project assignment discussed in Chapter 5. Before turning to an examination of the teacher education students' work, we set the context: the elements of the mathematics methods course in which the assignment was situated.

THE MATHEMATICS METHODS COURSE

Between 1991 and 1996, we designed and taught a series of courses in which the use of multimedia records of practice was a central element. We designed these courses collaboratively with the same group of graduate students who had worked with us in our classrooms, collecting the records and investigating teaching: Ruth Heaton, Kara Suzuka, Margery Osborne, Nan Jackson, Virginia Keen, and Jim Reineke.[2] Heaton, Suzuka, and

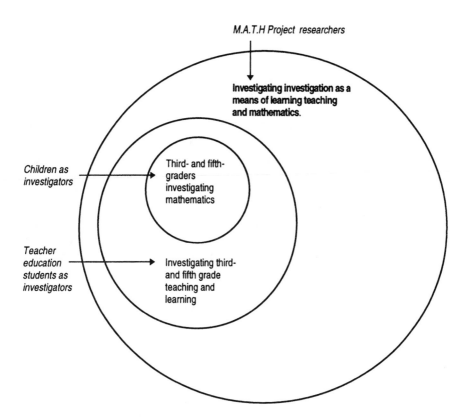

FIGURE 6.1. Layers of investigation: Mathematics, the teaching and learning of mathematics, and teacher education.

Osborne also taught courses themselves. Although the electronic multimedia environment was not yet up and running at the time of the first course in 1991, we designed activities using videos of lessons, photocopies of student work, and the teachers' journals as the centerpiece of that course. By 1992, we had assembled the hardware and software to support the use of the records by a whole class of teacher education students in a multimedia computer environment. All subsequent courses made use of this multimedia environment and shared a common pedagogical and technical design. Across these courses, we worked with our graduate assistants as more experienced partners in teacher education and research on teaching, inventing new pedagogies as we used new technologies, and piloting them in courses. Together we evolved problems, tasks, and structures for interacting with teacher education students, and these moved around back and forth among us. In this chapter, we draw on data we collected about the work of teacher education students in these courses.[3]

We designed the courses to help prospective teachers learn about the teaching and learning of mathematics, and develop understandings, skills, and dispositions that would assist them to go on learning from their own practice as teachers. The course assignments and in-class tasks were aimed at creating opportunities for prospective teachers to encounter the "big ideas" in both mathematics and pedagogy. Three discrete contexts grounded the work: (1) the mathematics methods course itself, (2) the multimedia learning environment described in Chapter 5, and, when possible, (3) the teacher education students' field placement classrooms. Each of these contexts offered a "text" for teacher education students' learning about teaching. The mathematical and pedagogical tasks we developed for the course were designed to support integration among the multimedia environment, the students' field placements in elementary classrooms, and the course itself. For example, during many class meetings, we did mathematics, exploring problems in depth, discussing and debating alternative methods and solutions. Later we also would treat these classes as instances of teaching and learning, and stand back from them to analyze issues of content, learning, and the roles of students and the instructor. In this way, we were creating opportunities to examine practice from the inside and from multiple perspectives. In their field placements, students observed and worked with elementary children. They interviewed children; designed, taught, and analyzed classes; and talked with classroom teachers about their teaching. Each of these tasks, whether in the mathematics methods class on campus or in the field, was designed to be complementary with the kinds of work that students would be doing in the multimedia environment.

Using the teacher education course itself as well as field placements as sites for learning, is a common part of mathematics methods courses on many campuses. Each offers important opportunities for teacher education students' learning. We assumed that the student learning environment we had designed would complement, not replace, the other two contexts. However, we also hoped that their work in the environment would restructure and enhance what prospective teachers learned *across* these contexts. Since the use of the multimedia environment provided a common classroom for everyone to examine, we used multimedia investigations as the anchor for students' work across the term.

TEACHER EDUCATION STUDENTS' INVESTIGATIONS

In Chapter 5, we watched the unfolding of the investigation assignment in one teacher education class. Beginning with watching a clip of videotape from the third-grade class in September, an instructor guided a group of prospective teachers from their initial reactions to the tape to the formulation of questions and conjectures. These questions and conjectures provided a partial field from which students were to identify a focal question for their own investigation. Here we resume with a glimpse of how the investigation project evolved and then turn to a closer look at what a collection of these projects reveals.

What happens once the teacher education students have formulated the topic or question for their project? In groups, or sometimes individually, they begin perusing the records of practice, collecting examples that inform their question. They copy and paste examples of children's work and excerpts from the teacher's journal, and they mark and preserve segments of video. They pursue their investigations for 2 to 3 weeks, alongside other work for the course. At some point, the instructor will ask students to present a piece of their work for public discussion. This provides a forum for shared investigation of the big ideas in teaching, with deliberate use of particulars as the ground on which to explore these ideas. As the students design a presentation about their inquiry, they can use the multimedia records of practice to give a shared referent to their comments as they display items—students' work, clips of video, teacher notes—to their classmates directly from their electronic notebooks. They can plan and design what they want to say and show, and then use their notebook to control and make the presentation, showing video, transcript, and other data to support their points. Sometime after these presentations, the final projects are due. The teacher education students appraise what they have learned from their forays in the environment and write about what they have learned about their original question and what they think now, both about the investigation topic itself as well as about what was entailed in pursuing it. What do they think they now "know" and what do they think is possible to "know"?

In all, we analyzed 68 investigations. Fifty of the projects we analyzed were conducted by groups of three to five teacher education students; 18 were the work of individuals. In all, 190 teacher education students' work is represented in the analyses on which this chapter is based. The investigation projects were located in electronic notebooks shared by the students who worked together. The pages included sections of reflection and writing by group members, collections of examples from the records of practice, and interpretive commentary and conclusions. They varied in length and design as well as in what students had collected to work with. Some were as short as three pages; they ranged to as many as 80 pages. On average they were about 21 pages long. Most investigations used all types of records: video, lesson transcripts, teacher's journal, children's notebooks. Most used the graphic tools to make figures or diagrams, or otherwise enhance the material and their commentaries. Some students amassed extensive collections of examples, while other collections were much leaner. More interesting than the physical features of the finished projects, however, were the questions students pursued and how they pursued them.

What Did Teacher Education Students Investigate?

Among the 68 projects we analyzed for this chapter, almost two-thirds focused closely on the teaching or on the teachers represented in the multimedia records. For example, one group asked, "How does the teacher choose the problems she will pose to students?" Another asked, "What does Deborah do if someone gives the wrong answer?" Still another set out to investigate the teacher's decisions about when to move forward with a lesson, when to pause, and when to back up. Some were quite particular to specific interactions or incidents. A few groups studied a long one-on-one interaction between Deborah and a third-grade student named Cassandra, in the context of a problem in which Cassandra attempted to share a dozen cookies equally among her five family members. This interaction was notable because Cassandra had five people in her family and was stuck trying to figure out how to divide the two leftover cookies among five people. Her task was considerably more complex than was the task of children who had three or four people, and she struggled. Ball's decisions about working with the girl intrigued several groups of prospective teachers.[4] Several groups of teacher education students focused on how the teacher decides whom to call on, how wrong answers are handled, and whether the teacher "ever tells" students anything. Two examined classroom "management styles," another looked at "how the teacher orchestrates classroom discourse," and several focused on the "classroom environment" and the effect of particular teacher actions on the development of that environment, or culture.

Of the 68 projects, although most dealt with students in some way, only seven focused directly on students. The questions in these seven projects were specific to particular children: small case studies of individual children or of types of incidents or "problems." For example, three projects investigated specific children and their participation in class. Children who appeared not to be paying attention or engaged in class were the focus, as were children whose performance and learning were questionable to the teacher education students. Examples included: "Daniel's participation: Does it increase over time? Why or why not?" and "Is Tembe learning?" Others included two on the behavior in class and learning of two different boys, one on a particular episode with one child who was struggling with a central idea about fractions, and another on a particular child's reaction to the teaching "style" in this class ("How does Mrs. Ball's[5] teaching style—reinforcement or lack thereof—affect Tembe?").

Some teacher education students located their inquiry in the intersection of teaching and external policy factors. One student did a lengthy investigation by herself of "covering the curriculum," asking how the teacher can meet the district objectives if all she does with the students is one problem a day.[6] Three projects used the National Council of Teachers of Mathematics (NCTM) Standards[7] as a template for examining the teaching and learning in the two classrooms. The Standards, required reading in all of the sections, offered a set of lenses for what to pay attention to and enabled the teacher education students to see how these ideas showed up—or were absent—in the classroom. Several other projects took similar advantage of the NCTM Standards without making the documents the main focus of their investigations.

What Kinds of Questions Shaped the Teacher Education Students' Investigations?

First, it is notable that the overwhelming majority of questions (80%) did not take account of the subject matter of the lessons—mathematics—at all. That is, they investigated questions that focused on teaching and the teacher's role, on classroom environment, and on students' engagement and participation. Not a single investigation probed a piece of mathematics, although it is fair to say that probably the assignment did not incline prospective teachers to think that such an inquiry would be an appropriate interpretation of the task. A few questions framed a pedagogical issue in the context of a mathematical one. One project probed the teacher's moves in a particular discussion of a comparison of 4/4 and 4/8. Another examined a specific student's understanding of fractions. A third focused on what the classroom culture reflects about "what mathematics is and what matters in developing and learning it." And several projects began with questions about manipulatives, visual representations, and other tools used to explore and express mathematical ideas.

Several projects were framed with theoretical concepts and terms that students had read about or heard about in other courses: wait time, reinforcement, resistance, discovery learning, learning styles, and higher-order thinking. None of these came from the content of the methods course, but arose either from the prospective teachers' other course experiences or from ideas they had encountered elsewhere.

A few investigations pondered questions that were philosophical or foundational. One probed whether "revising one's thinking" and "learning" were the same thing. Another asked about the role of language as a means to shape classroom culture. Two considered what was implied by using the concept of "culture" to view and describe a classroom. But most focused on issues that were closer to the daily realities of practice—how to decide whom to call on, how to choose problems, how to manage a classroom, how to engage students, and others of the same ilk.

One underlying assumption of our work was that prospective teachers could learn more than about us, our classrooms, our particular students, and specific incidents that occurred in that context. A premise was that work in these multimedia records of practice could afford opportunities to learn big ideas about teaching and learning. Therefore, we were curious about the context of students' launching questions. Were investigations framed specifically to a particular aspect of our classrooms or to a specific child in one of those classrooms? Or did teacher education students' questions represent general curiosities or concerns?

Coding the initial questions for the specificity to context revealed that 29 out of 68 investigations appeared to ask questions particular to our classrooms. Some were specific to a single moment or child. An example of this was the investigation of Ball's interaction with Cassandra around the cookie-sharing problem: "What does Deborah think Cassandra understands about fractions? What is she trying to get Cassandra to understand? How does Cassandra respond and how does she feel about participating?" Another example was, "Does David's participation in class increase over time?"

Still, most of the investigation questions that we coded as specific focused on an issue particular to one of the two classrooms but seemed to seek a kind of generalization, across the year, the teacher's career, or the child's personality. In other words, although these investigations asked about particular features, people, interactions, or experiences, the questions focused on issues beyond what was evident in any single piece of evidence. The questions were aimed at general conclusions. Examples included, "What disciplinary and motivational techniques do Lampert and Ball use to develop the classroom culture?" "What are the math notebooks used for?" "How does the teacher introduce students to new topics?" "Is Harooun shy?" Each of these questions entails looking for patterns across time and individuals, in a search for something more than the interpretation of a single interaction or event.

A few investigations were more general to begin with. One group asked, "How does the word *culture* relate to a mathematics classroom?" Or, closely related, "What does classroom culture seem to reflect about what mathematics is and what matters in doing, using, and learning mathematics?" Some students asked about "teaching diverse learners," and others began with questions about how teachers can motivate and engage students. These general questions were almost all situated in cases that fit their focus. For example, one group was interested in writing in mathematics and used the children's mathematics notebooks as a site to explore how writing played a role in these classrooms.

In the case of the specifically framed questions, we do not know whether teacher education students' interests and intentions were located in the more general issues of practice lurking behind the particulars. For example, the group pursuing the question about "Ball's and Lampert's disciplinary and motivational techniques," may be interested in developing a general repertoire of classroom management ideas as a product of their investigation. The groups who scrutinized Cassandra's experience with the cookie-sharing task could well have been seeking to understand more about what role a teacher can play in helping an individual child. Studying Harooun could well be an opportunity to problematize the notion of "shyness." Harooun is, after all, from Indonesia, and it is quite possible that cultural norms affect the impression of "shyness." But pursuing the question, "Is Harooun shy?" will not automatically be educative if all the students do is seek culturally based evidence of the kind with which they are familiar to determine whether this third grader was "shy." To know what they learned, we would have to know not only what the teacher education students did, but also what they made of it. We will turn to consider this in the next section.

How Did the Investigations Proceed?

What happened with the investigations that began, as most of them did, with specific questions? Some moved from the very particularistic focus to reach for insights beyond, but grounded in, the specific case. One example of this was Andrea, the student who, on her own, asked how the district objectives could be met if the teacher did only one problem a day. She began her investigation with a question about "coverage" in a classroom represented in the records, wondering, "Does the teacher cover the curriculum doing just one problem a day?" As she began to work on this, however, she found that the idea of "covering" was much more complicated than she had assumed. Looking at the evidence in ways that changed the focus from one lesson to larger issues of learning and teaching, she began to wonder what coverage might mean. She was drawn to read Lampert's journal and noticed how much attention there was to students' thinking, to anticipating what students might make of specific mathematical tasks, and to interpreting their responses in class and written work. Looking also at students' notebooks, Andrea began to think that coverage was relative to perspective. Students were not actually covering the same material. Andrea was fascinated and wrote page after page, scrutinizing specific children's work. Perusing transcripts and video, as well as the teacher's journal, Andrea also realized that single class periods often contained several related but distinct ideas.

At the end of her 76-page investigation project, Andrea concluded:

> I have found that my original question of "What is being covered?" has blossomed into something more than I originally realized. My first idea was what was basically being covered was the mathematical material and concepts. However, to my surprise, I was wrong. I think that "covering" means much more than just material. It means, most importantly, *engaging the students within the curriculum.*

She continued by saying that coverage also entails opportunities to review and practice "previously learned skills" and to build on "existing knowledge." Andrea seemed to work from a relatively limited question, "What is being covered?" into the complexities entailed in answering it. In so doing, she helpfully complicated her understanding of what it means to figure out what is being taught and what is being learned. Because of the discursive and connected nature of the class' mathematical work, she saw that many lessons defied simple synopses of what was being taught. And because children were engaged differently, she saw that what was being learned is still more complicated to ascertain. Certainly her learning cannot stop here. But she has made progress from her starting point: What appeared as a specific question about Lampert's class became a general inquiry into the notion of "curriculum coverage."

Another example of an investigation that began with a very specific focus but seemed to move into a more general set of issues was the project mentioned above entitled, "Is Harooun shy?" This group started with a curiosity about a particular boy who seemed to get a lot of reminders from the teacher to pay attention and who, on the couple of videos they had watched from September lessons, rarely spoke in class. They wondered about him: Was Harooun bored? Lost? Was he indeed unengaged at times? Perhaps he already knew the material, they thought. They set out to figure out what was going on with this one child. Their question was about what he was learning, a very specific focus. Yet by the end of their project, these three prospective teachers seemed to have shifted their thinking to reflect on what it means to know something about a child, the quest on which they had embarked. They felt much more tentative and explained that they did not think they could evaluate what the child was learning from one unit. "We would need to talk with him, see his homework, and so forth." Their conclusions were filled with multiple possible interpretations of his actions and demeanor in class. Like Andrea, this group seemed to leave their project with a greater respect for the role of context and interpretation in knowing.

These teacher education students proceeded from a seemingly idiosyncratic question to a set of issues much larger than one child and figuring out whether he might be considered shy. The way they thought about "investigating practice" was transformed in the course of doing it. (We return to this project later, to look more closely at its evolution.) Other students who began with specific questions about what was going on in our classrooms did not experience the same transformation. Some investigations that began like this remained at the level of the specific case. Take, for example, another group that focused on a particular child. They wanted to understand what this child "really knew" about fractions, because, from watching one video, they were not sure what he understood. This group looked at several videos, read the teacher's journal, and studied the child's own notebook. By the end of their project, they had some further ideas about what he understood, but said nothing that made it seem that they had learned something more general than about this particular child. Perhaps they learned something about how to learn about children, or about the ambiguity of conclusions about children's thinking, but there is no evidence of this in anything they wrote. Looking at their project alone is not enough to tell.

Where Did the Investigations Lead?

Overall, of 68 investigations, 42 concluded with answers to the questions. Examples included projects that analyzed the classroom using the NCTM Standards, projects that cataloged ways that the teachers established and maintained classroom culture, projects that examined the participation of particular children, and projects that examined wait time or other techniques for classroom management. In some of these cases, teacher education students were working to "show" or prove the underlying assumptions of their question as much as they actually were asking something. One group, for instance, set out to show that "wait time" may discourage students who actually know the answer. They said they wanted to use their investigation to show their classmates "what to avoid."

One group of five teacher education students worked on classroom management. Their project became a process of finding examples in the records of practice that illustrated positively or negatively the principles of classroom management that they held to be important. Three headings from their project included: "How to Begin Classroom Management," "Student Disengagement and Its Implications for Classroom Management," and

"How to Deal with Disengaged Students Without Disrupting the Overall Classroom Environment." The investigation was carried out as an evaluation of the teaching. Ball was referred to as doing "quite a good job" at times. At other times, the teacher education students in this group offered ideas about what she might have done better. They suggested things for the teacher to do that "would have been a lot more helpful." The five students who worked on this investigation each wrote their own conclusions. Aisha's were quite typical and showed that she seemed to be animated as much by ideas she had developed on her own, outside this class, as by her investigation.

> The conclusions that I have reached for now are several. I have learned that a good teacher does not force a student into a certain behavior. I feel this is disastrous for disengaged students because that student may already be frustrated, and full of anxiety. Forcing a particular behavior may close that child down even further. I did not see this in my research; however, this is what I feel is a strong possibility. Furthermore, handling disengaged students in a careful, smooth, and delicate manner is both productive for the teacher, other students, and the disengaged student as well. The teacher can maintain her classroom without power struggles arising from a forced classroom environment.

Although she speaks of what she "learned," Aisha's ideas about classroom management included several principles for what good teachers do, and her investigation gave her a chance to use these ideas in the context of an example of practice. She had an answer not only at the end, but throughout. Her project partners similarly illustrated their beliefs more than they challenged or revised them.

Twenty-six projects concluded with revised questions or ways of framing the issue, along with new ways to pursue it. These prospective teachers recognized problems inherent in their original focus—for example, a group focused on "high-level" and "low-level" students became aware that "ability" and "level" were too difficult to appraise—or their investigation led them from their initial question to a new set of significant questions. The investigation entitled, "Is Harooun shy?" was one of the latter ones. The 26-page project, conducted by four prospective teachers, sought to understand one small boy in Ball's third-grade class, a boy whom all four thought quite shy. They were curious about why he was not speaking in class and why he seemed so removed and reserved.

Their investigation was filled with their efforts to understand Harooun, to know better what he is thinking when he speaks. Almost immediately, they encountered the challenges of making sense of what students are saying. In Harooun's case, they wondered about whether the "language barrier" was at the heart of what made it difficult to understand what he was thinking. They wondered whether it was a weak understanding of mathematics. They disagreed about this.

> Harooun was asked to read a problem from the board. From watching the video, he seemed hesitant, and we couldn't even hear him very well. We're not sure if it was due to a language barrier or his uncertainty of himself.

The alternative interpretations held within the group help to complicate their view of Harooun and of their original question: "Is Harooun shy?" As they wrote about their investigation, they recounted the information they encountered and their increasing uncertainty about the "right answer" about Harooun.

> We now think that maybe because it was the beginning of the year, Harooun did not want to say anything because he was afraid of saying a wrong answer. Possibly, he did not know the other kids in the class and was uncomfortable speaking in front of them all.

The group examined Harooun's participation in particular class discussions, puzzling about what he was thinking. At one point, they scrutinized a few moments of video so closely that they discovered a substantial error in the accompanying transcript.

> Now that we have listened to this again, we realize that he didn't say, "people next"; he said "paper clips." We were trying to understand why the teacher hadn't said anything when he read "people next" since it didn't make sense in this problem. Now that we listened to the video without looking at the transcript, we noticed that he did say "paper clips" which makes much more sense. . . . It seems like his language has improved from earlier videos where he had much more difficulty reading from the board. We are still not convinced that just because he can read it better that he is actually comprehending the questions though.

Their quest to understand Harooun continued. They saw Harooun go to the board late in the year to defend a solution and they were fascinated.

> We found it interesting that Harooun finally came up to the board to prove his answer. Do you think he did this because he was fairly positive that his answer was right? He did not seem really shy, but when Mrs. Ball wanted him to explain his drawing he said, "Who me?"

Was he shy or just afraid to talk in front of class? Maybe his language barrier made him unsure that he would be able to explain his idea well in English. We know it would be near impossible to find this out without coming out and asking Harooun, but we wonder if he thinks in his own language or English. We thought it might also have to do with the fact that this example is from the end of the year (May 31). Maybe throughout the year he has been able to build up some confidence and gain the language skills to explain his point to the class.

For this group of prospective teachers, the simple hypothesis-turned-question with which they had begun their project evolved into a close examination of the young student. And at the conclusion, they had no answers.

After researching our question for the past few weeks, we have come to the conclusion that there is no one right answer to our question. Each question we asked just brought about more questions, instead of finding the "answer." Although we didn't come up with an "answer," we did discover a lot about Harooun's learning of math. This is illustrated in our discussions within this journal.

In their evaluation of the project, they wrote that "each question we asked brought about more questions, instead of finding the 'answer.'" In her comments to the group, the instructor noted this comment and also observed their increasing use of words like "perhaps," "maybe," "possibly." She commented, approvingly, that their project revealed "a deep appreciation for the complexity of trying to understand a student. . . . Rather than affixing labels, you tried on many conjectures as you tried to learn about Harooun."

WHAT DID WE LEARN FROM PROSPECTIVE TEACHERS' WORK IN THE ENVIRONMENT?

The teacher education students' investigations provided windows to their thinking and ideas. For example, situated in the concrete particulars of practice, some prospective teachers revealed their strong likes or dislikes of specific children. That these were not—to them—"real" children may have made it possible for these reactions to surface, but in this instance and others as well we were able to see aspects of their thinking that had been less visible in class discussions about teaching.

We saw what they were inclined to focus on, their assumptions about the teacher's role in students' learning, and their preferences. Like open-ended mathematics problems for elementary mathematics students, the investigation project offered instructors some more detailed pictures of their students' thinking. As they looked at particular children, specific teacher moves, actual tasks, and interactions, prospective teachers made comments that were concrete in a way not engendered by the often distanced and abstract discourse of teacher education. In many teacher education classes, students discuss teaching and learning in general terms. Claims such as, "Teachers should create a safe classroom environment," or "Students' prior experience shapes their interpretation and learning," are often not situated in practice and become little more than empty slogans. In the context of the investigations in the multimedia environment, teacher education students' talk was more concrete, more connected to actual phenomena, and as such made it possible to communicate with more precision than is often the case.

Overall, in considering what we can learn from examining prospective teachers' work with the records of practice on an assignment that evolved from their own questions, five patterns stood out.

- The projects were quite uneven. Some were long, used considerable and varied data, and entailed extensive commentary and analysis. Others were brief and less examined. We did not see patterns whereby some sections had much weaker or stronger investigations than others. This variation was across classes, not between sections.

- Teacher education students' initial questions tended to reflect strong normative assumptions. For example, their questions were grounded in notions about a "good" classroom environment, a "helpful" teacher, or "encouraging" teacher–student relationships. The prospective teachers were inclined to use these ideas to frame what they saw in the records of practice and to exemplify or illustrate their ideas. Only rarely were these challenged by doing the investigation. Since the assumptions framed the inquiry, merely looking at video and children's work would not automatically unseat them. It was more likely that the collection and interpretation of material would reinforce the entering assumptions.

- Still, teacher education students also tended to change their minds about empirical matters once they examined the data. When they thought boys were being called on more than girls, or that students were not understanding fractions, or that there were differences between "levels of ability," most teacher education students revised their initial ideas in light of the evidence.

- The relationship between particulars and generalizations was tenuous. Sometimes teacher education students made huge leaps from specifics to much broader claims. They made assertions about what teachers "should" do on the basis of an analysis of a single relationship, task, or incident. At other times, they remained seemingly stuck in the particulars. One group studied "student motivation" by completing four detailed investigations of children. These cases were done carefully, with much exploration of multiple sources and considerable interpretation and analysis. Yet the conclusion was little different from where the group started—in generalities about motivation.

> This project has emphasized the importance of motivation in the classroom. As future educators, we will focus upon this issue of motivation and be sensitive to the diversity of learners in our classrooms. We feel that if we can strive to focus upon students as individual learners we can prepare ourselves for a positive future in education.

Moreover, their reflections centered on the importance of working together and how well their group collaborated. Another group, focusing on "wait time" and the effects on students of not being called on while the teacher is waiting, examined instances of this and then made general claims about what teachers should "make sure to avoid" (i.e., discouraging motivated students by not calling on them).

• Prospective teachers' investigations focused little on the mathematics, except when prompted by instructor. No projects focused solely on mathematical content, and only three projects looked closely at curriculum or at particular tasks. Although there is much to investigate about the mathematics of the third or fifth grade, this was somehow not prominent on the teacher education students' list of what to pay attention to in teaching. Possibly they did not see the multimedia environment as a site in which to probe mathematics. Instead, they were inclined to see teaching and learning through pedagogical and psychological lenses.

CONCLUSION

This chapter has explored one of the major tasks we and other instructors used in mathematics methods courses over the past few years. The task was designed to offer prospective teachers the opportunity to identify a topic or issue of concern to them and to investigate it in the materials. In this chapter we have taken a broad perspective on what we have seen prospective teachers do with this assignment. The investigation project is an example of a task where a great deal is left to be designed interactively by both students and instructors. As tasks go, the balance of design is weighted toward what happens when students are actually working on it. In this way, it is well conceived to accommodate teacher education students' varying interests and the ways in which their ideas and interests may well evolve as they interact with the materials. The assignment is bounded in advance more by what material is available than by the structure of the assignment itself. The task offers the possibility of involving teacher education students in genuine inquiry, in investigations that they have framed.

However, the fact that so much is left to be designed interactively means that a large burden is carried by the teacher educator. As the teacher education students begin to identify areas of interest, the teacher educator must help them to frame their interests into questions that can be investigated. The instructor also must interact with students as they pursue their investigations, offering comments, asking questions, and otherwise helping to shape the task. Each task can be quite different from the next, and the instructor is in the position of appraising the potential and appropriateness of the task as it develops.

In looking over the 68 investigations conducted by teacher education students, the tasks vary in their formulation, their likely fruitfulness, and their focus. They vary in the balance of theory and assumption they reflect, and in the role that could be played by empirical data in their exploration. They vary in their relative specificity and generality. And they did not all prove to be fruitful. How much of that is inherent in the particular investigation as articulated in the initiating question, and how much is rooted in the ways in which the instructors and students worked with it, is not the point here. In some cases, the framing and evolving task were not well specified and thus were hard to bite into in helpful ways. In some cases, the task seemed potentially fruitful but the teacher education students did not seem to bear down on it effectively. The investigation assignment, by design, is a complex curricular task with high demands for both instructors and students. Most of what counts is left to be designed and specified as it unfolds.

The teacher educator has a challenging role to play with the investigation assignment. Working in the complex terrain of practice, the teacher educator is actively constructing curriculum as the course unfolds. At each moment, the instructor must gauge where a particular group's work has taken them and where it might take them. Considerations of content—what there is to learn about practice, students, and ways to help them learn particular things—all these are at play in the teacher educator's interactive work.

With so little of the investigation assignment specified and designed in advance, the work of the teacher educator is more complex. Some teachers have been overheard to say, "The best things happen when I don't plan," a position favoring spontaneity and adaptation in teaching. Some educators claim that teachers who design detailed plans in advance may be less able to "hear" their students for they are more wedded to their plans. However, it is also possible to make the claim that more anticipatory design of curriculum frees the teacher to do just that—to *anticipate* what students may think or say. More contingencies can be imagined and planned for. Even highly specified tasks can be focused on investigation. The investigative nature of the work need not be diminished by designing it more in advance.

The goal is to develop experiences for teacher education students that are educative. On the one hand, that implies building on what learners bring with them and what they will need to do in the future. On the other hand, this means designing for learners' active, critical, generative engagement with the curriculum, including tools, materials, activities, and discourse. Seeing all of teaching as curriculum construction in effect merges curriculum with pedagogy. This view challenges the conventional conception of curriculum as something to be developed and then implemented. While all curriculum is jointly constructed, the critical question for the development and facilitation of educative experiences is what parts can be profitably specified in advance and how do you design for curriculum construction in practice?

Our explorations turned increasingly in this direction. In our quest to develop opportunities for prospective teachers to investigate teaching in ways likely to be educative, we wondered what might be possible if the task were more specified. In Chapter 7, we discuss a redesigned example of the original investigation assignment and examine closely one prospective teacher's work on it. In Chapter 8, we return to an examination of the construction of a curriculum rooted in the investigation of records of practice and its entailments for the teacher educator and for teacher education students' opportunities to learn.

CHAPTER 7

A Design for a Pedagogy of Teacher Education

We continued to think that the multimedia environment offered significant potential as a site for a new pedagogy of teacher education. Work in the environment could offer the possibility for teacher education students to ground their learning in concrete particulars of teaching and learning as well as to use a shared text of practice to do so. It could offer the possibility to develop an appreciation for what it means to know something in teaching as well as to acquire skills at knowing and making knowledge claims. Outside the demands of interactive teaching, prospective teachers could grapple with some of the challenges with which they must deal as teachers: Are students learning? What is important in establishing a classroom culture? Is the curriculum being "covered"? We wondered, however, how to develop more fruitful opportunities for prospective teachers to investigate teaching and learning in the records of practice.

LEARNING WHAT COUNTS IN DESIGNING TEACHER EDUCATION

Our work has taken the vision of using our practice as a site for a different kind of study into the reality of experiment and analysis. Two big themes frame what we have been learning, one that focuses on curriculum making and the other on pedagogy and the teacher educator. Reciprocals of each other, these themes are tied by our concern for what it takes for experience in the multimedia environment to be educative.

When we set out to collect a year's worth of material from our two classrooms, we knew we were embarking on an ambitious project. We made our way through the steps of organizing the materials and designing software to make them usable. But as we then worked with the materials in teacher education, we realized we were facing perhaps the biggest challenge of all. The materials we had collected and assembled did not make a curriculum for teachers' learning. They were merely records of practice, with a promising potential to be made into curriculum.[1] What lay ahead was the design of tasks that could structure opportunities for prospective teachers to learn from interaction with these records of practice.

As we said in Chapter 6, the goal in designing tasks using multimedia records of practice in teacher education is to develop experiences for students that are educative toward the purpose of learning teaching. On the one hand, that implies building on what learners bring and what they will need to do in the future. On the other hand, it means designing for learners' active, critical, generative engagement both with the material and with the big ideas in teaching. The teacher educator has a challenging role to play in developing such experiences. Continuing to investigate the interplay of curriculum design and pedagogy seemed to us crucial in taking the next steps in our work.

In Chapter 5, we examined some of the issues entailed in moving from a collection of multimedia records of practice to the construction of opportunities for teacher education students' learning. As a first step in figuring out how to use multimedia records of practice in the preparation of teachers, this aspect of our work has helped us to understand what it takes to change the culture of knowing in teacher preparation from transmitting theories and methods to investigating practice. It has given us a deep appreciation for what teacher education students might do with records of practice and how they interact with the materials. In this chapter, we look closely at one student's work in her mathematics methods course, using her experience to speculate on the interplay of what students bring to the study of teaching, the design of tasks that afford opportunities to learn, and the teacher educator's role in making those tasks educative. Here we pay particular attention to what it is about the tasks that are assigned that makes it possible for them to be used fruitfully by instructors and their students. In Chapter 8, we will look more closely at the design of the teacher educators' role, analyzing what can be learned by looking closely at this case and making analogies with our work as mathematics teachers in elementary classrooms.

DESIGNING TASKS

In addition to preparing students to work at investigating teaching by formulating their own questions, instructors working with the records of practice, whether in the multimedia environment or not, have developed and tried a host of tasks to orient students toward pedagogical inquiry. Examples include:

• focusing on one child and developing a mini-case of what that one child seems to be doing, learning, and feeling in class over some period of time—perhaps the whole year, or perhaps a particular lesson or unit

• probing what is being "covered" in a series of mathematics lessons over several days

• trying to figure out what children are learning by examining their written work and their talk in class

• examining the role played by the teacher within a certain class period, or over a longer period of time: What are the moves the teacher makes? What seem to be her purposes?

• exploring and describing the "culture" of the classroom and its evolution over time

• considering whether and how key ideas from the NCTM Standards are interpreted and used in the classroom

In this section, we consider what is entailed in designing such tasks by analyzing one example. The example we examine was designed to help prospective teachers consider *classroom culture.*[2] As was evident in their questions and observations in response to the September 18 videotape, prospective teachers naturally tend to become interested in issues related to what we call "classroom culture," although they do not refer to it in these terms. More frequently they muse about how the children treat and speak to one another, or about the teacher's demeanor and persona. Classroom culture is also an idea that has attracted the attention of many researchers and reformers. It is an element of pedagogy with which most elementary teachers explicitly concern themselves. Whether called "classroom culture," "climate," "learning environment," "community of learners," or "context," this dimension of classroom life is widely seen to be one of the core dimensions of practice and hence an important idea for prospective teachers to learn.

The task as we have used it over time involves teacher education students first in creating a collection of items from the records of practice in the multimedia learning environment that they think exemplify key elements of the culture of the classroom. The second part of the task asks them to formulate a conjecture about some aspect of the teacher's role in establishing and maintaining these elements of classroom culture, as they interpret it from their investigation of the materials. Third, they write a commentary tracing the reasoning underlying the conjecture and showing its connection to the items they have collected. Next, they make a presentation to the rest of the class, showing some of their examples and explaining their conjecture about the teacher's role in establishing and maintaining the classroom culture. At the end, they write about what they think they have learned about methods of teaching mathematics.

What underlies the anticipatory design of this task in terms of considering the content to be learned, insights about what learners bring to learning this content, and means to engage learners in learning the content?

Considering Content

A central structure of classroom work to which teachers must attend, classroom culture, is the focus. The task is designed to unearth, name, and analyze elements of classroom culture in this classroom. What constitutes what we call culture? What do these elements look like in practice? Why do we think of this as "culture" and what are other ways that these elements might be conceptualized? The task concomitantly focuses attention on classroom culture as an evolving dynamic in which teachers play critical roles. What are the roles played by the teacher in the classroom represented in these materials? This focus emanates from the knowledge of practice: that understanding what constitutes classroom culture and how it can be developed in a classroom is crucial to the work of teaching.

Considering Prospective Teachers as Learners

The task is based not only on concern for the concept of classroom culture but also on careful consideration of what prospective teachers are likely bring to examining it. Unused to this idea, they nonetheless are aware that there are aspects of classrooms that shape the environment for learning. They are aware of tone, comfort, patterns of interaction, and so on, but are not likely to have organized these ideas conceptually. Moreover, they are likely to have ideas about what teachers do to shape the environment, such as the roles they make and enforce, their tone of voice, their manner and style, their pacing, and how they encourage or discourage students' participation, engagement, and learning. But prospective teachers are also unlikely to consider the creation and maintenance of classroom culture as an articulable dimension of the teacher's role.

Considering Engaging Learners

A third component of curricular thinking is to consider the means by which these learners—prospective teachers—can be engaged in learning this content—classroom culture and the teacher's role in creating and maintaining it. Prospective teachers need opportunities to parse the idea of classroom culture: What are its elements? What do these elements look like in practice? The task asks them to collect specific examples from the materials that make up the culture of the classroom. These examples then become the "text" for analyzing the practice of teaching. The student shares this text with other class members and the instructor and can present it over and over again in the multimedia environment, appreciating its multiple aspects. Prospective teachers need to be helped to focus closely and concretely on what teachers do to shape the culture of the classroom. So the assignment structures their work to turn their attention to specific investigation and identification of what the teacher is doing. Beyond producing a collection of examples, prospective teachers also are guided by the assignment to consider what they have collected, to look for patterns, to make conjectures about what they are learning. As they talk and write about what they are seeing, they move back and forth between the particular and the kinds of powerful big ideas that can inform thoughtful practice.

What distinguishes this second mode of curriculum development from the first, discussed in Chapters 5 and 6, is that it occurs in anticipation of any particular class or group of teacher education students; it is not constructed in and from any specific students' responses. The designs are built on general and particular knowledge of elementary teacher education students, drawn from our own work with several groups of students using these materials and the experiences of other instructors with the multimedia environment, as well as from the growing body of research on prospective teachers' ideas, beliefs, and ways of thinking. Like the interactive development of tasks, however, these designs depend on pedagogy to bring them to fruition. The task is still only partially developed in advance of its enactment. The teacher educator plays a major role in guiding students' work on the task in productive directions. In this sense, teaching and curriculum development continue to be fundamentally intertwined, just as they were in the earlier investigation assignment. In this example, however, more design occurred in anticipation; less was left to be developed in practice. We turn to a close examination of how this version evolved, looking through the experience of one prospective teacher.

BACKGROUND FOR THE CASE

The work we present here was done by Patricia Portland,[3] a teacher education student enrolled in an elementary mathematics methods course taught by Lampert at the University of Michigan in the fall semester of 1994. We analyze the tasks that Patricia was assigned in terms of the kinds of opportunities to learn teaching that they were designed to provide. We consider this case as an instance of a prospective teacher's learning teaching in which we used technology as a resource to turn our classrooms into sites for inquiry into practice. As we have seen, whether this new resource contributes to learning teaching depends on the nature of the teacher education pedagogy that surrounds it: the tasks that prospective teachers are assigned and the role played by the teacher educator. The heart of the analysis we present here will focus on Patricia's work on the "culture" assignment. In order to understand her work and her instructor's work in that context, we situate it in relation to other tasks that were part of the mathematics methods course. We draw on several pieces of Patricia's portfolio in our data analysis.

- Her handwritten journal in which she wrote her thinking about doing, teaching, and learning mathematical work involving fractions early in the semester
- Her handwritten work on mathematics problems having to do with fractions done early in the semester
- Her first case study in the multimedia environment (done with a partner early in the semester)
- The first stage of her second case study in the multimedia environment (done alone around the middle of the semester)
- The final stage of her second case study in the multimedia environment (turned in at the end of the semester)
- Her self-evaluation at the end of the course

Some of these pieces of work involved using hypermedia technology and others did not.

Looking across the elements of Patricia's portfolio, we see interesting relationships between her examination of the mathematics of fractions and her study of the teacher's role in guiding classroom discourse. The portfolio also illustrates consistent and progressive elements of the role that Lampert played as the teacher educator, attempting to provoke a shift in how Patricia thought about knowledge, both in relation to teaching and in relation to mathematics. We analyze how Lampert responded to Patricia's work in order to make her experience in the class and in the multimedia environment educative in learning to teach. We consider how Patricia's sense of what she needed to know in order to teach developed across that semester in conjunction with her increased appreciation of what it means to know fractions, gained in part from trying to describe what children understand, while looking at video, transcripts, and notebook pages in the multimedia environment.

A FIRST LOOK AT CULTURE
IN THE MATHEMATICS CLASSROOM

The first assignment in the course in which Patricia was enrolled was de-signed to familiarize students with the kinds of information that would be available to them and the computer tools they could use to browse, collect, and annotate it. Working in pairs, students were assigned the task of "get-ting to know one child in the third-grade class with the idea that you might be this child's teacher at some point." They were assigned to work in the "Beginnings" portion of the environment, where the information is all drawn from the first month of school in Ball's third-grade class. The assignment directed students to browse some materials in the environment and choose a particular student as their focus. They were told to "make a conjecture" from the perspective of a mathematics teacher about what this student would be like. We include excerpts from that work here both to introduce the reader to Patricia and to illustrate how the multimedia environment was used in her work on a task we often used to begin the mathematics methods course.

Before we turn to look at Patricia's work, we consider the task itself: What are its purposes and possibilities? What is entailed in doing it? What resources does it draw on, and how do its components contribute to the opportunity that it presents? Asking teacher education students to "get to know a child" is a direct intervention on the frequent inclination of many teacher education students to focus on the teacher and what the teacher is or is not doing. "Getting to know students" is a hidden part of the teacher's role; except for giving tests, learning to know students is not made up of a set of observable practices. This task deliberately turns the prospective teachers' eyes toward the student. Although they are not inclined to attend so closely to children, this task is likely to be appealing, for prospective teachers "like kids" and so it can be easy to interest them in this task. That the task is situated in the beginning of the school year makes it an authen-tic pedagogical challenge, because it is something all teachers need to do. The teacher education students are doing a task similar to the one that Ball herself faces in her own class in September. The task asks them to imagine that they are the child's teacher, a gambit aimed at helping them look at the child pedagogically, rather than some other way, and to consider, What is crucial to pay attention to in getting to know students if you are going to be their mathematics teacher, and why? The context of the task is a real one; moreover, it is designed to guide teacher education students to look at a child closely, and from the perspective of a teacher—not a baby-sitter, camp counselor, or older sibling, which are the usual ways in which they have looked at children in the past.

The task also is structured to guide the ways in which students work collaboratively with one another, with the aim of making a "conjecture." As in the investigations assignment, asking students to make a conjecture is intended to foster the idea that knowledge is not certain but is speculative, and that all speculations are not equally good. It also is designed to suggest that in teaching, teachers construct knowledge—in this case, of a child—rather than simply being taught it. This has implications for bringing learning to teach and teaching itself into closer proximity.

Asking students to work in pairs has at least a couple of underlying purposes. One is that when students work in pairs, they discuss the child, the evidence they uncover about that child, and their emerging conjectures. Talking about teaching, learning, and children is one of the things that teacher education students need opportunities to do. They do not come to teacher education with a well-developed vocabulary for describing teaching and learning, and are not used to close discussion and analysis of children. A second purpose grows from the need to articulate interpretations of the child to each other, and learning to probe and even disagree with one another's claims. Working with someone else can create a need to be persuasive, which in turn can help students focus on the evidence and making sense of that evidence. When the task is structured in this way, it becomes more than the simple rehearsal of a task that these students some-day will need to do when they have their own classrooms. It is also an opportunity to examine their individual approaches to the task and to compare their approaches with those of their peers.

As we will see in a moment, Patricia and her partner bring many assumptions and habits with them to the work of learning to teach. What they bring is both similar to what we know is typical of intending teachers and particular to these individuals. Even though this task is more structured than the investigation task, it still offers the instructor insight into how students look at children—what they see and how they interpret it. Lampert does not intervene in the work that Patricia and her partner do on this task. Her role is helping them to surface and examine their assumptions.

In working on this task, the students have access to the multimedia records from September in Ball's classroom. Patricia and her partner begin by laying out their understanding of the task and how they will go about it. They write in their electronic notebook:

> Tembe is a fifth-grade boy from Kenya. We chose him because we were interested in the possible cultural influences on his classroom interaction.

These students have a tentative notion that the fact that Tembe is from Kenya might have an influence on how he interacts in class. Here "culture" seems to mean Tembe's culture of origin, which they assume is different enough to affect how he interacts with the other students in the class and the teacher.

They look for all the references that Ball as the teacher made to Tembe in her daily journal by searching its text. They cut the following excerpt (in which Ball refers to Tembe) from the teacher's journal and paste it into their electronic notebook:

> In response to my, "What do the rest of you think about what —— said?" I found them quite ready to say that they agreed or disagreed and to give some sort of mathematical reason in the response to my "Why?"
>
> They wait longer for one another than I would have predicted. But I don't think they are in the habit of listening to one another (for the most part) or to speaking to one another. I felt they were speaking to me and when I asked Nathan or Mark, for example, what they thought about what someone else had said, it often seemed that they hadn't been really listening.
>
> They were able to confer, to "compare notes," and to share materials in small groups with no explicit direction from me. I did not comment on this to them today—I probably should have.
>
> It was not a terribly animated class, but neither were they disengaged. I'd say Mei, Cassandra, Lisa, Jeannie, Betsy, and Sheena were the most attentive/engaged—and Tembe and Devin the least. That would be my guess. It'd be interesting to know what the observers thought or what the tape reveals.
>
> I'm not sure if I should continue to the 3-coin version of the problem. Will it be too hard? I'd like to see how working on the 2-coin version affects (if it does) their work on the 3-coin one.

Beneath this, the only comment Patricia and her partner write is:

> Tembe is not engaged/attentive in class.

Although Ball, as Tembe's teacher, wrote somewhat tentatively in her journal that she was surprised at the students' general level of engagement, and that Tembe was among the "least" engaged, Patricia and her partner are more assertive and definitive. Ball seems to be hedging her bets, actually making a conjecture to interpret her observations, whereas Patricia and her partner use the statement in Ball's journal as evidence for the "fact" that Tembe is "not engaged."

Another excerpt from the teacher's journal that Patricia and her partner copy into their electronic notebook has Tembe making a connection and offering a solution. In figuring out the number of ways to arrange three items, he sees that lining up three children is the same problem as arranging three digits to form different numerals. He explains that "it's like the numbers," meaning it is like what they had gotten when they arranged three digits—6 three-digit numbers.

> When I asked the permutation of 3 questions framed in another context (suppose Sean, Chris, and Harooun lined up to go to the library and Mrs. Rundquist told them she'd let them go again as many days as they could make different lines—how many days would they be able to do this?) Many people thought 3 (this was articulated by Riba). Tembe suddenly brightened and said it would be like the numbers so it'd be 6. His explanation actually persuaded Riba to change her prediction.

Patricia and her partner make the following annotation on this excerpt:

> Tembe attentive and comes up with the correct answer; explanation confusing.

In contrast to the earlier annotation on the teacher's journal (of September 11), here they label Tembe "attentive" based on their reading of the evidence in the teacher's journal of September 12. They pick up on the teacher's calling Tembe's contribution an "explanation" and they label his explanation "confusing." It is not clear that they even know what the "explanation" is. In contrast, they label his "answer" as "correct." They seem to view the appraisal of answers as separate from whether or not they are supported by comprehensible explanations. The annotations made by these students could be interpreted in two ways. Either they think the explanation is confusing to the participants in the lesson, or the explanation is confusing to *them*. It is not clear from what they wrote. In any case, they do not go on to seek more information from the records in the multimedia environment, either to support the assertion that the explanation was confusing to the participants or to try to clear up their own confusion about what Tembe was actually saying. It is not clear that they understand his explanation, "it's like the numbers." If they looked back to the previous days where the children were working on permutations, Patricia and her classmate would see the connection. But they do not look and it is not clear why. Their comment is in the form of a straightforward judgment, both of his answer and of his explanation. It is typical of what teacher educators hear from students who make a few observational visits to an unfamiliar classroom. They see a given student as either attentive or not, and for them, these categories are straightforward opposites. They do not empathize, either with Tembe or with the teacher, which might have led them to make a different interpretation. In this, their first foray into Ball's classroom, they are meeting both teacher and students for the first time. As they look at more records of Tembe's and his teacher's activities, they will have the opportunity to develop a multifaceted impression of the players in this classroom drama. Across her work in the semester, we will see how Patricia begins to imagine them as people acting in relationship to one another rather than as mere objects of study. This shift is fundamental to appreciating teaching as actions carried out in deliberate response to students. But at this point in the semester, the interpretation she and her partner produce follows a single train of thought about the student they are trying to get to know: Is he attentive or not? This is how they imagine they will decide what to do as teachers.

As they go on to investigate more records in the multimedia environment within a task structure that requires them to return to and re-examine their interpretations using different sources of information, Patricia and her partner have the opportunity to get to know Tembe better than they would on a single class visit. In addition to reading the teacher's journal to look at her perspective on Tembe, Patricia and her partner look at Tembe's notebook and copy some pages from it into their electronic journal. They put student pages and teacher comments from several days next to each other. They reflect on this plan of work at the end of their project: The language of "conjecturing," imposed by the task structure, gives them the opportunity to express uncertainty and learning at the same time.

> In our notebook, we attempted to correspond dates within Mrs. Ball's notebook to dates within Tembe's notebook. At the end of each excerpt, we highlighted key points concerning Tembe's performance in the class. Our conjecture of Tembe is placed at the end of the excerpts. The conjecture will include our reflections on the three sources of information: Mrs. Ball's journal, Tembe's journal, and clips from the video.

First, they paste in a piece of the front cover of Tembe's notebook, noticing that he has decorated it with "doodles" (see Figure 7.1). Then they look at a page of Tembe's work from September 11 and 12, the same days on which they had read about him in the teacher's journal (see Figure 7.2). They interpret what they see as a confirmation of their interpretation of what the teacher said, although they state it as fact, not interpretation.

FIGURE 7.1. Front of Tembe's notebook in Patricia's electronic journal.

> 9/11 Tembe not attentive and 9/12 Tembe attentive according to Mrs. Ball's journal and this seems to be reflected in his handwriting.

Looking further in Tembe's notebook, they find more confirming evidence on September 21 (see Figure 7.3). Here Tembe has written the date and the problem but there is no evidence of his work on the problem. There is a "doodle" in the lower left corner that is scribbled over and just under the problem, hardly decipherable in a little box, is the answer. In describing Tembe's work for September 21, Patricia and her partner write: "Answer written very small but correct. Did he come up with the answer? Doodles more than 9/12." Comparing Tembe's work for September 12 and September 21, Patricia and her partner seem to imply that Tembe could not *both* doodle *and* "come up with" the answer. In their interpretation, less "doodling" on September 12 is connected with the teacher's observation that he was more attentive.

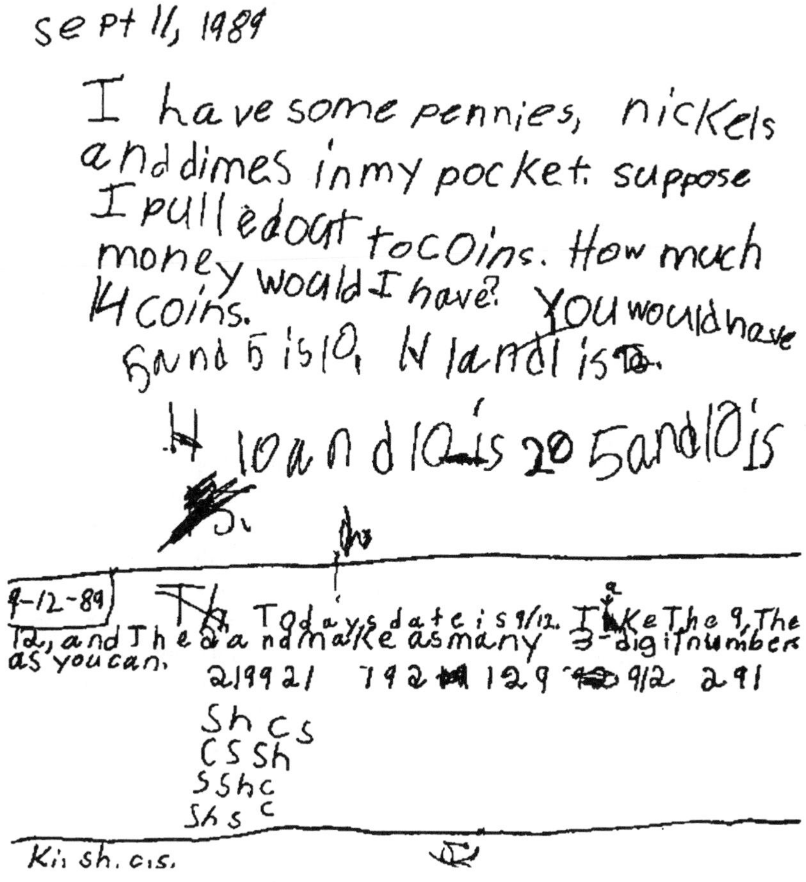

FIGURE 7.2. Page from Tembe's notebook, September 11, 1989, in Patricia's electronic journal.

The study of Tembe concludes with the following:

CONJECTURE

After reviewing and analyzing the sources concerning Tembe's performance, we suspect that Tembe is a bright boy, but easily distracted and
discouraged. He often has the correct answer, but he either does not
know the reasons for the answer or he has difficulty verbalizing the
methods by which he found the answer. Based on the transcripts, his

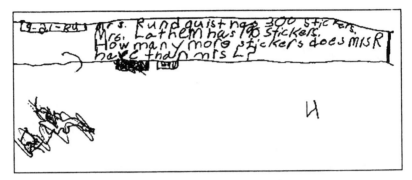

FIGURE 7.3. Page from Tembe's notebook, September 11, 1989, in Patricia's electronic journal.

answers were very short and when Mrs. Ball asked for an explanation of his answer, his response was full of hesitations ("ums") and insecurity (quiet voice, vague words). This tells us that Tembe is not confident with either his knowledge of math or his verbal skills. If the former is true, then Tembe needs to know the why's and how's of his mathematical knowledge. If the latter is true, this might reflect a cultural difference. Perhaps his family encourages the value of listening, rather than speaking. We would need to observe Tembe's performance and interaction in other classes in order to make a conclusion on the culture issue.

We had also found a connection between Mrs. Ball's journal and Tembe's journal. On the days Mrs. Ball described Tembe as being attentive, his journal entries were written neatly and were far more comprehendible than on the days that Mrs. Ball described Tembe as the least engaged/attentive in the class. We noticed that on the days when he was least attentive, he doodled more, which may indicate boredom or frustration with the problem at hand.

The video did not reveal a lot to us about Tembe's performance. He was not on camera frequently. This may indicate that Tembe does not actually participate as actively as some other students, such as Betsy.

In order to make more comprehensive conclusions, we would need more observation time and over an extended period.

The structure of this task affords these students the opportunity to be more tentative than usual because they are creating an evolving multimedia document rather than a finished "paper" to be handed in on a certain date. Their work will be evaluated on the basis of its evolution rather than in terms of a final product. The structure of the multimedia notebook also makes it possible for the "evidence" on which they base their argument to be present both to them as they analyze and reanalyze and to their instructor as she responds to their thinking. Having looked at this student from several angles and over several days, Patricia and her partner become increasingly tentative in their conclusions about the effect of Tembe's "culture" on his classwork. They add the idea that he may not understand the mathematics that is under discussion since he gives only short answers. But they interpret his not being on the video as evidence that he is not "active," suggesting that they believe only students who talk in class are "participating." This is a very common belief among intending teachers. The sort of work that Patricia did in the multimedia records helps her instructor learn some of how she currently thinks and what she assumes.

Patricia and her partner finish their study of Tembe with the idea that one of two possible interpretations can be called "true." They write, "Tembe is not confident with either his knowledge of math or his verbal skills. If the former is true, then Tembe needs to know the why's and how's of his mathematical knowledge. If the latter is true . . ." Having attempted this first task in the multimedia environment, they seem to see themselves as searching for certainty. They appear to believe that with enough evidence, they will be able to state a fact about Tembe, and that a teacher should know what to do with Tembe on the basis of this factual knowledge. At the same time, we see some signs of increasing speculativeness and some appreciation of the uncertain nature of knowledge in teaching.

LOOKING MORE DEEPLY AT THE LINK BETWEEN CULTURE AND MATHEMATICS

The second assignment in the course used the records in the multimedia environment to investigate the pedagogical problem of "establishing a classroom culture." The assignment followed the outline given in Appendix C. Throughout Parts 1 and 2 of the task, students were given a great deal of latitude in defining their investigations, and they were not expected to formulate a clear question for investigation until they had looked at some of the multimedia records and discussed them with a colleague. The structure of the task was such as to suggest that their interpretations of the data would evolve as they talked them through with someone else, and their questions would become more refined as they looked at more data. The role of the teacher educator in the second assignment is interactive. Periodically throughout the semester, Lampert commented on students' work using electronic annotations. The students' work on their investigations was evaluated at two points, over the Thanksgiving break, after the question to be investigated had been formulated, and then at the end of the course in the third week of December.

First we will examine what Patricia did on this assignment between November 1 and November 15. Then we will look at some other work that Patricia did in this course as she worked on tasks more directly engaging her in mathematics. Finally, we return to the investigation assignment to see how she integrated her work by the last weeks of the course. Patricia starts her investigation wondering about what might be meant by "classroom culture" and then picks a lesson from the third-grade class to look at in the teacher's journal where Ball is musing on what problems to assign (she doesn't tell us why she starts here). She adds a few annotations to the journal to point out her interests. Her electronic notebook entry begins with:

> Mrs. Ball's third-grade fractions
> Culture of class?
> A culture of the class could mean the diversity within the class (ethnicity, gender, age, etc.)
> A culture of the class could mean how the students act (in relationship to peer or teacher norms, values, etc.)

After this, she pastes in an excerpt from Ball's journal and annotates it [italics] (see Figure 7.4). The format of exploration gives Patricia a choice about where to begin and how to formulate the question she will pursue in relation to the information available. From any starting point, she can construct her journey through this classroom and through the terrain of practice and move across it in many directions on both the specific and the conceptual level, weaving between them as she goes along.

The starting point she has chosen is a set of mathematics problems about sharing collections of discrete objects (paper clips, small cookies), which Ball has posed to the third-grade class. In the teacher's journal we see three problems, and on the left some notes about each one. Part of the problem set (part 2b) is personalized in that each child is supposed to solve it using the actual number of people in his or her family: Given a dozen cookies, how would it work to "share them equally"? Here the third graders are asked to tell how many cookies each member of their family would get and also to tell how they know how many each person would get.

At first, Patricia does not comment on the problem set itself, but she comments on what she thinks the teacher is doing in her journal. She then goes on to look at the video for this day and writes a commentary, which follows:

Video # 11 → April 23, 1990
Comments from video

Mrs. Ball types the problem into their notebook because it would be a lot of writing for them to do. Then she explains how she would like them to work on the problem. First, *alone*, then in small groups. Why does she want them to work alone first? What does this say about the culture of the class?

Ball explains exactly how she would like them to present the problem. For example, she doesn't leave much room for them to work in between her typing, so they should "work out" the problem on a separate page. What is she suggesting about the problem? About her norms/values?—that she values "how" the students reach an answer? rather than just seeing their answer?—Raising hands with questions about where to "work out" problem—Ball has specific intentions about where they write the problem.

Reading the problem out loud, so everyone understands "the words"—third-grade culture—may not understand all of the words? maybe Ball doesn't want their reading level to interfere with their ability to do the math problem?

Notice that Harooun has difficulty reading—Cultural difference?

Interesting that Ball did not want them to confer before working on the problem, yet they do clarify the problems together before working alone. Is this because the classroom culture is usually one that allows and encourages discussion? A lot of students seem comfortable speaking in class.

Students begin to confer with one another and Ball gives them a lot of freedom.

Circular versus rectangular cookies—equal pieces necessary—Cassandra who Ball is working with does not question that Ball uses rectangular cookies, nor does she ask why to use equal pieces.

An interesting characteristic of Patricia's commentary is that it is full of questions. These questions range in levels of focus from specific inquiries about the lesson under consideration to more general questions about this teacher's practice to even more general questions about the work of teaching. At the end of this commentary, we see Patricia's first mathematically focused observation. She is noticing that in the lesson, the teacher found it appropriate to discuss whether circular or rectangular cookies would be used as a representation. The question has to do with the work of a particular student, Cassandra.

In the role of teacher educator in this case, Lampert responded to Patricia's commentary with praise for her questions, adding even more

D. Ball wants to see how students will solve the problem.

4/23/90, Monday

problems:

-> **estimation 20 x 5**
-> **invented strategies**
   for 19 x 5 ——>

If I want to give 5 paperclips to each person in our class, will a box of 100 be enough? How do you know?
10x5 + 9x5? (Can we get this? Maybe the minicomputer?)

• adding 19+19+19+
  19+19
• trying to multiply
  19
  x5 ?

2a. I have one dozen small cookies. If I want to share them equally with my family, how many would each person get? How do you know?

-> **getting needed**
   information, i.e.,
   how many people
   in my family
strategies for division

b. How would this work out in your family—how many cookies would each person get? How do you know?

possibilities of inverting
i.e., Benny can give 2 cookies to each person and will have 2
left over—how many does he have?

I experimented with typing the problems on paper and gluing them into the students notebooks.

I asked the students to work independently on the problems before conferring.

This went pretty well, with only Harooun and Daniel and Devin seeming stuck.

D. Ball is experimenting with teaching methods to get an
understanding of how students understand fractions (what methods they
will use, what pictures they will draw, etc.)

FIGURE 7.4. Annotated page from Ball's teaching journal, April 23, 1990, in Patricia's electronic notebook.

questions. The multimedia environment includes the capacity for instructors to annotate their students' work, posing questions, making suggestions and connections, pointing out conflicting data, probing, focusing, and extending the work. The points at which the annotations appeared in the electronic notebooks were indicated by a symbol that could be customized with the instructor's initials. The instructor has an important role to play in mediating between the particular instance of practice that a student is analyzing in the multimedia environment and larger questions about teaching and learning. In addition to having her look closely at Ball's practice and the work of her students, Lampert asks Patricia to construct some general arguments for and against what Ball does in this instance. This creates an opportunity to think inside and from the perspective of practice rather than simply analyzing it from the outside. Another thing Lampert tries to communicate to Patricia is that she did not have the answers to the questions that were on Patricia's mind, but that she did have other perspectives that could contribute to what Patricia could see. Lampert also challenges Patricia to think carefully about what she includes as evidence in her narrative. As in the scenario in Chapter 5, the teacher educator must take responsibility for moving students away from the kind of talk about teaching that college students are inclined to do when they bring examples into class from their field experiences, commenting on what they liked or didn't like or what they agreed or disagreed with about the class. The instructor seeks rather to put the discourse at the intersection of theory and practice. There is a deliberate attempt to move out from the particulars of the lesson under consideration to reflection on big pedagogical ideas. The words that Patricia uses are themselves made an object of inquiry as Lampert asks her to be more specific in her descriptions of Ball's thinking and action.

In Figure 7.5, we see what Patricia's commentary on the video of Ball's teaching looked like after Lampert added her annotations. The annotations appear in a separate box when the reader clicks on the symbol in the text. In the first annotation, Lampert presses Patricia to think more closely inside the reasoning of the teacher. She writes to Patricia:

> Why might this method of beginning to work on the problem make sense? What are some arguments against doing this?

Here the annotation asks Patricia to try to think what the teacher might have been thinking, rather than agreeing or disagreeing with the teacher's approach. Lampert challenges Patricia to go beyond solving the problem of whether students should work alone before they discuss their work, to looking at the context in which a teacher might decide the social configurations of classroom activity. In Lampert's second question, Patricia is asked to consider alternatives and reason about other approaches that the teacher might have taken. Here the level of the problem under consideration is raised still higher, beyond trying to figure out Ball's practice to trying to figure out how to reason about action in teaching.

The next annotation gives positive recognition to Patricia's tentativeness and questioning approach to her investigation.

Video # 11 → April 23, 1990
Comments from video

Mrs. Ball types the problem into their notebook because a lot of writing for them to do. Then she explains how she would like them to work on the problem. First, **alone**, then in small groups. Why does she want them to work alone first? [ML] What does this say about the culture of the class?

Ball explains exactly how she would like them to present the problem. For example, she doesn't leave much room for them to work in between her typing, so they should "work out" the problem on a separate page. What is she suggesting about the problem? About her norms/values? --that she values "how" the students reach an answer? rather than just seeing their answer? -- [ML]

Raising hands with questions about where to "work out" problem-- Ball has specific intentions about where they write the problem.

Reading the problem out loud, so everyone understands "the words" -- third grade culture--may not understand all of the words? maybe Ball doesn't want their reading level to interfere with their ability to do the math problem? Notice that Harooun has difficulty reading--Cultural difference?

Interesting that Ball did not want them to confer before working on the problem, yet they do clarify the problems together before working alone. [ML] Is this because the classroom culture is usually one that allows and encourages discussion? A lot of students seem comfortable speaking in class. Students begin to confer with one another and Ball gives them a lot of freedom. circular versus rectangular cookies--equal pieces necessary--Cassandra who Ball is working with does not question that Ball use rectangular cookies, nor does she ask why to use equal pieces. [ML]

FIGURE 7.5. Patricia's electronic notebook entry with instructor annotations.

> I like the way you tentatively try out your ideas here, focusing mainly on good questions to ask.

In the third annotation, after Patricia describes what the students are doing together as "clarifying," Lampert asks her to explain further what she means. Here there is attention to making the use of a particular word a deliberate act. Preservice teachers need to develop language with which to describe and analyze practice. The grounded nature of the materials provides an opportunity for instructors and students to develop finer analytic and descriptive tools in reference to shared particulars, as in this case. Lampert points Patricia toward fine distinctions in her wording that reflect important pedagogical issues.

> Do you mean they "clarify" as a whole-class discussion? How might this be different from "conferring"?

Finally, at the end of Patricia's commentary, where she comments on the question of whether the cookies are to be represented as round or rectangular, the annotation serves the purpose of underlining this as an important issue. By asking Patricia to look again at her own comment about the choice of representation, the instructor turns her toward an issue that does not come up on its own very often: links between pedagogical choices and content: Why is the distinction between using round or rectangular cookies an important pedagogical decision? Lampert's annotation on this point reads:

> Why does this seem important to include here?

In further commentary, on a piece of video from the next day's lesson, Patricia doesn't say anything about this issue of number of pieces versus equal pieces as the focus. Instead she returns to the issues of "paying attention" and "participation" that were prominent in her earlier case study of Tembe. Since these topics are interwoven with the mathematical content in the journal entries that represent Ball's pedagogical reasoning, Patricia has the opportunity to examine strategies of interaction in close relationship to the subject matter to be taught. As Patricia goes on to describe what is happening in the video, it seems as if she cannot get away from this set of connections. She comments, in quick succession, on issues of teacher expectations, mathematical content, mathematical discourse, representations of rational numbers, and student understanding.

Patricia has an opportunity to wonder about what was going on and what the teacher was intending. She is working in a task environment in which it is appropriate to ask why, without the idea that someone in authority is going

Video # 12 → April 24, 1990

Asks Mark to give his answer about 2 people in his family—Ball antici-
pates that other students cannot hear him, so she has him repeat it—
Showing that she wants everyone to listen and participate.

Ball does not indicate whether answer—12 divided between 2 family
members is six—is correct or not. Instead she opens the problem up for
discussion. "Does anyone agree or disagree?" She asks how Mark
figured out the answer (drawing, thinking in head, etc.). What are her
goals? Why does she set up a discussion-centered culture? Why can't
she just say, "Right, good answer."

Cassandra shows an overhead of her "work" on the problem "how
to divide 12 cookies among 5 family members?" D. Ball probably wants
to make sure that Cassandra understands the problem which is why she
presents her answer to the class. However, I wonder if Cassandra
understands why she uses rectangular cookies, rather than circular
cookies. Does she?

Why does Ball let Cassandra explain her answer herself? Cassandra's
explanation is confusing to me. I wonder if the other students are
confused as well. Why does Ball believe that this is the best classroom
culture to achieve her math goals for students? What about Tembe, for
example; he seems to have no clue what is going on. So does this
culture simply benefit a few students, or does it accommodate all the
students? What about the ethnic and cultural diversity within the class?
Does this affect the math culture created by Ball?

to answer her, but rather with the expectation that she will be able to examine more information and revisit her assertions. It is also worth noting here
that she returns to Tembe, the student whom she studied in her first multimedia investigation. She integrates two different senses of the word *culture*
here—one that means Tembe comes from a different culture because he is
from Kenya, and the other that has to do with Ball creating a "classroom culture" for teaching and learning mathematics. Here she is confronting the
overlap between these and seems to be wondering how they interact.

As she looks at the teacher's journal (see Figure 7.6), she sees that on
this day the teacher seemed to be seriously concerned with the way one
student represented her solution, using "circular cookies" instead of rectangular ones. The teacher's focus on the shape of the drawing puzzles
Patricia, but she identifies this teacher's journal entry as central to her interests. Examining the mathematics in the context of a pedagogical act gives
her room to think about questions like: What *is* a representation? and Why
does it matter if it is round or square?

Patricia's journal entry, reproduced in Figure 7.6, shows how she integrates her own thinking with investigating in the multimedia records. She switches from blue to red in her commentary here,[4] suggesting that she too recognizes a turning point in her investigation. On this page, Patricia has copied a piece from the teacher's journal where Ball writes about a student who does not understand why rectangles might be a better representation than circles in the problem she is working on. Patricia annotates Ball's journal, focusing on the social and personal aspects of Ball's pedagogical reasoning. She has identified a pedagogical strategy she thinks might be worth exploring further, which she calls "scaffolding," and she sees this strategy as linked to the classroom culture and that as linked to the teacher's goal: developing understanding of fractions and developing self-confidence. Patricia writes in a way that begins to express an appreciation of the teacher's multiple goals and how they overlap in different

From D. Ball's journal, April 24, 1990

I added language to her explanation. (At some point it might be interesting to compare how I help different people give their explanations.) What I'm trying to see here is if Cassandra can give a successful explanation implying fractional remainders, will her understanding of the mathematics be enhanced? It's a questions about the role of explanation in learning, about the role of "self-concept" or confidence in understanding, about my role in supporting her in doing that. I was very directive, shaping and guiding her explanation rather than so much questioning—eliciting of ideas in order to make sense. I said things like, "The part I don't understand is why you're dividing the cookie into fourths when there are five people" and, even more directive, "Those aren't halves—these are halves—drawing ① —what are these: ⌷⌷⌷⌷?" It's an interesting dilemma, for I want Cassandra to be able to give public explanations of her ideas for all the reasons outlined above (develop her understanding, develop self-confidence) but I want it to be hers, something she owns and understands. In trying to support her—even the scaffolding metaphor seems to apply here—I direct her more, with possible consequences in terms of her own ability to confront ambiguity and stuckness. No—I don't think that's right. What is difficult varies for each child and one challenge is to stretch each one similarly.

D. Ball's goal here is to see if oral presentations will help students' understanding of mathematics and fractions. She also makes it clear that although she is teaching mathematics, she also wants to foster the students' social and personal development (i.e., self-concept).

FIGURE 7.6. Patricia's annotations on Ball's teaching journal from April 24, 1990.

contexts: with different children and different mathematics. Through reading Ball's journal, Patricia has been getting to know her as a person with a host of concerns about her students. Patricia also has the opportunity to recognize that Ball is concerned about both her students and the mathematics; Ball's thinking reflects those dual concerns, even though her actions do not seem at times to Patricia to express them.

Once Patricia has declared what she wants to explore for her project, the instructor's role is again to raise questions about the meaning of words, about evidence, about the nature of practice. In her annotations on the above work, Lampert pushes Patricia to re-examine the basis on which she makes interpretations or claims. Lampert asks, "What happens when goals lead to conflicting practices?" suggesting that Patricia should reflect both on what happens in Ball's practice in this instance and on what happens more generally *to teachers* when their goals conflict. The latter consideration takes Patricia into the realm of pedagogical theory.

In the next work she does on her investigations, Patricia looks closely both at Cassandra's thinking and at the teacher's thinking about Cassandra as a learner. She makes a brief comment about the "rectangle/circle issue" as an aspect of teacher–student interaction, but she does not engage the question of which representation is more useful from the perspective of the mathematics problem on the table. In another part of what she has written, Patricia observes:

> Cassandra doesn't seem to understand *why* rectangles are better than circles because she keeps attempting to use circles. Is this important? Why does Ball let this go and simply tell her to use rectangles, when on other occasions, Ball takes the time to let the students figure it out? Does she have some underlying purpose and she sees the rectangle/square issue as a mere technicality?

After this entry, Lampert's annotation reads:

> What do you think? Is there information in the multimedia environment that would help you to think more about these questions?

These questions suggest to Patricia that she define her terms carefully and examine the assumptions embedded in them, and that she use records in the multimedia environment to inform her further deliberations. The intention here is to push her to rethink and revise the knowledge of teaching that she brought to the experience of investigating practice.

At this point, Patricia writes in her notebook:

> Later Ball opens the rectangle/circle issue to the class. They decide that circles are difficult and that Cassandra's circular drawing did not divide

the five pieces evenly. However, the students still did not decide whether using circular cookies was possible.

She then examines more multimedia records, including the excerpt from Ball's journal of April 24 shown in Figure 7.7.

The multimedia work that we have just analyzed was done just before Thanksgiving break. After that hiatus, Patricia returned to complete her investigation. At this point, there were only a few weeks left in the term, and the teacher education students in the methods class were asked to shift gears in the investigation process. Until this point, they had been looking at records of practice and commenting on what they saw there in relation to an initial, not very well-formulated question about a problem of practice. In the next phase, they were to prepare a "report" of what they had learned, including responses to the annotations that had been made along the way by the teacher educator.

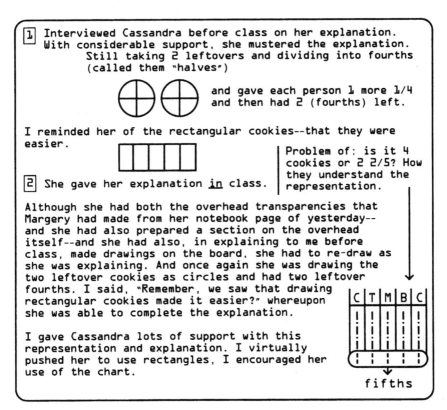

FIGURE 7.7. Excerpt from Ball's teaching journal in Patricia's electronic notebook.

Before we consider the final draft of Patricia's project, in which she responds to these annotations, we look at another kind of intervention on the part of the teacher educator, this time aimed to help students develop a more explicit kind of knowledge and understanding of fractions—the topic of the teaching and learning under investigation.

Turning More Directly Toward the Mathematics

One of the tasks that was common to the pedagogy we described in Chapter 5 was having the teacher education students keep a weekly journal. The structure of the journal was that the instructor would suggest a topic to write about or a mathematics problem to work on each week at the end of class. Students were to respond in writing between classes and be prepared to discuss their responses in the next class session. Early in the term, Lampert posed the question to her teacher education students: "What does it mean to know fractions?" Her question was intentionally vague and designed to elicit students' interpretations both of "knowing" and "fractions." Patricia wrote:

> October 5, 1994
> To *know* fractions means that you have an understanding of how to move from a whole to parts and back to the whole again. You would know the relationship that the part(s) have to the whole. For me "knowing" fractions requires some sort of visualization—drawing a picture or a shape so that I can see the parts (or fractions) of the whole object. I think that understanding fractions also requires an understanding, a conceptualization of what it is to be whole. What makes something whole (numbers and objects)? What makes something a part?

A couple of weeks later, the journal assignment was to work on the "cookie jar" problem, a problem that had been developed and used across courses.

> There was a jar of cookies on the table. First, Ken came along. Ken was very hungry because he hadn't had any lunch, so he ate half the cookies in the jar. Martha came next. She had missed dessert, so she ate one-third of what was left. At that point, Karen came by and she took three-fourths of the remaining cookies. Then Dorothy came jogging along and took one cookie to munch on. If one cookie was left at that point, how many cookies were there in the jar to begin with?

This problem is used in many of the courses we have taught. It is adapted by Lampert for Patricia's class by using names of teacher education students in this section. The problem focuses on the centrality of the idea of "the unit" in fractions. Ken, the first person to take cookies from the jar, takes half of the original total, but Martha, who is second, eats one-third of what is left—one-half of the original amount—after Ken has taken his. So Martha takes one-third of one-half, or one-sixth, of the original amount. The teacher education students must think carefully as they consider what Karen takes: Three-fourths? Of what? In each instance, the person is taking a fraction of the remaining cookies, an element of the situation that also eludes many of the students. For example, after Martha takes one-third of the one-half that remains after Ken, what is left? Many teacher education students do not notice that what they need to take into account is how many cookies are left, not how many have been taken. So if Ken took one-half, and Martha took one-third of the one-half that was left, then Martha takes one-sixth of the original amount. Together, then, they have eaten one-half plus one-sixth, or four-sixths, or two-thirds, of the cookies that were there to start. So Karen takes three-fourths of the remainder, which is one-third of the original amount.

Another feature of this problem is that it lends itself to several different solution methods and forms of representation. It is solvable algebraically (C = total number of cookies):

$$C = \frac{1}{2}C + \frac{1}{3}(C - \frac{1}{2}C) + \frac{3}{4}([C - [\frac{1}{2}C + \frac{1}{3}(C - \frac{1}{2}C)]]) + 1 + 1$$

It is also solvable using a geometric representation to reason about the relationships of the parts, for instance, by beginning with a rectangular whole and partitioning off sections to represent the amounts taken by each person. Figure 7.8 shows the area represented by one cookie (lower right-hand corner), and so allows the solver to reason to the total by considering the spatial relationship between that one cookie and the whole rectangle, which represents all of the cookies that were in the jar to begin with. Seeing the power of a geometric representation is illuminating for the students, and this form of representation as a solution approach usually is tried by someone who thinks of him- or herself as "not good at mathematics." It is a way to approach the problem that makes readily accessible the underlying importance of considering "the unit" in reasoning with fractions. It represents how a cookie can be one whole share (Dorothy's), one-half of what was left when Dorothy came along, and one twenty-fourth of the total. The students who have been more traditionally successful in mathematics tend to use algebraic solutions, which, although they work, are clumsier than some of the more elegant representational tools. Other solution strategies

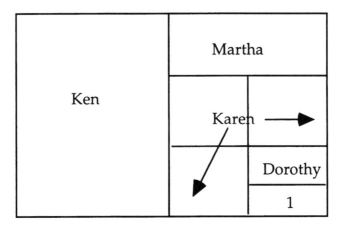

FIGURE 7.8. Area representation of the cookie distribution.

and forms of representation include working backwards: reasoning that 2 was one-fourth of what was left after Martha took hers because Karen, we are told, ate three-fourths of what was left, and the one that Dorothy ate plus the remaining one therefore would have to constitute one-fourth. This solution method can be continued, by noting that the drawing in Figure 7.9 must be two-thirds of what was left after Ken ate one-half, for Martha, we know, ate one-third of what was left. The drawing in Figure 7.9 can be replicated two times to represent that reasoning, as shown in Figure 7.10. This offers prospective teachers both another geometric representation as well as a different strategy for reasoning (working "backwards" from knowing that the remainder is a constant, 1).

The cookie jar problem offers the opportunity for teacher education students to work on several key elements of mathematical understanding. As with the "three-coin problem" in Chapter 5, they work from a concrete problem scenario to a big idea about fractions (the importance of the unit) as well as some important ideas about representation and solution methods. Algebraic forms of representation can be used, probed, and compared,

FIGURE 7.9. Representation of Dorothy's share.

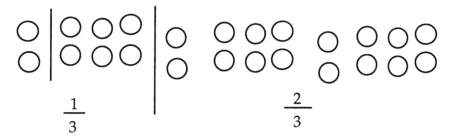

FIGURE 7.10. Representation of Martha's share.

and connected with geometric ones. They have an opportunity to "crack" a complex problem in their own way and then to examine and come to understand others' methods. Often, after such a discussion, prospective teachers will report learning to appreciate the efficiency or elegance of a representation or strategy different from the one they used.

The opportunities to learn are not only centered on mathematics: A second potential lies in experiencing a mathematics lesson different from ones that they remember from their past. They are encouraged to represent their thinking, to discuss their reasoning, to listen to classmates' ideas. The teacher's role, here enacted by the teacher educator, includes asking probing questions, offering challenges, and pushing students to make connections and comparisons.

Another, less obvious, opportunity is the experience of learning to listen and make sense of others' ideas, a task even more central to being a mathematics teacher than to being a mathematics student. Teacher education students may complain that they see no value in hearing others' ideas when they already have "the right answer." Instructors seek to help them understand how much of their work as teachers will involve them in just that: listening to people whose thinking differs from their own, trying to interpret it, and trying to appraise its mathematical appropriateness and potential. Thus the experience of learning and doing mathematics in this way comes full circle to serve simultaneously as instruction in mathematics and quintessential preparation to teach mathematics.

In her work on this problem, Patricia uses a version of the "working backwards" method, illustrated in Figure 7.11. When she talked about her work in class, she explained that she was taught this method in another course (Mathematics for Elementary School Teachers). Several other students used the same procedure. It involves using a conventional heuristic and symbolizing parts of the problem, but no diagrams. First Patricia does something she labels "WRONG." She starts again using the same method, this

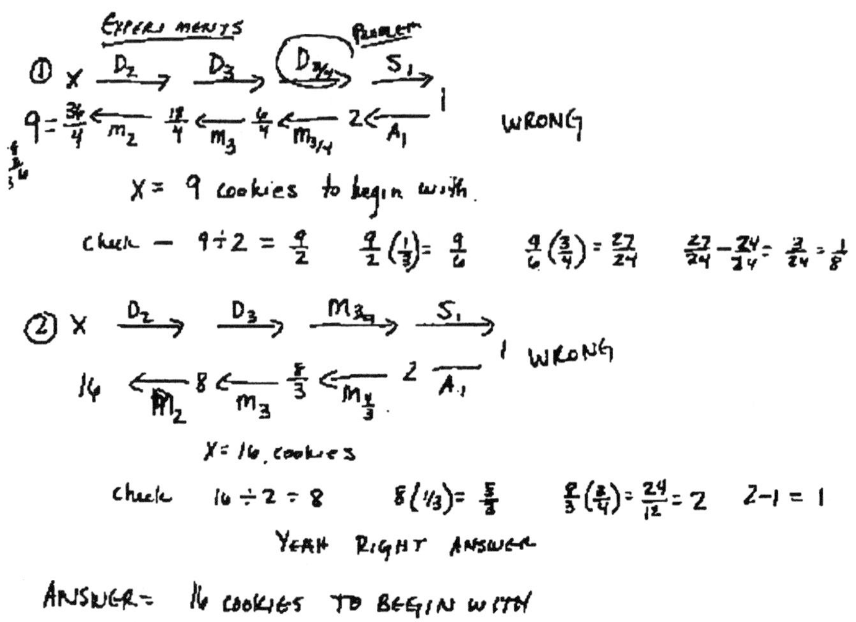

The handwritten work shows:

$EXPERIMENTS$ — $PROBLEM$

① $X \xrightarrow{D_2} \xrightarrow{D_3} \overset{\frown}{(D_{3/4})} \xrightarrow{S_1}$

$9 = \frac{36}{4} \xleftarrow{m_2} \frac{18}{4} \xleftarrow{m_3} \frac{6}{4} \xleftarrow{m_{3/4}} 2 \xleftarrow{A_1} 1$ WRONG

$X = 9$ cookies to begin with.

check — $9 \div 2 = \frac{9}{2}$ $\frac{9}{2}\left(\frac{1}{3}\right) = \frac{9}{6}$ $\frac{9}{6}\left(\frac{3}{4}\right) = \frac{27}{24}$ $\frac{27}{24} - \frac{24}{24} = \frac{3}{24} = \frac{1}{8}$

② $X \xrightarrow{D_2} \xrightarrow{D_3} \xrightarrow{M_{3_4}} \xrightarrow{S_1}$

$16 \xleftarrow{M_2} 8 \xleftarrow{m_3} \frac{8}{3} \xleftarrow{m_{\frac{4}{3}}} 2 \xleftarrow{A_1} 1$ WRONG

$X = 16$ cookies

check $16 \div 2 = 8$ $8\left(\frac{1}{3}\right) = \frac{8}{3}$ $\frac{8}{3}\left(\frac{3}{4}\right) = \frac{24}{12} = 2$ $2 - 1 = 1$

YEAH RIGHT ANSWER

ANSWER = 16 COOKIES TO BEGIN WITH

FIGURE 7.11. Patricia's version of working backward strategy.

time doing something she labels "YEAH RIGHT ANSWER." She does an algo-
rithmic "check" by sticking the "answer" back into the procedure. She does
not return to the original scenario to see whether the answer also "checks"
there.

These assignments are designed, like the early assignments in the
multimedia learning environment, to surface what teacher education students bring to the experience of learning to teach. Here, for example, we
see that although Patricia had some notion that drawing is important to
someone who "knows fractions," she does not use drawing herself when
she is assigned a problem that involves fractions. We also see the struggles
she herself has mathematically, information useful to her instructor in planning how to design the class discussion of this problem so as to help Patricia
and her classmates each develop their own understanding of the mathematical ideas and elements entailed by the problem.

In the class following the assignment of "the cookie jar problem," the
teacher education students present their different approaches to this problem and attempt to convince one another of their solutions. During that discussion, Patricia and others work hard to understand a drawing like that in
Figure 7.12, which one of their classmates put up on the board. In the course

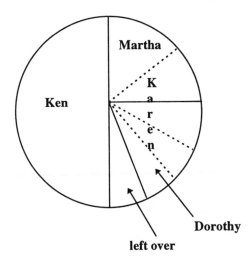

FIGURE 7.12. Cookie distribution as represented by Patricia's classmate.

of this discussion, Patricia reconsiders her "working backwards" solution and announces that the answer she thought was "right" was now "wrong."

She draws diagrams like those in Figures 7.13 and 7.14 in her journal during class. Next to the circle, she writes in her journal "be able to explain." She also writes on this page, "We realized that Dorothy's and Alicia's methods were not so different from one another. They both 'undid' or worked backwards to solve the problem." What Patricia writes and draws here is a recording of what happened in class. We need to look at her later work to get some insight into what she might have learned from this class debate.

After they discuss the cookie jar problem and work it through thoroughly and in a variety of ways, Lampert shows the class a videotape of fifth graders working on another kind of fractions problem that will take them into the same conceptual territory. In the video, the teacher can be seen drawing a diagram (see Figure 7.15) on the board as one student speaks about how she has drawn and divided circles to represent the meaning of dividing a larger number by a small one. The fifth graders have been asked to represent the computation "3 divided by 16" and then try to figure it out. The girl who is talking as the teacher is drawing on the board is attempting to divide each of three circles into 16 pieces to prove her assertion that each share would be "three sixteenths."

For fifth graders, there are two big mathematical ideas to be investigated in working on this problem: the relationship between division and

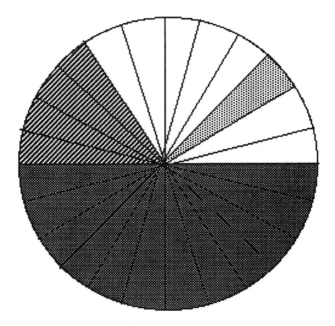

FIGURE 7.13. Diagram in Patricia's journal.

fractions and the issue of "remainders" in division. On the day before the lesson on the video, the fifth graders had worked on representing "3 divided by 15." Here, when they produced a scenario like "three pizzas need to be shared among 15 people," they could solve the problem by dividing each of the three pizzas into five slices. (An alternative, of course, is to

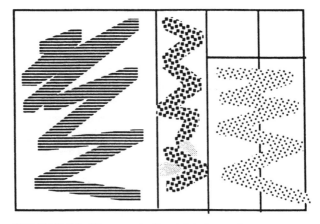

FIGURE 7.14. Diagram in Patricia's journal.

divide each pizza into 15 slices and give each person three. But this solution is much messier!) When the division was changed from 3 divided by 15 to 3 divided by 16, there was not such a "neat" solution because 16 is not "evenly divisible" by 3.

One of the fifth-grade girls, whose scenario had been "share 3 pieces of cheese among 16 mice," says she has discovered that if you divide each piece of cheese into five slices, "One little mouse wouldn't get any!" Another girl says she should have divided the three pieces of cheese into six slices, and there ensues an interesting debate about what to do with the two extra slices. Some of the fifth graders think it will "work" to divide each of the left over slices into eight pieces, and they are challenged to explain to their classmates how they have figured out that it will be eight. Another issue for debate was what each of the "little pieces" should be called. (Each of the big pieces, it had been agreed, was "one-sixth" of a piece of cheese.) The diagram shown in Figure 7.16 was up on the blackboard during this discussion. One student said the little pieces should be called "one-sixteenth," another argued that they were "one-eighth," and still another argued they should be called "one-forty-eighth." This debate led the fifth-grade class, and the teacher education students who were watching them work, into the fundamental question of how to think about the unit on fractions.

As in the cookie jar problem, prospective teachers were grappling here with at least two core ideas in fractions that they likely never considered before. One idea is that fractions are always fractions of something, and so the unit matters. Understanding when and why each of the little pieces can appropriately be called one-forty-eighth, one-eighth, or one-sixteenth is crucial in understanding fractions. Understanding that all three names for the quantity can be considered right is important, as is knowing what each means in this context. Moreover, most prospective teachers have considered fractions only as part of a single-unit whole, such that three-sixteenths

FIGURE 7.15. Teacher's representation of a student's talk about "three divided by sixteen."

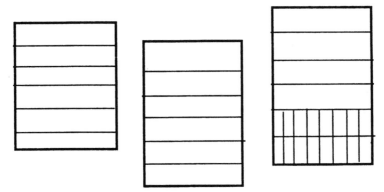

FIGURE 7.16. Teacher's representation of the left-over "little pieces" in a student's solution.

represents the result of taking a single whole, dividing it into 16 equal pieces and then "taking" three of those. The idea that 3/16 might mean three wholes divided equally into 16 pieces, and that the result of that division is in fact represented as 3/16, is new to them, as is the idea that it might mean three wholes divided into *18 pieces* so each share is 1/6 plus 1/48. Across the two problem contexts, the teacher educator seeks to expand, deepen, and better articulate prospective teachers' explicit and conceptual understanding of fractions. Prospective teachers' knowledge of fractions is challenged and developed from a simple regional part–whole representation of 3/16, as shown in Figure 7.15, to a conception of fractions that includes connections to division (3/16 as 3 divided by 16), fractions as parts of discrete sets, and fractions as continuous measures of any size whole. In addition, these problems offer the opportunity to explore alternative mathematical representations, particularly real-world contexts, and algebraic, numeric, and geometric representations. Not only can they develop a richer sense of alternative representations of a concept or a problem, but they also can compare the representations to investigate their mathematical translation and equivalence. Prospective teachers also can be helped to consider the strategic value of one representation over another in particular problem contexts. Representations make some aspects of the mathematical structure of a problem more visible, while obscuring others, an insight central both to doing mathematics and to teaching it. For example, sometimes an algebraic representation compresses, and through strategic use of mathematical notation, makes accessible certain key feature of a problem or an idea. Sometimes an algebraic representation does not illuminate, but may even complicate or hide a central relational or conceptual feature of a problem. Learning to analyze representations critically, both mathematically and pedagogically, is part of what working on these two problems can afford prospective teachers.

Having watched and discussed the "3 divided by 16" video, the teacher education students were asked to do the following assignment in their journals before the next class meeting:

Think about the following interpretations of 3 divided by 17:

3 PIZZAS DIVIDED AMONG 17 PEOPLE
3 DOLLARS DIVIDED AMONG 17 PEOPLE
3 DOZEN DONUTS DIVIDED AMONG 17 PEOPLE
WRITE OR DRAW AN EXPLANATION OF HOW YOU MIGHT
DO EACH OF THESE "FAIR SHARE" PROBLEMS.
NOW TRY DIVIDING THE SAME QUANTITIES OF PIZZA,
MONEY, AND DONUTS AMONG 15 PEOPLE. WHAT DIFFERENT
MATH GETS CALLED INTO PLAY?
NOW TRY DIVIDING THE SAME QUANTITIES OF PIZZA,
MONEY, AND DONUTS BETWEEN 2 PEOPLE. WHAT DIFFERENT
MATH GETS CALLED INTO PLAY THIS TIME?

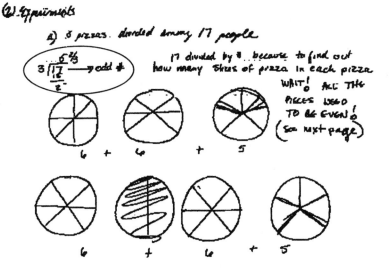

FIGURE 7.17. Patricia's work on the pizza problem.

In order to give the teacher education students the same opportunity as the fifth graders had to engage with the mathematics of division and fractions and to examine the relationships among these ideas, while at the same time having them recognize the control the teacher has over the issues that come up in a problem, they were challenged to work on "3 divided by 17." The mathematics they needed to engage would have some similarities to and some differences from what they had watched on the video. Like the second girl in the video, they might see a relationship between 3 and 17 that initially suggested that each quantity be divided into five pieces, but then they would come up *two* short. If they followed the lead of this girl, and then divided each quantity into six pieces, they would have 18 pieces all together and have to figure out what to do with the *one* extra. This gives the teacher educator the opportunity to challenge them to think about what it is about the numbers that makes it work out that way and to come up with conjectures about what would happen with other numbers: 18, 19, 20, and so on. Mathematically, she moves the students from the particular to the general. The task requires students to work with pizza, which is a unitary object that can be sliced; dollars, which can be traded for quarters, dimes, nickels, and pennies; and dozens of donuts, which present some features of each of these kinds of quantities, so that they would investigate different kinds of representations and construct some ideas about how representations and computations interact. It intertwines the mathematical with the pedagogical in that there are important things to notice about the relationships between the numbers and kinds of quantities, but there are also fundamental questions to consider, which a teacher might think about as she designs the tasks to be assigned to the class.

Figure 7.17 shows a page from Patricia's journal on which she worked on this problem. She begins by doing the computation (which is shown enlarged in Figure 7.18). It is not clear what she means by the label "odd

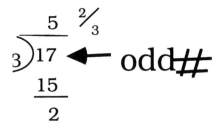

FIGURE 7.18. Patricia's computation as labeled.

#" next to the number 17 in her division, but this phrase is commonly used unconventionally to refer to division problems that do not "come out even." After doing this calculation, note that she draws three pizzas and divides them into 6 + 6 + 5 pieces. In her drawing, the pieces are not equal to one another, either in the two pizzas divided into sixths or the one divided into fifths. To the right of the calculation she "explains" what she did: "17 divided by 3 because you find out how many slices of pizza in each pizza. WAIT! All the pieces need to be even! (See next page.)" She does come back to the problem later. But first, on the same page as she worked on the pizza problem (part a), she works on "3 dollars divided among 17 people" (part b) and "3 dozen donuts divided among 17 people "(part c). Then, on the next page, she starts the pizza problem again. She rewrites the problem, draws one circle, and then writes:

> I am going to come back to part a) because I'm having difficulty with the number 17.

A few pages later, after working on a problem that was assigned in a later class, she writes (no drawing):

> 3 pizzas divided by seventeen people—each pizza divided into 17 pieces (even)—each person receives 3 pieces

She seemed satisfied with this solution, while she remained puzzled by her work on part c—3 dollars divided among 17, because

> Pizza can be broken down into almost any number of pieces and so can donuts. Money, however, cannot be broken down below 1 cent so I'm not sure what to do with the leftover 11 cents.

She does not consider whether it actually is possible to divide a pizza into 17 equal parts, or how one might do that.

Patricia's approach to the mathematics of rational numbers is typical, not only among the students we have worked with, but among American teachers broadly sampled.[5] By Patricia's own definition of what it might mean to know fractions (written in her journal on October 15 and cited above), she does not demonstrate "knowing" in her work on these problems. She does not demonstrate what she calls "an understanding of how to move from a whole to parts and back to the whole again." She is not able to "visualize" either the cookie jar problem or the pizza problem in a way that enables her to come up with a reasonable solution that is also expressive of an understanding of the quantities and relationship among quantities that fractions represent. Her "conceptualization of what it is to be whole" is limited, as she is unable to move flexibly from one perspective on the whole to another. Understanding how to answer the questions, "What makes something whole (numbers and objects)?" and "What makes something a part?"—which Patricia considers to be central to knowing fractions—is at the heart of being able to solve and explain one's solution to the cookie jar problem and the "3 divided by 17" problem.

By posing these mathematics problems as a journal assignment, the instructor gives students the opportunity to work as long as they like, together or alone, in a relaxed environment, before bringing their thinking to class and seeing what others have done with the problems. By the end of the term, Patricia will have seen several of her classmates attempt to explain their solutions and their thinking, and she will have seen the instructor function as a person who supportively questions everyone's reasoning. This teacher education pedagogy mirrors the mathematics teaching that Patricia is examining in the multimedia environment, adding another example of a teacher trying to establish a particular kind of "classroom culture" for her to consider. She also will have had multiple opportunities to try to figure out how others think, to puzzle about others' solutions and claims, and to try to make connections between how she thinks and how they do.

Looking at a conventional quiz that was administered in the second month of the term, we have some evidence that Patricia brought her mathematical investigations and her pedagogical investigations together. The first question on the quiz was:

> A delivery person has 111 cakes to distribute equally among 24 bakeries. Show two different ways that the cakes can be cut up so all 111 cakes can be used.

Like the problem of distributing 3 pizzas equally among 17 people, this problem confronts Patricia with the question of what to do with the leftovers, and the use of fractions as a way to represent her solution. Figures 7.19 and 7.20 show what Patricia did with this problem. Patricia's performance on this problem shows an improvement in her understanding of fractions since she tried dividing pizzas into 17 pieces. She moves flexibly back and forth among the concrete domain of cakes and bakeries, her graphic representations, and her numerical representations. She recognizes that it matters that the pieces be "equal" and even though the numbers are as "messy" as the numbers in the pizza problem, she confidently produces two alternative solutions. Of course, we cannot pinpoint what caused this improved understanding, but the nature of the change seems related to some of Patricia's work in the multimedia environment.

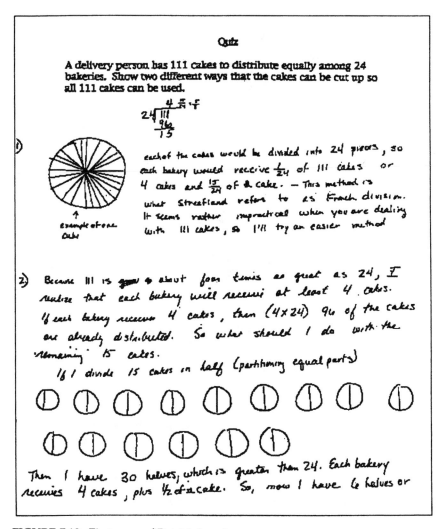

Quiz

A delivery person has 111 cakes to distribute equally among 24
bakeries. Show two different ways that the cakes can be cut up so
all 111 cakes can be used.

$$24\overline{)111}$$

each of the cakes would be divided into 24 pieces, so
each bakery would receive $\frac{1}{24}$ of 111 cakes   or
4 cakes and $\frac{15}{24}$ of a cake. — This method is
what Streefland refers to as French division.
It seems rather impractical when you are dealing
with 111 cakes, so I'll try an easier method

example of one
cake

2) Because 111 is _ + about four times as great as 24, I
realize that each bakery will receive at least 4 cakes.
If each bakery receives 4 cakes, then (4×24) 96 of the cakes
are already distributed. So what should I do with the
remaining 15 cakes.
If I divide 15 cakes in half (partitioning equal parts)

Then I have 30 halves, which is greater than 24. Each bakery
receives 4 cakes, plus ½ of a cake. So, now I have 6 halves or

FIGURE 7.19. First page of Patricia's quiz.

Field assignments also can serve to extend the contexts in use in the
course. In the semester in which Patricia did the work, complications interfered with finding sufficient field placements so she and her classmates
did not work in the field as part of their mathematics methods course.
Usually, however, the field is an integrated and important context in this
course. An instructor might ask teacher education students to design and

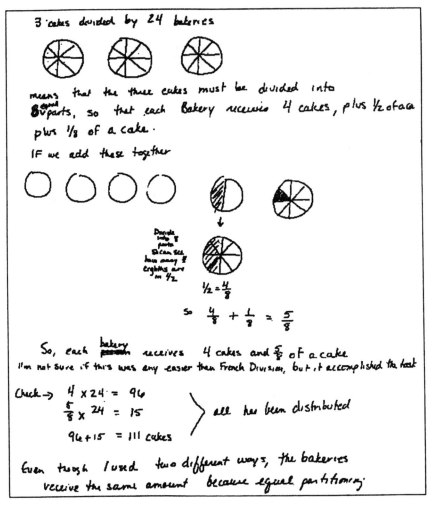

3 cakes divided by 24 bakeries

means that the three cakes must be divided into 8 equal parts, so that each Bakery receives 4 cakes, plus ½ of a ca plus ⅛ of a cake.

IF we add these together

Divide into 8 parts
So I can see how many ⅛ eighths are in ½

$½ = \frac{4}{8}$

So $\frac{4}{8} + \frac{1}{8} = \frac{5}{8}$

So, each ~~bakery~~ receives 4 cakes and ⅝ of a cake
I'm not sure if this was any easier than French Division, but it accomplished the task

Check → $4 \times 24 = 96$
$\frac{5}{8} \times 24 = 15$ ⟩ all has been distributed

$96 + 15 = 111$ cakes

Even though I used two different ways, the bakeries receive the same amount because equal partitioning.

FIGURE 7.20. Second page of Patricia's quiz.

teach a lesson on fractions, for example, building on the work done in class and adapting it for the ages of their children. The instructor might have prospective teachers examine textbooks at the level of their field placement classroom to see how curriculum is developed for fractions. In class, they might share the results of their investigations of curriculum materials, both to look critically at the development of ideas about fractions over time and to get a sense about curriculum materials across grades. They might interview their teacher about how he or she teaches fractions, and why, or they might design prompts about fractions and interview children in their classes. Again, they might pool their data across levels to get a broader sense of how children below and above third grade reason about fractions, as well as to compare Ball's third graders with others.

Returning to Patricia's Investigation of "Classroom Culture"

As we noted above, the final project in this course is designed to be an opportunity to revisit and integrate several earlier issues, questions, and assignments. For Patricia, it serves to bring together the mathematics of fractions, with which she has been struggling, and her concerns about making the classroom culture one that offers all students an opportunity to participate and learn. For her final report, Patricia restates her question about classroom culture in a way that is directly linked to learning mathematics. She introduces her report with a summary of the work that will follow.

Question: How does the classroom culture that D. Ball creates in her fractions unit reflect the kinds of mathematical skills and thinking she values?

> Deborah Ball establishes an interesting classroom culture for her third-grade fractions unit. The culture of her classroom seems to operate according to a theoretical framework. What D. Ball values about mathematical skills and thinking establishes the structure and content of each fractions lesson. While D. Ball definitely values the understanding of mathematical concepts and the application of those skills, she creates a culture which also supports the personal and social development of the students. She encourages discussions, debates, and oral presentations, and these serve to indicate what and how the students understand fractions. In my analysis, I attempt to evaluate D. Ball's goals and values, how she creates a culture which supports these values, and how successful this method is within the third-grade classroom. My analysis illustrates and interprets four distinct days in the multimedia environment from the beginning, middle, and end of the third-grade fractions unit.

By the time Patricia comes to write this report, she has had the opportunity to view teacher action over time in relation to teacher thinking over time. She has been able to revisit each of the teacher's actions several times and keep closely attached notes for each visit. She is aware that her own thinking has developed, and she includes some writing she did earlier in the term as well as her "final analysis" in her report.

My final analyses will be in blue characters. I interwove my analyses between the examples I pulled from the environment.

In her summary, Patricia is operating at the level of pedagogical big ideas. We have seen how the teacher educator worked with her, the task, and the multimedia environment to support her development at the nexus of theory and practice. A few pages into Patricia's project, she again copies the same excerpt from the teacher's notebook that appeared in her earlier work, but her annotation, presented in Figure 7.21, focuses squarely on the "fairness" issue (fractions mean *equal* pieces) in a way that was absent from her earlier draft. In her annotation of the next section (see Figure 7.22), Patricia says that the teacher's goal is *to see if* oral presentations will help students to understand. In the way she has constructed this annotation, she demonstrates her own understanding that the knowledge on which the teacher acts is tentative rather than factual. She seems to be viewing the teacher as a deliberate actor, testing out her ideas and acquiring knowledge about teaching in the context of teaching.

After these excerpts from Ball's journal, Patricia has a section in her investigation she calls "Analysis." The title of the analysis section is "The Culture of Fairness in Fractions." This title is telling because it pulls together the culture of *mathematics* (a culture in which parts of a whole must be equal parts) with the culture of *teaching and learning* (a culture in which the teacher

From Deborah Ball's notebook: April 23, 1990

```
One interesting thing to me about her clever solution was
that, contrary to what I've tended to assume, Cassandra
didn't seem to focus on the pieces being "fair" i.e., equal
in size: What mattered more, it seemed, was having the right
number of pieces. Is that an artifact of the representation
or if she were dealing with real cookies would see deal with
it the same way? I remember some arguments last year when we
worked with division and fractions where this "number of
pieces" frame dominated so that 4/8 and 4/16 seemed the same
to some people. This will be interesting to watch for when
we get more deeply and directly into fractions soon.
```

*"Fairness" is an important issue in fractions. By Cassandra's
explanation on April 24, 1990, the students are introduced to
why fractions need to be "fair" and why this means "equal parts."*

FIGURE 7.21. Annotated excerpt from Ball's teaching journal of 4/23/90 in Patricia's electronic notebook.

From D. Ball's journal, April 24, 1990

I added language to her explanation. (At some point it might
be interesting to compare how I help different people give
their explanations.) What I'm trying to see here is if
Cassandra can give a successful explanation implying
fractional remainders, will her understanding of the
mathematics be enhanced? It's a questions about the role of
explanation in learning, about the role of "self-concept" or
confidence in understanding, about my role in supporting her
in doing that. I was very directive, shaping and guiding her
explanation rather than so much questioning--eliciting of
ideas in order to make sense. I said things like, "The part I
don't understand is why you're dividing the cookie into
fourths when there are five people" and, even more directive,
"Those aren't halves--these are halves--drawing ① what are
these: ☐☐☐☐☐ ?" It's an interesting dilemma, for I want
Cassandra to be able to give public explanations of her
ideas for all the reasons outlined above (develop her
understanding, develop self-confidence) but I want it to be
hers, something she owns and understands. In trying to
support her--even the scaffolding metaphor seems to apply
here--I direct her more, with possible consequences in terms
of her own ability to confront ambiguity and stuckness. No--I
don't think that's right. What is difficult varies for each
child and one challenge is to stretch each one similarly.

*D. Ball's goal here is to see if oral presentations will help
students' understanding of mathematics and fractions. She
also makes it clear that although she is teaching
mathematics, she also wants to foster the students' social
and personal development (i.e., self-concept).*

*I think this paragraph in D. Ball's journal is a key to what I want to explore
for my project. How does D. Ball "scaffolding" help create a particular
classroom culture, and does this culture achieve her goals: develop
understanding of fractions and develop self-confidence? For whom will
Ball's type of culture work? Does it work for individual students or the class
as a whole?*

FIGURE 7.22. Annotated excerpt from Ball's teaching journal of 4/23/90 in
Patricia's electronic notebook.

guides but does not tell students how to use the tools they have available to solve problems).

Unlike Patricia's earlier work, this analysis interprets the teaching and learning that occurred in Ball's classroom as a continuous and cumulative process that happened over time. She is investigating the mathematical territory around the meaning of a fraction and the pedagogical territory of representation, every so often wandering into related "big ideas" like the importance of the unit or the role of self-confidence in mathematical reasoning.

The Culture of Fairness in Fractions

During Cassandra's explanation to D. Ball on April 23, 1990, D. Ball does not explain why Cassandra should use rectangular cookies. She simply asks if it is okay if she changes Cassandra's drawings to rectangular cookies [see Figure 7.22]. Similarly, D. Ball has Cassandra create rectangular cookies in her explanation to the whole class on April 24, 1990. D. Ball does not explain why it is "easier" to use rectangular cookies. Initially, I thought that D. Ball was ignoring the issue because she wanted Cassandra to be able to solve the problem without the difficulty of dividing circular cookies, although this may have been part of the goal for D. Ball because she wants students to build their self-confidence with mathematical thinking. The students definitely gain self-confidence when they solve a problem and rectangular cookies do make the solution easier. However, D. Ball telling Cassandra to use rectangular cookies without explaining why is similar to D. Ball giving the students a problem without saying why or how to solve it.

Here Patricia is taking the long view of Ball's teaching actions and giving them meaning in terms of the flow of events across several lessons. She continues:

She wants the students to decide their reasoning and present it to the class. She guides the students and Cassandra by implying that it is better to use rectangular cookies. Only after the math period on April 24, 1990 did D. Ball ask the class why rectangular cookies are easier to divide than circular cookies. By having the students discuss and experience through real problems why rectangular cookies are better, the class begins to be introduced to the idea of fairness in fractions. Cassandra learns to divide cookies among her family members, and in the process, she learns that fractions are parts of a whole and that these parts must be equal parts of the whole. Sean says that the pieces wouldn't be equal in Cassandra's original circular picture, so rectangular cookies make it easier to divide the amount evenly. Understanding equal parts is an essential component of learning fractions.

When Patricia says, "By having the students discuss and experience through real problems why rectangular cookies are better, the class begins to be introduced to the idea of fairness in fractions," she is making a statement about the complexity of the concepts underlying an understanding of fractions. She points out that the third graders are *beginning to be introduced* to those concepts, not being taught a strategy to remember for coming up with right answers. In this analysis, Patricia expresses empathy for both the teacher and Cassandra. She "understands" what is going on here by adopting both of their points of view, among others. She is no longer the outsider who labels students' work and teacher actions with simple categories like "engaged/not engaged" or "right/wrong."

With regard to the mathematics, Patricia seems to have gained a degree of appreciation for the teacher's way of thinking about the issue of round versus rectangular cookies. Her own struggles with the fractions problems in the methods class and her growing attention to representation as an aspect of mathematical thinking may be related to her work on this project.

Patricia's Reflections on Her Own Learning

The last task of the final project that we have been analyzing was:

> Reflect on how your investigation of classroom culture might impact on what you would do or think about doing as an elementary mathematics teacher.

Implicitly, this task is an invitation for the students to consider what kind of knowledge might be useful to them as teachers. In responding to this task, Patricia writes in a way that is unusually explicit about how she thought about mathematical knowledge and pedagogical knowledge at the beginning of the course, and how she thinks about it at the end. She takes it as an opportunity to reflect on herself both as a knower of mathematics and a knower of teaching. Although Patricia's capacity for representing her own learning is unusual among the students we have taught, we include it here to give a glimpse of what is possible to see with teacher education students who work inside the approach to teacher education we have been describing.

Patricia begins by explaining how, at the beginning of the semester, she did not think that this methods course was going to challenge her understanding of what it means to know mathematics. What she believed about "knowing" mathematics was linked with her assumptions about how one would teach it and learn it.

Part 5: Multimedia Environment Impact on Me

Exploring and analyzing D. Ball's third-grade fractions unit has caused me to reconsider all of my preconceptions about teaching and learning mathematics. When I entered the Education 411 class, I expected it to be very objective and very boring. I did not realize that fractions, or any mathematics for that matter, could be discussed, conjectured, or debated. I did not know that there are different ways of learning mathematics that require innovative teaching methods. After reading the *Professional Standards for Teaching Mathematics* and the *Curriculum Standards for Teaching Mathematics*, I have discovered that learning mathematical knowledge and concepts is a process, not a challenge that is overcome and beaten.

In the next segment of her conclusion, Patricia writes about the kind of knowledge she thought she would need, and expected to get in the methods course. She refers to her early writing about "what it means to know fractions" (quoted above), as she talks about her changing conception of what she thinks a teacher needs to do and what she needs to know in order to do it. She says she focused in that writing on "the skills of learning" and not on "the process of understanding." It is difficult to interpret what she means here by skills, but it is clear that the conception of "knowing math" she had when the course began did not include discussion, debate, and collaboration.

When I began Education 411, I expected to learn objective methods for teaching mathematics. I did not anticipate, nor want to alter my perception of what it means to know or teach mathematics. I liked hating math because it gave me an excuse to ignore my difficulty with it. Besides, I thought, how difficult can it be to teach elementary students mathematical concepts and knowledge? The first part of the course allowed me the opportunity to explore how I learn mathematics and how other students learn mathematics. In my analysis of "what it means to know fractions," I concentrated on the skills involved to know fractions (i.e., must know equal parts of whole, must know unit, must know numerator, must know denominator). It seems that I focused on the skills of learning fractions, rather than the process of understanding. In the second half of the course, however, I began to see the implications of mathematical learning on teaching. What sort of classroom culture can I create to develop students' understanding? This course has enlightened me to a whole world that I never would have considered.

Patricia makes further links as she considers how thinking about mathematics differently leads to thinking about teaching differently.

Math is discussion? Math is debate? Math is collaboration? I admit that I was skeptical in the beginning, but now I see how it all comes together. I see that math does not have to be dry and impersonal and antisocial. Using the "methods" that I have learned in the multimedia environment and the 411 class discussions, I have begun to reconsider my initial conceptions. Not only can students develop their math abilities in a culture similar to D. Ball's third-grade fractions unit, but students also learn to be communicative and positive peer collaborators. It seems that the job of teaching mathematics to elementary students is more complicated than I thought. Nevertheless, if I rely on student insights, reasoning, and cooperation, I will probably be a more successful math educator.

In the end, Patricia puts a value on students' capacity *to think for themselves* (insights, reasoning, and cooperation). She also exhibits a greater tendency *to think for herself* about both how to do *and* how to teach mathematics.

What Might Patricia Have Learned in Her Mathematics Methods Course?

In Chapter 3 we described some of what we know about what preservice elementary teachers bring with them to teacher education. They have had, for the most part, thin and often unsuccessful experiences with mathematics. They bring many assumptions about the teacher's role, what children are interested in, how a teacher helps children learn, what is important about the environment of a classroom. Many of these ideas are common, for they develop from preservice teachers' experience as students themselves in American classrooms. Patricia is no exception. So an important question to ask is the skeptical one: What is she learning from all this work in her mathematics methods class, using the multimedia environment as a site for an investigation of teaching, discussing that inquiry with others, and complementing all that with her work out in schools?

Because we are inclined toward conjecture rather than certainty, we conclude this chapter with some questions about what she *might* have learned. The information we have offers us some glimpses of changes in Patricia across time in Lampert's class. For example, she begins her work in the multimedia environment with an investigation of one child, Tembe. At the outset, she and her classmate are quite definite in their appraisal of him. They reach conclusions relatively easily. He is, according to them, not very engaged most of the time. They make similar assumptions about Tembe's classmates: If the children do not talk, the prospective teachers think they are disengaged. By the end of her project on classroom culture, Patricia is far more tentative. She asks far more questions and makes far fewer conclusions. She makes proposals and conjectures, and she considers context; she seems to realize and appreciate that she does not—and perhaps cannot—know some things here, and perhaps even not in real time in a real classroom.

In her concluding reflection on the course, Patricia writes of having encountered perspectives on mathematics she has never thought about. She suddenly sees mathematics as involving debate, discussion, and collaboration. She has seen the light: "Math does not have to be dry and impersonal and antisocial." Patricia seems relieved at this. She had thought, prior to this course, that mathematics was "boring." Not any more. Now she sees it as more engaging and complicated. Patricia also had thought that mathematics teaching would be easy: "How difficult can it be to teach elementary students mathematical concepts and knowledge?"

These changes that Patricia reports are good but also worrisome. That she now understands mathematics to involve discourse, representation, and reasoning seems worthy. That she makes no mention of the place of skills—something she thought *was* mathematics before she took this course—gives us pause. Is Patricia developing a new imbalance in her conception of mathematics, from a skills focus to a arena of debate and interaction? We cannot know what she means when she says in her reflection, "Math is discussion? Math is debate? Math is collaboration?" we do not know whether she now sees reasoning and talking as the core of mathematics. We do not know what her ideas are about what constitutes mathematical discussion or debate, and what counts as evidence to verify a solution or establish the truth of a claim. We do not know whether she recognizes that "skills" are fundamental to doing mathematical argument. Moreover, we are concerned that Patricia does not mention feeling that she herself has become more competent in mathematics. When she says she now believes that she can "rely on student insights, reasoning, and cooperation," we wonder what she will do with those processes to turn them toward students' learning of mathematics.

Patricia now also thinks teaching is much more complicated. She is, it seems, taking it and preparing to do it much more soberly. She has developed a grounded appreciation of how much thinking it is going to take to do it well, how much more uncertain some of her moves and decisions will be than what she likely expected. This is good news, for a more complex view of the work can help her be a more self-aware learner in teacher education.

But we also wonder: What does she mean by saying teaching is complex? In what features of practice is her appreciation of its complexity rooted? Does she just think it is "hard," or has she learned some specific recurrent dilemmas or challenges? Has she learned a slogan ("teaching is hard") or does she have a set of ideas with which to learn to teach and to teach? And does she understand that in teaching, as in mathematics, not all solutions are equally worthy, not all reasons equally sound? Is she developing a sense of pedagogical and professional norms, and a sense of how to examine an issue, analyze it, and determine a move or interpretation that she can justify professionally?

CONCLUSION

As with the students whose investigations we analyzed in Chapter 6, we wonder about how particular or general Patricia's learning is. She studied the classroom of one third-grade teacher. Because of the term during which she began as a teacher education student, she did not have a field placement simultaneously with taking the mathematics methods course. While on the one hand we celebrate her discovery that students can think and talk about mathematics, we worry that she does not raise any questions about how specialized the context is in which they do that. She did not make any observations about the age of the students or question whether this kind of talk might be easier to do among third graders than seventh graders. There are many things that teacher education students can study in the multimedia environment, but they cannot get much of a perspective on how "typical" the children are or where the teacher fits along a spectrum of pedagogical accomplishment. We see that Patricia has examined the thinking that Ball does as she constructs her actions, but we wonder how much Patricia appreciates what it takes to learn to do that well. At the end of this course, we sent Patricia off to do student teaching the following semester, hoping that some of the habits of thinking about teaching would stay with her as a continuing learner.

We can make no claims about whether Patricia learned more with these new technologies in the context of a new pedagogy of teacher education. She did learn *differently* than she would have in a conventional methods course, and perhaps she learned in a way that will have an impact on her knowing teaching in practice. When we compare her work with that of the students whose projects we examined in Chapter 6, we see that she is guided by her instructor to focus in ways that few of the other students did. For example, she considered the mathematics in the context of teaching questions, something we had come to realize would not happen automatically. The assignment also focused her work on classroom culture, an idea her instructor knew to be central to practice and yet not an idea that a single one of the 68 investigation projects had focused on. In Chapter 8, we turn to the questions that have surfaced from our analyses of curriculum, pedagogy, and student work.

CHAPTER 8

Investigating Teaching
in Teacher Education

We now turn to new questions, questions born of our opportunity to investigate teaching in the context of teacher education and to explore what
it might mean to ground teacher preparation in the study of records of
practice. Three headings capture our current challenges: one focuses
on what we have yet to learn about teacher education students' experiences and learning, a second on the central problem of learning big ideas
through the examination of particulars, and the third on what such
rethinking of teacher education raises for the development of teacher
educators.

THE CHALLENGE OF WHAT WE DON'T KNOW
ABOUT STUDENTS' LEARNING

Our perusal of the 68 investigations, of Patricia's work, and of the work of
her peers—in order to figure out what teacher education students might
have learned—places us in the position in which preservice teacher Andrea
found herself. We are, in a way, seeking to know "what was covered."
Clearly, examining the assignments alone does not answer that question,
for so much about the opportunity to learn is left, by design, to be constructed as it is enacted. So we look at the students' projects. What does
that yield? What do we still have little insight into?

Our examination of teacher education students' work reveals a number of useful patterns in prospective teachers' and their instructors' use of
the multimedia environment. We see what they investigated and see them,
guided by their own assumptions, wending their way through a thicket of
records of practice. We see what kinds of questions predominate and we
can examine the nature of those questions. Visible also are some of the
assumptions, preferences, and inclinations of prospective teachers. At times
we see signs that their work in the multimedia environment has pushed
their thinking beyond where it was when they started. We also see how

they use the records of practice to reinforce the beliefs they bring with them into teacher education.

Despite this, there is much we do not yet know about what this work offers or helps to create. Repeatedly, instructors commented to students that they would like to see more of the *processes* of their work. We want to be able to understand not only the questions, sites of inquiry, information, and conclusions. In order to understand prospective teachers' reasoning and ideas, it would help if we had more insight into the things they do not record: video they looked at and rejected; discussions in their groups about interpretations of particular children, events, and teacher moves; struggles they had with a bit of mathematics or a child's statement.

We also do not know what these teacher education students took from their work, what conclusions or questions really found their way into their thinking, or what may have grown from initial work they did here. Did Andrea continue to develop her ideas about "coverage"? Did the group who focused on Harooun continue to problematize "simple" terms like *shy*? Did the groups who worked on classroom management find their ideas shifting once they got out and tried to manage classrooms themselves?

Further, we do not know whether and when students learned from one another. Did listening to one another's presentations, or working together in project groups, influence what they learned? Did they change one another's resources for interpretation? Did they develop habits of mind from one another? Was there value in the group design of the work, beyond the obvious practical value?

Maybe there are other trajectories of growth that we do not know how to recognize or track. For example, perhaps it is not the particulars of their investigation topics and conclusions that stay with these beginning teachers. Perhaps they collect from their work material for the composition of their teaching selves. Maybe it is through the focused opportunity to study a teacher in practice that they develop elements they use in constructing the way they talk with children. Possibly they take with them images of qualities as elusive as the rhythm and tone of classroom discussions, a stance of respect toward learners, a seriousness of manner, a kind of attention to students, commitment, patience-in-action, or other matters of manner, person, and role.

Similarly, we do not know whether their learning may have been impeded by some aspect of their work with the records of practice. Might the weight of "real" data have convinced them prematurely of ideas that they would do better to hold as conjectures? Or did the fact that the teachers in the materials are university faculty—even, in some cases, their own instructors—affect positively or negatively their thinking about what they were seeing?

THE CHALLENGE OF AIMING FOR BIG IDEAS
THROUGH THE STUDY OF PARTICULARS

In the lesson she taught on September 18, Ball designed the problem about the three coins very deliberately. Her journal entry for the day shows that she explored the problem's mathematical contours as she prepared the lesson: How did it work out with only two coins? Or with four? Or if quarters were part of the collection as well? In addition to maneuvering her way around the mathematical territory opened by this problem, she noted the things she thought this problem would enable her to learn about her third graders, on this early day in September. She also had considered what this problem might communicate to her students about what it would mean to do mathematics in this class this year. Once the lesson was underway, she further designed the task in action. In fact, the first time she set out to do it, the day before the lesson we looked at, she decided no more than 3 minutes into it that the problem was too difficult for her students with three coins, so she reduced the constraint to two coins. Even at that, her role in the discussion was crucial in developing the enacted curriculum. The construction of curriculum for mathematics education does not stop at the classroom door, but is distributed across the pedagogical life cycle of a curricular idea. The teacher plays a significant role in shaping what gets taught and studied as it happens.[1]

In our work on teacher education, we now come full circle, having gained a deeper appreciation for how this idea plays out at a new level. When Patricia's investigation focused on Ball's decision to have students work alone before they worked in small groups in the video of a third-grade lesson Patricia had watched, Lampert inserted a comment that suggested not only different questions, but different *kinds* of questions: "Why might this method of beginning to work on the problem make sense?" and "What are some arguments against doing this?" Here Lampert takes Patricia into the terrain of pedagogical decision making where theories about the interpersonal dynamics characteristic of 8-year-olds and the social construction of ideas bump up against practical questions about how much time to spend on one thing or another or how to arrange the chairs. When Patricia comments on the attention Ball pays to whether she should use round or rectangular cookies, Lampert asks Patricia to reflect on why such a choice is important. Lampert constructs and chooses mathematics problems for her teacher education class to work on that have them traveling the terrain of mathematical representations of fractions over and over again. She asks questions as they talk about their work that foster mathematical as well as pedagogical inquiry.

As with the third graders' work with coins, teacher education students' work in the multimedia environment relies heavily on the instructor's capacity to navigate the terrain under investigation, interactively construct-ing curriculum with students. One important part of this role, as we have seen, is the construction, selection, and use of tasks. A second is helping learners to study something more than the particulars at hand, to develop ideas that have heft and generativity beyond the immediate context. It is precisely this movement from the particular to the general and from the familiar to the new that makes the work educative, as opposed to simply an "experience" or the completion of tasks. Whether in mathematics or teaching, how does a teacher help students move from the particulars of a learning context to more general understandings that can support their ongoing learning and practice? Building from the investigation of particu-lar records of teaching to knowledge of teaching more generally, is analo-gous to the challenge faced in helping children learn mathematics from their engagement with particular problems or materials.

Let's consider this analogy more closely. In the elementary mathemat-ics class, Ball begins her work with the third graders with a pile of coins and a concrete question: "I have pennies, nickels, and dimes in my pocket. If I pull three coins out, what amount of money could I have?" (see Fig-ure 8.1). But she does not stop with having posed this problem. She moves out from there to have students think about the multiple possible combi-nations. Coming up with one solution that works—for example, "You can make 15¢ by using three nickels"—is different from coming up with mul-tiple solutions. The first entails simple arithmetic, the latter an engagement with the numerical patterns that produce additional combinations. Based on students' experiments and discussion at this level, the teacher broad-ens the focus still further with a question about mathematical argument and evidence, asking the students to construct knowledge and formulate

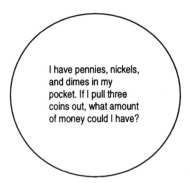

I have pennies, nickels, and dimes in my pocket. If I pull three coins out, what amount of money could I have?

FIGURE 8.1. The "Three Coin Problem" at the level of particular solutions.

an assertion that is removed from the specific problem with which they began. She asks them, "How do you know if you have *all* the possible solutions?" This question is a quintessentially mathematical one that is crucial to ask in many mathematical contexts. By posing it, Ball creates the opportunity for her students to engage a mathematical issue that is more general than anything about the specific problem at hand. She has constructed a task that makes adding groups of coins an opportunity to learn several things: addition combinations, looking for multiple solutions, determining the completeness of a solution, and the intellectual habit of asking about the completeness of any solution. In the way she interacts with students, she asks questions and redirects their work in an effort to turn the opportunities afforded by the task into experiences that have educative value beyond the solution of the particular problem. She pushes them to new queries beyond those they are already inclined to pursue and focuses their attention on mathematical issues larger than the context of this problem (see Figure 8.2). In teacher education, instructors face a similar task: how to move students from the particularities of the teaching text under examination to questions about teaching that are larger and conclusions that are more general. In the end, deeply probing the work of one lesson is likely to have little effect on the ways in which prospective teachers think about knowledge for practice or on what they know or can do beyond the present context. What is needed is to help them formulate ideas, methods of inquiry, and habits of mind that they can take with them into any context.

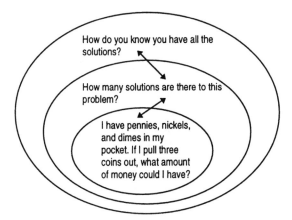

FIGURE 8.2. Three levels of the "Three Coin Problem" moving out from particular to general.

Returning to the segment of mathematics teaching we saw from September 18, we observe that Ball faced several issues: who to call on, what questions to ask, who to push further, where to take the mathematics, how much to tell the children about combinations, and so on. As they examine this piece of teaching, prospective teachers could work on questions of managing a mathematical classroom discourse (see Figure 8.3). But simply figuring out what is going on in Ball's third-grade class one September morning is not adequate to prepare teachers for practice. Although a fine-grained analysis of this lesson, these children, and this day of Ball's teaching has initial interest and produces some knowledge of the context, it would not be educative to stop with that analysis, if our purpose was to educate students for teaching. This is no different from the issue of third graders learning to produce some, but not all, solutions to the coin problem. Prospective teachers need to learn more than immediate and local interpretations. As they investigate the many particular problems that arise in the lessons in the multimedia environment, they "travel a wide field of thought crisscrossed in every direction."[2] These journeys are designed to be opportunities to learn things that can help them teach and continue to learn as teachers (see Figure 8.4).

To design such opportunities, the instructor at times may need to make explicit connections with the mathematics work teacher education students did in the course and with the issues that were raised as students talked about their field placements. In doing this, the instructor would seek to help the teacher education students begin to see their investigations of the particulars of one specific third- or fifth-grade classroom as a medium for a much broader investigation of teaching and learning crucial to developing knowledge of and for practice. To be educative, their work must be

On whom is Mrs. Ball calling?

What role is she playing in this discussion?

How do children find out if they were right?

FIGURE 8.3. Pedagogical problems at the level of the particular.

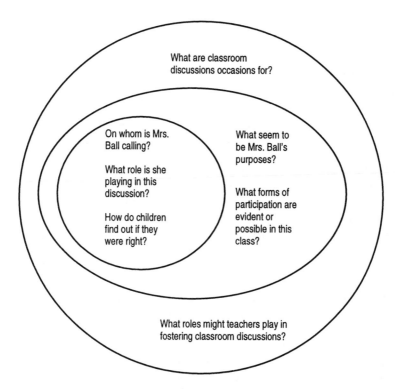

FIGURE 8.4. Three levels of pedagogical problems moving out from the particular to the general.

situated across multiple levels rather than in the mere study of one class or the vague generalities in which so much knowledge about teaching is expressed. How the instructor manages the interplay among grounded particulars, broader contexts, and bigger ideas is crucial in making this sort of work educative.

THE CHALLENGE OF LEARNING AS A TEACHER EDUCATOR

In Chapter 3, we considered three arguments for the lack of impact of conventional teacher education: the discontinuities between the experience that teacher education students bring with them and the formal education they are offered, the institutional and programmatic contexts of teacher education, and the assumptions about knowledge in teacher education programs.

In our work on turning records of practice into a multimedia environment for educating teachers, we have attempted to incorporate a more fruitful set of assumptions about what and how teachers know in practice. We have built in many opportunities for teacher education students to expose the ideas and assumptions that come from watching teachers through several years of formal education, and for teacher educators to respond to them. But it is only with the articulation of our understanding of the crucial role of the teacher educator that we can begin to address the problem of institutional and programmatic context.

We have argued that the teacher educator interactively guides investigations in the multimedia environment toward the big ideas of practice, having chosen tasks that have the potential to engage students in fruitful inquiry. This speculation suggests that in order to use records of practice in ways that are educative toward the purpose of learning teaching, teacher educators need to both know teaching and know how to do the kind of teaching that negotiates between students and content. If, as the literature suggests, most of the people who teach teachers do not think of themselves as teacher educators, and even those who do are unlikely to have a deep knowledge of teaching, then much needs to change before we can take the next step with the approach to teacher education that we have been investigating. Educating teacher educators in a way that will prepare them to use materials like those we have gathered is not happening in today's graduate schools of education. Very few prospective teacher educators have the kinds of experiences that we reported in the early chapters of this book. We end this stage in our ongoing investigation of teaching and teacher education with a question about what sort of policies and programs could be designed to support an appropriate education for teacher educators.

Experience and Education

LEARNING TO TEACH

David Cohen

The relationship between learning to teach and experience with teaching is an old and troublesome puzzle. Many teacher educators and teachers have argued for more pre-professional work in schools, thinking that it would add practical experience and redress the emphasis on theoretical work in university teacher education. But many university scholars see practical experience as the problem, arguing that intending teachers' extended exposure to conventional teaching, both as students in school and as practice teachers, hardens them against efforts to improve teaching. Experience with teaching figures both as the salvation of teacher education and as its greatest enemy.

EXPERIENCE AND ITS PROBLEMS

Once upon a time American teachers had little but experience, for they attended grammar school and then went to work, learning what they could about teaching as they taught. Horace Mann and other reformers billed that as a disaster and pressed for more formal academic preparation. During the ensuing century and a half, most efforts to improve teacher education focused on adding or modifying academic preparation. Learning to teach by experience was an enemy in these endeavors, for it was thought both to produce rudimentary classroom work and to keep professional status low. Reformers argued that more formal schooling for teachers, in institutions of higher education, would save them from drowning in primitive experience and being kept in a state of professional subservience.

Efforts to devise better clinical experience blossomed a bit near the end of the nineteenth century, when a few normal schools organized teacher education around the study of exemplary classroom work in laboratory schools. More clinical education also became a particular dream of some Progressive educators, in part because Dewey and others saw that unless teacher education was informed by knowledge of good practice, intending teachers would be more likely to learn the wrong lessons in conventional classrooms. In these cases, educators tried to offer carefully supervised experience in controlled settings as an antidote both to what teachers had learned as students and to what they might learn from ordinary teaching experience.

But by the turn of the twentieth century normal schools began to be captured by the developing system of higher education, and teachers' professional preparation moved into college and university classrooms, closer to academic disciplines but further from practice.[1] In the 1920s and 1930s the Bank Street College of Education and a few sister institutions found ways to use classroom practice as a focus for teacher education, but they were only a small eddy in the rising tide of academic professionalism. The force of that tide was multiplied by state laws that tied certification and licensing to the completion of specific college or university coursework, and the growing influence of teacher unions later strengthened those links by tying salary schedules, tenure, and seniority to university coursework, certification, and licensing.

Hopes for expanded clinical studies rose again in the 1980s and 1990s, as some reformers and academics tried to invent professional development schools or other arrangements that would root teacher education more deeply in experience with good teaching. But the old arguments remained lively, for efforts to create "alternative routes" to teaching also blossomed during the same period. These programs vary in many respects, but all seek to break the grip of university professional preparation by placing candidates who have little or no pre-professional education in classrooms as full-time teachers. Experience, often little supervised, is offered as an antidote to the monopoly that higher education has had on professional learning.

Everyone in these arguments agrees that experience with practice is important, for candidates need above all else to become competent beginners. To do so they must learn how to teach as well as learning about teaching. How much they need to learn depends on how complex and intellectually ambitious one thinks teaching is, and there is much disagreement about that. But even if one thinks it is only moderately complex, intending teachers would have a great deal to learn—including knowledge of how children think about academic matters and how to manage their thinking in classrooms, familiarity with instructional materials, knowledge of how to frame assignments in the subjects to be taught, knowledge of what good, poor, and indifferent student work would look like, and much more.

The entries on that little list imply that knowledge of how to teach is somehow different from the disciplinary knowledge that one teaches. Scientists want to find the truth about the structure of the atom or the genetic content of DNA. Historians want to know what life was like for African-Americans on southern plantations, what Jefferson thought about cities, and why Catholic Americans felt compelled to organize their own school systems. Such knowledge is essential to teaching and learning—there could be none without it—but as commentators on education have known, at least since John Dewey pointed it out, knowledge that is organized and held from disciplinary perspectives is not sufficient for thoughtful instruction.[2] In addition to disciplinary knowledge, historians who teach should know how to help students cultivate historical imagination, think historically, employ historical research methods, know and use sources, and make defensible arguments about the past. To do such things these teaching scholars should know how to use knowledge in ways that will engage students, provoke work on serious problems, and open opportunities to learn the art and craft of historical studies. As disciplinary researchers, they must know how truth is established in their subject, but as teachers, they must know how to help others learn the truth and how to find it for themselves. Knowledge of disciplines thus would be held and used in somewhat different ways when scholars seek the truth and when they help others learn how to seek it.

Critics and defenders of university-based teacher education accept the validity of learning disciplinary knowledge in traditional form—the "content"—and disagree chiefly about the role of direct experience in learning how to teach content. But a hard-and-fast distinction between disciplinary knowledge and learning to teach probably is unwise. I argued just above that learning to teach prominently includes learning both how to use disciplinary knowledge pedagogically and learning how disciplinary knowledge is acquired. If intending teachers learned not only the disciplines they teach, but also how disciplinary concepts, operations, and arguments are learned and can be taught, they would be learning two faces of the same body of knowledge. They might, for example, do so in part by studying cases of how students in ordinary classrooms thought about particular mathematical concepts, how the students' ideas related to mathematical thought, and how teachers might respond to students' ideas. Learning about mathematics could be situated in part in learning how children think about mathematics, how they respond to different sorts of tasks and assignments, how to understand children's thinking, and how to frame better and worse assignments.

My point is not that real mathematics should be replaced with "methods," but that exploring the pedagogical content of mathematics—that is, evidence on how learners understand central ideas and procedures, and how teaching can influence and respond to learners' ideas—could enhance intending teachers' understanding of mathematics as well as their capacity to teach it well. Work of this sort would require that evidence of children's and teachers' classroom experience be made central to university instruction, but it is not necessarily an argument for more work in schools. Learning mathematics "in practice" might be done by bringing evidence about learners' work and teaching into university classrooms, where it can be studied in detail, rather than shipping university students out to schools where sustained study would be difficult to arrange in the midst of ongoing practice.

These comments suggest that the long-standing opposition between academic studies and practical experience turns on overly simple ideas about experience and where it can occur. For instance, if educational psychology courses centered on teaching and learning academic subjects in classrooms—including relevant psychological theory and research—intending teachers could learn a great deal about learning and teaching in schools through indirect experience while in the university. Unfortunately, educational psychology historically has focused on what psychologists took to be general laws of learning, research on motivation, and the like, just as mathematics and history courses for teachers focused on teaching some set of topics that disciplinary scholars see as central with no attention to how they might be understood, learned, or taught. Most pre-professional courses have been presented from the disciplinary perspectives that are thought to be suitable to universities, rather than from the professional perspectives that would be suitable to learning a practice. Instructional research and theory are no exception to this argument: They could bear on practice if university scholars chose to make professional work the center of their attention.[3] If teacher education were reframed from a perspective of practice, many overly simple distinctions—between disciplines and "methods," between theory and practice, between academic work and experience, and between school and university learning—helpfully would erode.

Efforts to expand experience in teacher education have focused much more on exporting intending teachers to schools than on importing knowledge of practice to universities. With a few exceptions, that export trade has been limited to the "practical" component of teacher education, which often includes observation and limited work in classrooms during one or more undergraduate years, and nearly always includes 6 or 8 weeks or even a semester of full-time school attendance and "practice teaching." Many teachers later report that this was the only useful element in their professional education and say that one of the main things they learned was how to manage a roomful of children.

But such apprenticeships have as many limitations as advantages. Most of the observational work that intending teachers do has been arranged to broadly familiarize them with schools and classrooms and introduce them to the teacher's role, rather than to help them learn deeply about what teachers and students are doing, and why, and whether it works. Similarly, practice teaching rarely has offered extended opportunities to design academic tasks, to learn to interpret students' responses, to experiment with modifying tasks in light of students' responses, to manage discussions, to carefully investigate the results of teaching in learners' work, and so on. Intending teachers have had as few opportunities to investigate other teachers' practice as to probe their own; hence few have learned very deeply about either practice or how to teach. Many report that they were grateful just to have acquired some "survival skills."

If one wants to understand the place that experience could play in teacher education, it is no less important to understand why imports from practice to universities never developed than to understand why exports from university teacher education to practice have been so limited. One reason for the latter is institutional barriers in universities: The development of university education curricula as departmental courses with various distribution requirements left little place for extended work elsewhere. More experience in schools would have required more than a few hours a day for a few semesters, but the schedule of courses and graduation requirements left intending teachers only bits of time to do anything else. That problem has increased as expanding requirements and courses have steadily pushed 4-year degree programs toward 5-year programs.

The growing emphasis on faculty research productivity and specialized disciplinary credentials not only reinforced the focus on work within academe, but also created barriers to the study of classroom experience within universities. To greatly extend clinical studies in schools would have required either that the supervising university faculty become capable schoolteachers or that practicing schoolteachers be allowed to instruct undergraduates off campus for credit. Such requests would have been met with hostility by academics who were trying to build research universities, disciplines, their own scholarly reputations, and faculty power. Appointing teachers to university positions or turning university faculty into competent schoolteachers and supervisors would have struck many as a return to the bad old days of academic disrepute, when higher education had weak standards and faculty had few special academic qualifications and did little research. In addition, the growing status of disciplinary teaching and inquiry meant that professional studies—including teaching and research on professional practice in universities—had low status, even in professional schools. For example, one mark of a high-status law school came to be its faculty's disdain for the study of legal practice; education faculty followed this dismal example by orienting their teaching and research to the academic disciplines rather than professional studies.

Even if universities had desperately wanted to increase learning from experience, there would have been an acute shortage of opportunities. One reason rarely has been considered: Few universities tried to import elements of practice from schools to academe. University faculty could have collected strategic examples of students' work from ordinary classrooms and used them as curriculum for the university study of learning and teaching academic subjects. Members of education faculties could have collaborated with faculties in the disciplines to study the teaching and learning of academic subjects, and used the results to inform teachers' university education. University teacher educators could have composed cases of classroom learning and teaching, and used them as part of the curriculum of teacher education. Intending teachers could have learned to role play students' responses to lessons, to learn more about how students think about topics and how teachers might respond. Education faculty could have established tutorial programs in which intending teachers taught schoolchildren a few important topics in the school curriculum, collected evidence on their learning, and used the results as part of the curriculum for teacher education. And university classes could have been used as laboratories in which to try out the teaching and learning of particular topics, so that intending teachers could learn some of what their future students would learn, enabling them to turn their experience as learners into curriculum for their education as teachers.

Experience means several different things in these examples: copying fragments of real experience in order to study it, imitating experience in order to learn what it is like, documenting experience in order to understand it, and mimicking experience in order to profit from something close to professional work. Each example suggests ways in which elements or versions of classroom work could have been imported into intending teachers' university education, but few have been tried—apart from a few small experiments. Many of the resources required seem trivial: pencils, paper, people, and bits of time; but some other resources, while even less costly, have been more rare: imagination and university faculty who understood that deep knowledge of teaching and learning should be at the center of teacher education.

One reason for the absence of such work is the nature of teacher education itself. Teacher educators have not required that entry to their field depend on expertise in teaching, nor have they required that advancement depend on teacher educators' research on teaching, teacher learning, or teacher education. Instead, teacher education has been treated as an embarrassment by faculties of education, a financial and professional necessity that ought to be avoided wherever possible. The education of teachers has been an academic pursuit in flight from itself, whose practitioners preferred to advance their careers by teaching and research in such presumably more prestigious matters as the educational subdisciplines of psychology and other "foundations" subjects like sociology and history, or by developing new subject-matter-oriented curriculum.[4] Under such conditions one could hardly expect either the cultivation of sophisticated practice in teacher education or the development of substantial scholarship on practice. University teacher educators' response to the developing academic status system turned them into the worst enemies of improved professional practice and research in their own field.

Lacking opportunities for intensive study of practice within academe, it made sense that advocates of improved professional studies would argue for the export of novices to classrooms, to learn from expert practitioners. But an obstacle to learning from experience of that sort was the shortage of such teachers. Most teaching in the United States has been reported to be didactic and intellectually conventional, as far back as evidence and commentary stretch. Lacking many good classrooms, education faculty could not have used practice as a site for many students' learning without a different sort of import trade—that is, reconfiguring their facilities so that good teachers worked in the equivalent of hospital operating amphitheaters, with hundreds of novices looking over the shoulders of one practitioner and her students. A few normal schools tried a version of that a century ago, but noone seems to have followed suit since.

Even if there had been plenty of able teachers near universities, schools would not necessarily have been able to use them well in school-based teacher education. Public schools have not been organized to offer teachers many opportunities to learn, whether from each other or anyone else; teachers' work is organized so that even the best already have their hands full. Most could not do much to educate novices unless their jobs were reconfigured to make room for it. But that would make teacher education into a leading purpose of schools, which would collide with established ideas about schools' operations, their relations with parents and sponsoring agencies, the design of curriculum and instruction, and teachers' time with students. The logistics of such teaching-cum-teacher education would be a special problem for many state university teacher education programs that graduate hundreds or thousands of teachers a year, for it would take many schools, with many talented teachers in each, to accommodate a graduating class of even 500 aspiring teachers.

Suppose for the sake of argument that there were enough exemplary teachers, and sufficient support in their schools that each could work with a few novices. Those teachers would still have to design classroom instruction for children that also could support on-the-spot teacher education. That would be difficult, for raw experience can be the enemy of learning. One reason is that it keeps whizzing by. Unlike books and films, real classrooms cannot be stopped while novices analyze or look again. Teaching and learning cannot be put on hold while intending teachers digest the prior 10 minutes, nor could teachers and students be asked to repeat the last part of the lesson so that onlookers could better understand it. If real experience were to be made into more than a chance for quick and superficial learning, teacher educators would have to somehow open it up to careful scrutiny. That would require teaching to be documented so that there would be an adequate basis for analysis. Experience would have to be turned into curriculum, and that would require teacher educators to refine, organize, and improve on experience. Such work would be much more complex than simply turning novices loose in schools with a bit of supervision.

Another limit on efforts to learn from live practice resides in learners' inexperience: The less one knows about what one observes, the less one can see, and the less one can see, the less one can learn. What learners know is a powerful influence on their learning, and naive novices know little about what to notice in the work of an exemplary teacher. Worse, if they had conventional schooling as students, they would be likely to suspect or reject the entire approach of an exemplary teacher. For example, novice cooks who had been raised on hamburgers, potatoes, and overcooked vegetables would have difficulty learning to cook by watching Julia Child prepare dinner for 20 people. Such novices would find the cuisine unfamiliar, and thus would not know what to notice; many also would find it repugnant and would doubt whether it was worth learning.

Cognitive psychology and common experience teach that learners' experience powerfully mediates learning. If so, experience can be the enemy of new knowledge and changed practice. One consistent thread in research on teaching and learning to teach has been the power of what Dan Lortie termed the "apprenticeship of observation."[5] Researchers report that intending teachers' experience as the students of conventional teachers has a powerful and generally quite conservative influence on their pre-professional learning and on their subsequent teaching.[6] These problems are compounded when raw practice is the medium for learning, because practitioners have few opportunities to open their work up for exploration, explanation, and debate. If Julia Child was trying to get dinner made for 20 hungry guests, she would have to focus more on the dinner than on novices' questions. In preparing for her television shows she could reorganize the preparation to make it cognitively more accessible to naive observers—in effect, to turn it into a curriculum of sorts—but that approach to dinner for 20 would have her guests eating and dozing in fits and starts through a long night.

If exemplary classrooms were to be the center of teacher education, it would be unwise to assume that naive onlookers would learn deeply if left to their own devices. Rather, one should assume that novices often would be mystified by what they saw, that many would reject it as strange or atypical, that most would understand it in fragmentary and incomplete fashion at best, and that many would conclude that what they saw and heard was not how they could or would teach. Most would fasten on the obvious and familiar things like "classroom management," much of which would be far from what exemplary teachers had chiefly in mind. Lacking carefully designed opportunities and incentives to learn from exemplary practice, most novices probably would not learn what teacher educators might wish. Conventional apprenticeships easily impede learning that departs from established practice.

To do better, the teaching from which novices were to learn would somehow have to be made into a curriculum for teacher education. Teacher educators who wished to improve practice would have to reorganize classroom experience so that it not only was accessible to novices but also would enable them to critically scrutinize prior ideas and assumptions about practice. To do that, teacher educators would have to turn teaching into the curriculum of teacher education, and that would be no mean assignment, especially if it were to be done in ordinary classrooms. Teaching children would have to become a split-level practice, in which lessons for children also were lessons for intending teachers. Either classroom teachers would have to instruct two very different groups of learners at roughly the same time, simultaneously deploying two different curricula and pedagogies, or they would have to work alongside teacher educators who used the teachers' work with children as a curriculum for intending teachers.[7] Neither would be easy.

Teacher educators and reformers who argue for more clinical experience often ignore these problems of instructional design and the cultivation of professional taste. They seem to assume that what was worth learning either would be evident to intending teachers or could be made so with some scraps of supervision, thus ignoring the barriers that experience can present to learning. Such easy assumptions ought to be replaced with several hard questions that might be part of any effort to reconfigure teacher education around experience.

- What sort of a practice is teaching, that we believe experience would be a good teacher?

- What sort of learning is entailed in becoming a good teacher?
- To whose experience do we refer in such sentences: exposure to the teaching of accomplished teachers, or one's own work? What part might each play in teachers' learning?
- What do we mean by experience in these sentences, and what reconfiguration would be needed to make it into curriculum for intending teachers?

These questions have not been the focus of much scholarship or thoughtful professional commentary. As a result, we lack much evidence that could illuminate teachers' learning from any sort of experience, let alone how they might learn better, how best to promote various sorts of learning, and where learning from experience might fit in teachers' education. Evidence, theory, and analysis on the questions above would help to inform thoughtful attempts to ground teachers' learning in practice, but all are in short supply. There appears never to have been a theory of teacher learning that would inform pursuit of such queries, or much interest in devising it. Similarly, there has been little systematic scrutiny of what we refer to as learning from practice, apart from intending teachers' reports of what they learned from practice teaching. Teacher educators have paid little attention to the development of intellectual foundations, either for curriculum in teacher education or for the organization of intending teachers' instruction. Despite the American passion for experience, or perhaps because of it, there has been little investigation of what we mean by experience, of how teachers learn from it, or of how experience might be reorganized to promote learning.[8]

That paradox is emblematic of the relations between experience and education for American teachers. There are large circumstantial barriers to using schools as sites for better clinical education, including the structure of universities, the relations between higher and lower schools, and the organization of schools. Yet circumstances were not controlling, for teacher educators could have imported experience into university teacher education in many different ways, had they the required imagination, scholarly interest in practice, and thoughtful attention to teachers' learning. Even if all circumstantial barriers to placing intending teachers in real classrooms disappeared today, tomorrow there still would be profound difficulties in using practice as the site for clinical education. One difficulty would be finding ways to teach children while also teaching teachers. Another would be the lack of much theoretical or professional guidance about teachers' learning, and still another would be the absence of scholarship on practice that could provide both curriculum and intellectual foundations for teacher education. Despite decades of complaint, many proposals for change, and some impressive but isolated efforts, learning from experience in teaching has been the subject of little systematic experimentation, investigation, or improved professional knowledge.

REDEFINING EXPERIENCE

Magdalene Lampert and Deborah Ball have made a significant contribution to solving these problems by bringing new technology to bear on old issues. They collected complex records of teaching and learning during an entire year in two elementary school classrooms. The records include video- and audiotapes of daily instruction, the teachers' daily journal entries, and students' work. These records were collected in multimedia computer environments, creating a rich array of vivid representations of teaching and learning. The records create opportunities to improve learning from experience because they enable educators not only to use complex records of living practice as a basis for both teacher education and research on teaching, but also to modify the records for more effective use as curriculum or research materials.

Such records demonstrate that educators can create vivid, full-length video and audio records of classroom work for a few minutes, days, weeks, months, or a year. Observers who worked in real time on the spot would find it very difficult to locate and preserve such things, let alone coordinate them in a usable dataset. Ball and Lampert added a rich array of other artifacts, including photographic records of the blackboard; transcripts of interviews with teachers and students about the lesson, including their conception of what was being done and their explanation of their work; observers' notes on lessons; other salient texts, including readings that address the subject matter in question; and discussions of scholars' earlier efforts to solve the problems that students were addressing.

Records of this sort could help both to break the monopoly that live experience has had on learning from practice and to enable reconsideration of what experience is and how we might learn from it. Multimedia records of practice, including full-length, high-resolution color video and audio records of classes that extend over weeks or months, can be extraordinarily vivid and convincing. Although they are not the "real thing," if well done they are a quite rich and very convincing thing. In fact, multimedia records probably are better than the real thing in some respects, because they are more complex than what any observer could see and hear in real-time observation of practice. A good multimedia record of a classroom can include exact copies of students' work, including the detailed traces of their thinking, false starts, and solutions that were recorded in their workbooks; video and audio records of interviews with students; similar records of students' work in small groups; interviews with teachers; observers' notes; teachers' journals; and more.

Multimedia records of practice thus can improve on experience in two crucial ways: by enabling users to see much more than could be seen in real time, and by creating opportunities to learn much more than could be learned in real time. One reason is that the records can have much higher fidelity than the most systematically recorded firsthand experience, because multimedia records can be less filtered through the recording viewer's sensibility than can oral or written reports. Cameras, of course, will record only what they are pointed at, and in that sense they are limited by their operators' judgment. But unlike the human eye, which is subject to the same limit, cameras can be set up to record much of what goes on in a classroom from several different angles. And unlike the observing eye, cameras would not be distracted from recording the entire field by movement in one corner of it, thus failing to record movement elsewhere. Because the methods of recording are mechanical and electronic, the fidelity and completeness of visual and aural records are potentially much greater than any human observation could be. Professional observers and social researchers record others' experience by dint of notes, checklists, or disciplined ethnographic techniques that issue results in detailed field notes. In all such cases classroom experience is transformed into the observers' impressions, the researchers' prose, or quantitative measures in various categories that the investigators devised. No matter how scrupulous the investigators' work, it loses fidelity and richness in the process. Consumers of the ensuing analysis have nothing approaching direct access to the experience from which the data and analysis were derived.

In contrast, multimedia records make it possible to analyze teaching and learning while still preserving direct, complex records of experience. Consumers of such materials could have access to primary records of teachers' and students' experience, along with observers' systematically recorded observations and any accompanying commentary or analysis that researchers or teacher educators thought useful. If a classroom had been recorded well, users of the multimedia records could have access to more aspects of teaching and learning, with more detailed and dispassionate coverage, than would be possible in even the most sophisticated firsthand observation. Users could check observers' analysis and commentary against the records, which would be impossible in the best ethnographic studies.

Multimedia records also are portable, for unlike firsthand observations they do not lose fidelity with time and transport. Observers can carry excellent records of experience away from schools, to be considered, investigated, or re-presented elsewhere. The records can be revisited over and over again, undimmed and undistorted by memory that fades or changes focus to follow the recollector's shifting interest. Teacher educators, intending teachers, or researchers can scrutinize the records at greater leisure, and in much greater depth and detail than would be possible in real time, and they can work with much higher fidelity to students' and teachers' experience. Although multimedia records are less vivid than raw experience in some dimensions—they do not permit one to smell classrooms, or feel the heat, or pick up chalk dust on one's shirt—they are more vivid in others. What they lose in smell, touch, and feel, they gain in fidelity and complexity.

Multimedia records also can be manipulated, which is another reason they enable us to reconsider learning from experience. Most simply, users can evade the constraints of real time by stopping and rerunning lessons, to see what was happening in more detail, at a more approachable pace. That is a sort of temporal enrichment, for by slowing time down or repeatedly viewing the same record observers can see more than ever would be possible in real time. A slightly more complex manipulation is to link various elements of records in a database; for instance, video and audio records of a lesson on two-digit multiplication could be linked to the written records of students' work in that lesson, to the teacher's writing about the lesson, to observers' notes on the lesson, and to students' comments about multiplication in a subsequent interview. Observers could consider all these elements of a single lesson together, something that would be impossible in real life; for even if an observer were able to collect all the artifacts just mentioned, they could not be linked in a database that permitted revisiting audio and video records of the lesson.

Links of this sort would greatly enhance opportunities to learn from experience. One reason is that observers would be able to regard the "same" bit of experience from the vantage points of several different participants, viewing learning from the students' perspectives as well as the teacher's. Another is that observers could use several different sorts of evidence to inform their work: teachers' journals as well as students' notebooks and papers, video and audio records as well as observers' comments. These things constitute a sort of relational enrichment, for by tying various threads of a teaching and learning together, observers could get much more perspective and much richer evidence. That would enable intending teachers and teacher educators to deepen their understanding of such crucial matters as the relations between teaching and learning.

An even more complex manipulation of multimedia records would reset the entire frame of experience. For instance, a group of lessons on ratio and proportion that occurred over the course of a month could be linked to related lessons on fractions and decimals that occurred several months later. In such cases, connected instructional topics can be considered together, and any given chunk thereby reframed simply by placing it in the context of others that share the same thematic elements. Such reframing would enable observers to see how students and teachers deal with different aspects of what might be considered to be a single mathematics theme, or with a set of closely related topics. That would enable observers to resituate particular lessons in somewhat different and perhaps revealing perspectives. In real life such reframing can be done only with some combination of memory and imaginative reconstruction, but the technology enables us to link or combine records without losing any fidelity. Such reorganization would enable a sort of topical enrichment, in which records were rearranged to escape not only the flow of time but also the topical flow of the curriculum.

The new technology thus enables us to slow, combine, relate, and reframe records of experience, organizing and reorganizing them in ways that can serve analysis and learning. We now can steal experience from real life, violating the rules of time, place, relations, and access that constrain learning in real classrooms. Observers can probe connections that could never be checked directly in real life, and they can dig much more deeply than if they were working with paper, pencil, and tape recorder in real classrooms. Educators can turn vivid and complex records of instructional experience into curriculum, without ever straining the schedules or capabilities of teachers, teacher educators, children, or intending teachers. We can reconstruct experience so that it fits intending teachers' puzzles and schedules, rather than the demands of real-time instructional performance.

VIRTUAL APPRENTICESHIPS

If experience with classroom teaching and learning were no longer hostage to real life in real time, the education of intending and experienced teachers could be grounded in classroom work without being located in schools. Practicing and intending professionals could study vivid, extended, and complex records of practice in circumstances that were conducive to intentional learning. They could become virtual apprentices, learning in and from practice by looking over the shoulders—and into the work and thoughts—of exemplary teachers and their students. Apprenticeship seems a fair term, because in the real world of real work, apprentices work alongside journeypersons. The new technology turns "alongside" into a matter of technical capacity rather than location. Intending teachers could work in proximity to master teachers and their students— although not under their supervision[9]—as they sat in a university classroom, a computer laboratory, or their own study.

Some readers may wonder whether it is fair to describe such work as apprenticeship. Intending teachers would not prepare and execute lessons under the supervision of a cooperating teacher. But consider the alternative. In university teacher education curricula, teaching, learning, and academic subjects are carved up into courses in learning psychology, pedagogy, mathematics, and the like. These are offered as preparation for teaching but rarely are organized in ways that ground learning in practice. For instance, the mathematics taught in universities is rarely related to the curriculum of elementary schools, for mathematics courses are the province of university math departments, whose members focus on generating new knowledge and transmitting what is known rather than on mathematical pedagogy. Intending elementary teachers often must take a math course or two, but these courses typically do not address them as teachers, for that would entail teaching about how mathematics could be taught and learned, and how it related to the elementary curriculum, which math departments would not countenance.[10] Intending teachers instead are addressed as students of mathematics, uninteresting and unwelcome students at that, who often are poorly taught by inexperienced and uninterested graduate students in mathematics.

That approach to carving up the curriculum would make a certain sense if universities were only engines for generating and transmitting knowledge, and if teaching were only an activity to be parsed out into convenient components for academic study. If students were apprentices of any sort, it would be as intending scholars. But if teaching is a practice to be understood and learned, then the typical university approach forecloses the chance of any sort of professional apprenticeship.

The Ball and Lampert materials open up a radically different possibility for the intellectual organization of teacher education. They contain records of pedagogy, mathematics, and learning in classrooms—which is to say, tangled together. The tangle does not defeat learning or analysis, but situates both differently than in conventional university studies. The mathematics on display in the materials is not a set of topics to be covered or chapters to be read, as in most university math courses for intending teachers, but records of teachers' math lessons and students' work on them. Intending teachers who used the materials would encounter mathematics in the context of students' and teachers' work. There is a topic structure, but the classroom work on mathematics is much more prominent.

Apprenticeship seems an appropriate designation for work of this sort, partly because the content is pedagogically embodied. Because the mathematics is being taught and learned, it opens up opportunities for learning about mathematics as it is implicated in classroom work. A version of such pedagogical embodiment could be achieved in a standard university course that used materials drawn from practice, but it would be emaciated in comparison to studies that were based on multimedia records of teaching and learning mathematics. Although intending mathematicians might disdain such work, it makes perfect sense for intending teachers.

Situating mathematics that way would enable teacher educators to build pedagogically more substantial math curricula for teachers, and that would increase the likelihood that intending teachers' mathematics learning would be connected to their math teaching. Such work would be less powerful if the lesson content were the usual school mathematics, but Lampert and Ball's materials represent mathematics as a way to frame problems and reason about them, not as a set of algorithms to be worked and facts and procedures to be memorized. Intending teachers who use the materials encounter students and teachers actively trying to make sense of mathematical problems, working on big mathematical ideas, disputing mathematical relationships, and explaining complex mathematical puzzles. The materials represent knowing mathematics as a matter of making sense of quantitative relationships and making mathematically reasonable arguments.

Work with such materials would be no small challenge for most intending teachers, for many appear to have superficial and mechanical knowledge of mathematics, even when they have majored in the subject to prepare for high school teaching. Intending elementary teachers additionally seem to consider themselves incapable of making sense of the subject—two respects in which they resemble most American adults. Although some are able to work mathematical procedures efficiently, few report much mathematical insight or appreciation. The mathematics in the materials would present intending teachers with opportunities to learn or relearn mathematics, to reconsider the nature of the subject and what it means to know it. The materials are especially useful here because they abound with evidence that other humans, even quite ordinary youngsters, can learn such things.

A related advantage of situating teacher education in records of practice is the rich evidence that they can offer about students' work. Intending teachers could become students of students' mathematical thought and work: They could begin to learn about learners' varied understanding of mathematics by studying how they attack assignments. They could begin to learn how students think about and express mathematical ideas by analyzing their questions and discussion in class. And they could observe how students' thinking changes in response to classroom work, by tracking workbook assignments. In these ways and others, intending teachers could learn about teaching from the learners' perspective. That could be immensely fruitful—teaching presumably is aimed at learning—but it is a perspective few teachers achieve. One reason is that most instruction in the United States is so frontal that it screens a great deal of students' thinking from teachers, and another is that most teachers appear to focus on activities and assignments rather than on learning. Materials like those that Ball and Lampert created enable teacher educators to refocus learning to teach on students' learning. It would be a bit of an exaggeration to say that novice teachers could apprentice themselves to learners, the better to understand learning mathematics, but it would not be an exaggeration to say that the materials would enable intending teachers to become close students of students' thought and expression.[11] That could be an enormous gain for both teachers and students.

Pedagogy is a third realm in which these materials could support apprentice-like relationships. Intending teachers presently have very limited opportunities to learn pedagogy from practitioners, let alone exemplary practitioners, even though pedagogy is the very core of teachers' craft. Most learn instead from experience as school and university students, and in practice teaching, that didactic teaching is the only way, even though they often are told in pre-professional courses that they should not teach didactically. University teacher education offers little opportunity to learn how good teaching works.

The Lampert and Ball materials make it possible to change that, by situating intending teachers' learning in the study of teaching itself. Novices could learn about teaching by analyzing the work of exemplary teachers.[12] They could study how such teachers frame issues, how they manage complex ideas and social interactions, how they explain their moves and judgments, what they need to know in order to help students make progress, and much more. Intending teachers who learned about teaching by studying rich records of the real thing could not be apprentices in the sense that these exemplary teachers would directly supervise them, but they could be apprentices in the sense that they learned a great deal from direct observation and analysis of how good teaching works, and why, and what it takes to carry it off.

One essential element of learning any practice is determining what exemplary work looks like, something that is difficult to do without extended observation and analysis that includes comparisons. Ball and Lampert's materials display records of teaching that is both exemplary and quite different from conventional practice; they depict teachers who are both intellectually demanding and respectful of students' ideas. Such records enable novices to learn how teachers can give priority to disciplined argument and evidence, and to the cultivation of rational discourse, while also respecting how students think, express themselves, represent mathematical ideas, and justify their views. Novices could learn how classrooms are managed around serious mathematical work, in contrast to being managed around activities or the idea of order. A crucial part of what would be learned in such work is, therefore, what demanding norms of professional conduct look like in practice. The teachers in these multimedia records could not step out of the video to correct novices' own efforts to do such work, but the records offer rich documentation of what classy professionalism looks like and opportunities to learn what it takes to sustain it. Learning about teaching in proximity to such vivid examples is certainly part of what one would want from an apprenticeship.

CONCLUSION

Apprenticeship conventionally includes at least three elements. Observation of capable practitioners is one; it offers a general orientation to the work, examples of what good work looks like, demonstrations of technique and the use of materials, and the like. "Practice" is another; it allows novices to try the work out, to get a feel for it and opportunities to learn from one's successes, errors, and revisions. Supervision is a third; it offers novices the chance to profit from a master's comments and examples.

The materials that Lampert and Ball have developed would enable those elements of apprenticeship that are associated with observation of capable practitioners at work. They also would enable novices to learn what exemplary professional work looks like, which many apprenticeships do not offer. But the materials would not support direct supervision of novices' "practice" by experienced teachers, which is a critical element of conventional apprenticeship. The materials would nonetheless offer novice teachers certain other opportunities to learn that have been either rare or simply impossible in most teacher education programs. One would be to conduct extended analysis of exemplary teachers' practice, which would enable a much richer appreciation of teaching and a greater understanding of what it takes to teach well. Another would be much deeper analysis of students' work and learning, which has been nearly entirely missing from teacher education. That would enable teachers to learn much more about how students make sense of mathematics, how they express themselves, and how teachers can respond usefully. Each of these learning opportunities has elements of apprenticeship, but neither has been developed within the boundaries of conventional teacher education.

Multimedia records thus would offer both more and less than conventional apprenticeships. The critical point is that the Ball and Lampert materials enable us to imagine a new territory for teacher learning, in which the nature of work "in practice" can be reimagined, developed, and greatly expanded. The result would not be a substitute for conventional "practice" at teaching, but it would broaden and deepen intending teachers' opportunities to learn about both teaching and how to teach. Of course, much remains to be learned about this new medium: While we know enough about it to see extraordinary opportunities to learn, we do not know enough to see more than the rough outlines.

We do know enough to anticipate some of the principal difficulties in using such materials; the simple summary is that even the best materials are not self-enacting. For example, while the materials could be a terrific resource for teacher educators, few either are exemplary practitioners or have much experience working "in practice." One could address these problems by building a curriculum for teacher educators that offered them opportunities to learn about how to use the materials with intending teachers. That probably would require the creation of a new layer in the materials, in which Lampert and Ball would create records of their work with intending teachers and then reframe that as curriculum that would introduce teacher educators to using the materials, to the issues that come up when intending teachers use them, to how other teacher educators used the materials, and the like. That would enable more teacher educators to use the materials and thus would perhaps make them more widely used, but it would require a considerable development effort, probably including new documentation of the records' use in teacher education, record building, and curriculum design and construction.

Devising such a curriculum for teacher educators would not guarantee that they would be able to use the present set of multimedia records. For users also would require extensive familiarity with a huge dataset and quite advanced computer and computer support capacities, and few teacher educators are masters of multimedia technology. An alternative approach would be to refashion some of the existing materials into a much more structured curriculum for intending teachers, and to create a parallel curriculum for teacher educators organized around intending teachers' use of that structured curriculum. That would reduce the knowledge and technical capacities required of teacher educators who would use the materials, but it would require some modification of the pedagogy of investigation that Ball and Lampert write about in this volume, in building both curricula. For curricula of the sort that I just proposed would require that the designers decide how they wanted to focus intending teachers' and teacher educators' attention, and then use the present materials as a data source from which to build new records organized around those issues. Although extensive investigation still would be possible within the new records, the broad terrain for investigation that the present materials offer would be restricted.

Reducing the technical requirements for using the records while building knowledge of how to use them would broaden the potential audience, and that would be a considerable advantage. Additionally, as they restructured the materials, the designers could build in additional layers that could greatly enrich the educative potential of the materials. As things now stand, for example, the materials offer intending teachers many opportunities to learn about teaching, but relatively few opportunities to learn how to teach. Analysis could be a partial remedy for that problem. For example, intending teachers could use the present materials or some more curricular revision to probe how Lampert and Ball were able to carry off their lessons—what they needed to know, how they managed ideas and social interactions, what choices they made, how they inquired about students' knowledge and ideas, and much more. Extensive analysis of such elements of teaching could enable novices to accumulate much more rich knowledge of how good teaching works than most experienced teachers now possess. Intending teachers would not literally learn how to teach, but would learn a great deal about what makes good teaching tick. Having done so they would be much better situated to learn how to teach that way themselves: Their understanding would be broader and deeper, they would have a greater repertoire of teacherly actions, and they would have a sense of the applicable norms of practice. If the redeveloped materials also were broadened to include examples of more conventional teaching and learning, novices would gain that much more intellectual leverage on what it takes to teach well.

Another way to enhance the materials' capacity to support learning how to teach would be to build into the materials assignments that engaged novices in solving typical problems of teaching. Users could, for instance, be asked to interpret a piece of student work in the records and to support their interpretation with evidence, in order to improve their capacity to understand learners' thinking. They then could be asked how they would respond to that work if they were the teacher and to devise a suitable next assignment. They could be invited to devise tasks that would assess students' understanding of a topic, to then role play students' responses to that assignment, and to revise the assessment accordingly. Work of this sort is worth mentioning partly because it would enable intending teachers to begin to build a repertoire of interpretations of students' work, of ideas about how to respond to that work, of suitable mathematical tasks for students of a certain age and competence, and much more. Such things would not be practice, but they are part of the intellectual and social infrastructure of practice that is now largely missing from teachers' education, but should be a substantial foundation for and accompaniment to learning to teach. The lack of this foundation would be analogous to educating physicians without ever exposing them to direct clinical evidence of health and diseases. Practice of this sort also would occur in a pedagogical context— an exemplary *genre* of teaching—and so the novices' work would be referenced to that genre. Ball and Lampert could even collect evidence on such work from early users and then include them, and some commentary, in redeveloped materials. Although such work would not be the same as "practicing" teaching, it would entail some important elements of such practice. It also would be situated "in practice" and in both respects would be more oriented to practice than is most work that novices do.

Even if we assume that all the materials were quite marvelously redeveloped, that teacher educators were well prepared to use them, and that intending teachers learned their lessons well, those better-educated novices still would have to find jobs in the existing schools. The virtual apprenticeships sketched above would be more situated in practice than is conventional teacher education, but since the practice these apprentices would have learned from Lampert and Ball would be so unusual, the apprentices would be far from conventional practice. Most of these better-educated teachers would nonetheless go to work in standard schools, so they would not be teaching the same arithmetic as most of their colleagues. The new teachers would know that, and their students, colleagues, and the students' parents would soon figure it out. The more wonderfully the virtual apprenticeships discussed here worked, the more they would prepare teachers for schools and careers that do not yet exist. That too would cause problems.

Teacher education cannot cure an entire school system, and it would be unfair to argue that Ball and Lampert should find ways to enable users of their materials to learn how to work to high standards with professionals who know little of such work and care for it less. But teacher education does not subsist in a vacuum; one would not want to prepare teachers to deal superbly with curriculum and students in ways that would set them up to fail in dealing with colleagues, administrators, and parents. The developments in teacher education that this volume describes hold enormous promise for improving American public education; but precisely for that reason, their success would depend as much on broad changes in public schools as on the improved teacher education that I have discussed.

Acknowledgment. I owe thanks to Magdalene Lampert and Deborah Ball, whose comments considerably improved this essay.

Appendix A

November 13, 1994

First, I would like to discuss the definition of classroom culture. Culture is what separates different groups of people. It is common ground that binds people together. I pondered the term "culture" for two years during my Peace Corps experience in Poland. Last Wednesday night, I heard the term "classroom culture" for the first time. In my understanding, it is a term for classroom environment. Yes, I do believe every class forms a different environment depending on the teacher, the students, moods, and material.

This can change daily depending on the factors of the classroom (students, teacher, material, moods, past classroom experiences, etc.). I feel more comfortable using the term "learning environment" because I feel culture is too strong of a word when discussing the way a class operates. Culture involves time and most classrooms don't spend long amounts of time together.

The environment of a class is largely dependent on how a teacher interacts with his/her students. A teacher is expected to maintain an organized class which allows and encourages students to learn. To accomplish this feat, classroom management is extremely important. Dr. Lampert's class seems to have a good rapport. The students work in groups of four and seem to be working well together. When they don't, Lampert takes care of the problem immediately. My first example is when Lampert sees Ellie out of her seat and collaborating with another group.

Lampert:	. . . what are you doing over here?
Ellie:	My three members in my group won't help me.
Lampert:	Hmmm?
Ellie:	My team members won't help me.
Lampert:	Your team members won't help you? The solution to that problem is not to get up and join a new team, I'm sorry to say. Let's go see what I can do about it.

Lampert returns to Ellie's group and tries to encourage them to interact more. She does this by reprimanding them and then by asking them to discuss the problem.

Lampert:	Okay, what's happening here? You're not finished. You're nowhere near finished. For one thing, you um need to talk to the other people in your group to work on this problem, okay?
Lampert:	Okay, this does not, it's, this is not an explanation, this is a procedure. Okay? Why do you multiply 3 1/2 times 4, that's what I want to know.

Then, she directs them into a discussion by asking key questions. She also asks another student to explain the problem to Ellie, since she doesn't understand.

Lampert:	Okay, do you, do you understand what, what Karim just said?
Ellie:	. . .
Lampert:	Do you think you could help her to understand? Maybe you could draw a diagram that would help her to understand?

This technique (students teaching students) works wonders. Dr. Lampert successfully guides Karim into discussing his answer with the group and explaining how he got his conjecture. To get the whole group working together, she has to remind a student to write a little bit faster (see video). Now that she has the whole group up to speed, she keeps an eye on them to make sure they are working together.

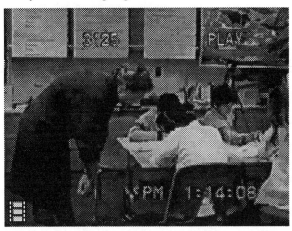

Casually walking around the room and listening to other groups discussing and persuading each other of certain answers, Dr. Lampert is able to make her presence known. By this, I mean she is available to help students when necessary and keep the students focused on their work. She continually guides conversations to keep up their interest and to help them help themselves in discovering an answer.

> Lampert: Okay, and why don't you also write down one hour equals 40 miles, one hour equals 40 miles.

Her language is important to note. She suggests the students do something, she doesn't tell them to do it. This provides them with the control. They choose whether to write it or not.

> Lampert: Okay. So here's your 12 and here's your 2 that you added together, okay? This is 3 times 4, or 4+4+4, and this is the extra 20. Now one of the things that I saw as I was walking around was something now I'd like to see a lot more of. I gave Karim a very special challenge. One member of his group said, "I really don't understand these kinds of problems at all." And I went over there and I said, "Karim, can you help this person explain? Can you explain,

help this person understand?" And he said, "Oh, yes, it's just 3 times, you know, 3 times uh 40, that's all." I said, "But what if the person doesn't know why you're supposed to times? How could you explain that?" And you know what he did? He said, "I know how I can explain that." And he drew a line in his notebook and he explained it, using that line. Karim, do you think you could come up here and show the whole class what you did? This is a picture of why you multiply to solve this problem. Okay?

In the example above, Lampert reinforces what she would like the students to do. Karim was given a "special challenge" and helped teach another person in his group. He is then asked to explain how he did that to the class. She uses him as a model for the class. He exemplified what she wants. She tells the class she wants to see more of this behavior (students teaching students). It is extremely important to focus on positive points and not the negative. This keeps the learning environment aware of what is going on and also lets students actually see the behavior the teacher wants in his/her class.

I have spent all of my time so far focusing on the compact disc LVO2 and have just read Dr. Lampert's journal. It was interesting to read that all the work on the problems of time/speed/distance hadn't quite worked until this particular day. What changed? She mentioned parent teacher conferences and paying attention. Also, the groups seemed to cooperate together.

Well —> today's lesson was a real turn around! For one thing, Tyrone was acting like math made some sense and there was positive interaction in his group.

THE MOST FASCINATING THING ABOUT ALL THIS WAS HOW MUCH OF IT WAS COLLABORATIVELY CONSTRUCTED BY THE KIDS, EVEN AS I HAD PLANNED TO BE MORE DIDACTIC. Was it because I knew better what to look for, & thus how to orchestrate?

Her comment, "Was it because I knew better what to look for, & thus how to orchestrate?" is interesting. Is the teacher solely responsible for the learning environment? Are his or her reactions, questions, seating arrangements, moods, etc., what the learning environment works from? From my experiences and my research so far, I think yes.

November 20, 1994

Lampert: 'kay, I'm wanna ask everybody to pay real close attention to this because lots of people think the answer is five miles. And Charlotte is explaining why she thinks the answer is seven miles. If you disagree with what she did, you're gonna have to convince her that the answer is five miles, so you better pay attention to this.

After reading through what I've written so far, my observations are still the same. Above is another example of the proper use of language. Dr. Lampert keeps everyone's attention focused. They will have to pay attention and explore Charlotte's problem and compare it to their own answer. Based on their conjecture, someone (and they don't know who at this point) will have to convince her of their answer.

Looking at this vid-bit, I think teacher management and language play a strong role in environment. The students listen to each other revise and change their answers. The students discuss their problems and their reasoning... how they figured it out... why they changed it... exactly what they did. This involves a lot of thought processes instead of just a simple yes or no. The students have to be prepared to explain and prove their reasoning which enables them to have a clearer understanding of what they are doing instead of just memorizing a formula. This discussion involves the whole class as a community and creates a sense of "whole" to figure out what's going on. Knowing they will say "I agree" or "I disagree" forces them to understand their own thinking and how to verbalize it. They are putting their own opinions on the line and have to defend them. It isn't a simple matter of "right or wrong."

O.K.... I have a few questions. One: I am not sure my notebook is going in the right direction. I think the question I would like to ask is: Is the teacher solely responsible for the class environment? Or is the teacher simply a factor in the environment? These questions seem a bit broad...but as a teacher, personally, I would like to explore how big the teacher's part is in the environment. For example: Does he or she create it? If so, how? How would I answer these questions? This is hard.... I can pull in my own experiences from my class, use examples of Dr. Lampert's class, and some from Dr. Ball's class, and maybe even examples from other teachers. Is this possible? My problem seems to be in a focus. Are my questions too general? Would I ever be able to formulate an answer? Do you want an answer or a thesis or conjectures with examples of what I mean? A lot of questions....

Now, back to the project.... Before I go any further, I would like to hear some input from you. Am I going in the right direction?

> Deliberately <u>do not</u> suggest using a diagram
> & see what they do. Also <u>not</u> saying:
>
> which is time, speed, distance.
>
> Getting 8.33333 will take us into a
> whole new territory [if I let it!]

These excerpts are taken from Dr. Lampert's journal. She proves that her language and actions have a definite effect on the environment. She deliberately doesn't suggest using a diagram to see if they can figure it out on their own what to do. She also talks about going in different directions, which can only happen if she lets it. Who has control of the environment? Is it solely on the teacher?

November 21, 1994

O.K.... to get back to my project...My conjecture...the teacher is responsible for the classroom culture. The learning environment changes course and direction through the students' actions and behavior, but the teacher guides and models how things should be run. How does the teacher talk with the students? What questions does the teacher ask? How does the teacher guide the conversation? Is the teacher a good guide? Is there a clear objective for the students? Will they be able to say "I can do...(whatever they have learned)" after the lesson? What is the attitude of the teacher to the students? Do the students feel safe, threatened, capable of learning? Does the teacher encourage them to express what they are thinking and feeling?... it looks like language plays a major role in the environment...

> I was surprised at their general
> sense of the concepts involved—the
> kids who participated, anyway.

This excerpt was taken from Lampert's journal. How to keep them involved... pair them up... teach each other... how to assess them? How does this affect the environment?

> While making the list, I was conscious of the
> issues listed above, conscious of this as
> "collaborative teaching," drawing heavily on
> what students were contributing but also
> shaping it to fit my own ideas about what
> they should be learning here. The real
> trick, it seems, is to do both, authentically,
> at the same time, so that students perceive
> their own thinking as legitimate, but also are
> disposed to listen and change their ideas.
> Lots of thought here about "language" in
> relation to "thought" —> how does what we
> say both express & affect our thinking?

This is another part from Lampert's journal.
    Kids need to feel like they are being taken seriously; if not, why should they say anything at all? Is there such a thing as collaborative teaching? The teacher has control in the end... they provide the ultimate direction through guiding... but kids having input is important. It helps them feel like they are accomplishing a goal, being taken seriously, and are guiding their own thinking. It also gives them a source of power... there isn't one figure with absolute control.

> I wondered if he was thinking: "Why is
> this teacher entertaining all these other
> ideas when I have clearly answered the
> question?" or "why doesn't she tell them that
> they are wrong and/or show them how to do it
> my way?"

This is a very subtle
pedagogical strategy —> i.e., not
confirming Shahroukh, entertaining all these
other possibilities and taking them seriously.

What are those kids who are saying nothing learning?

I think it's good for students to listen
to one another try to construct definitions,
and I also wanted to know something
about how they construct meaning & who does it
assertively.

Then there was also talk about a
"collective" sense of the class & an
"individual" sense of what a student does
or doesn't understand and how one plans in
response.
It is both collective and individual
back and forth.

...because I wanted to announce
the bathroom policy: don't go out during
large group. But 2 kids were already out.

Was this class a waste because of poor
planning? I made up the problem "on the fly"
with a variety of legitimate concerns, I
think, but because I was only half paying
attn. I thought the computation would be a lot
easier than it is.

I have comments to make on each of these excerpts from Lampert's journal...however, I'm still not sure if my question is too broad or not...I need
some guidance...I think I have a lot of pertinent questions, but am trying
to do too much?

December 4, 1994

These are from Dr. Ball's journal on fractions.

So I debated about whether to help Cassandra move from her drawing and her label "1/2," respecting her genuine attempt to distribute all the cookies equally—but giving her new tools to accomplish her goal. <u>She</u> was <u>NOT</u> dissatisfied with her solution but I thought I saw in it an opportunity to extend her thinking to encompass the notion of <u>fifths</u>, as well as to offer her an easier model to work from—rectangles (instead of circles). (This is all probably about 1:15 or so on the tape.)

So I suggested to her that we draw rectangular cookies and that I'd show her how I would draw dividing up those cookies so that all the pieces were the same size. I drew

and told her that one of those pieces would be called "one-fifth" and I wrote "1/5." I asked her if she could explain why we would write it like that or call it that and without any apparent difficulty, explained that it was because it was divided into five pieces. (She also later explained 2/5 as "two divided into five pieces.")

My experiment with her for tomorrow is to support her presenting her solution to the class by photocopying her journal page and making an overhead transparency for her to use. My thought—my question—is this: If Cassandra can successfully explain her solution to the class, will it help her develop her understanding of what she and I worked on together? Will having an already represented illustration (one that she has already herself made) help her to make her presentation more successfully than usual? How will she feel about it? I will interview her before and after class about it in order to delve into how this is all developing/affecting her.

Although she had both the overhead transparencies that Margery had made from her notebook page of yesterday—AND she had also prepared a section on the overhead itself—AND she had also, in explaining to me before class, made drawings on the board, she had to re-draw as she was explaining. And once again she was drawing the two leftover cookies as circles and had two leftover fourths. I said, "Remember, we saw that drawing rectangular cookies made it easier?" where upon she was able to complete the explanation.

I gave Cassandra lots of support with this representation and explanation. I virtually pushed her to use rectangles, I encouraged her use of the chart... (At some point it might be interesting to compare how I help different people give their explanations.)

December 7, 1994

My conjecture: the teacher creates and maintains the mathematical classroom (or any subject area for that matter) environment through communication and interaction. I am starting to sum up everything before I actually begin my analysis... I have to admit I haven't done all of this on the computer. I printed some things this past weekend and studied some transcripts at home so I could organize my thoughts better.

MY ANALYSIS

The teacher is expected to maintain an organized class which allows and encourages students to learn. How he or she communicates with students plays a key role in this assessment. Language and actions are the first areas that popped into my mind as I re-read my original notebook. How the teacher explores problems with the students and how he or she reacts to answers and questions is central to the environment. The teacher creates and maintains the mathematical classroom (or any subject area for that matter) environment through communication and interaction.

If you had a teacher who yelled every time you made a wrong answer, you would feel frightened to suggest anything in class. If you had a teacher who encouraged your ideas and nourished your thoughts, you'd open up in class. Students need to feel safe and capable of learning in order to verbalize their thoughts. They need to be taken seriously in order to develop an environment open to their suggestions and comments. The language a teacher uses with his or her students affects the language in the classroom. Here is an excerpt from Mrs. Ball's classroom.

Harooun:	Forty-eight dozen?
Ball:	Forty-eight dozen.
Harooun:	Yeah.
Ball:	Can you explain how you got it?
Harooun:	Umm—It says how many cookies are there in four dozens?
Ball:	Uh huh, and what did you do?
Harooun:	Uh, I did um, 12 dozens and 12 dozen, 12 dozens and I got, uh, 42 dozens.
Ball:	Forty-eight, I think you said?
Harooun:	Forty-eight, yeah.

Ball:	Okay, comments? He says the answer is—48 dozen. Could some people comment on that? Mark?
Mark:	Uh, I agree.
Ball:	That's the same thing that you have?
Mark:	Um hm.
Ball:	Keith?
Keith:	I disagree.
Ball:	You disagree?
Keith:	You said it's 4 dozen, not 48 dozen.
Tory:	No.
Keith:	This says 4 dozen. How many cookies are there in 4 dozen?
Tory:	Yeah, but...
Keith:	You said 48 dozen cookies. You said 48 dozen. Forty-eight dozen.
Tory:	Yes.
Ball:	What do you think the answer should be? Keith, what do you think the answer should be?
Keith:	The—It's 48 is 4 dozen, not 48 dozen. He said that it was 48 dozen cookies. It's 4 dozen cookies.
Ball:	And now how many cookies is that?
Keith:	Forty-eight.
Ball:	Forty-eight cookies?
Keith:	Yeah.
Ball:	Okay, Mark, do you want to comment?
Mark:	I wanna—wanna revise. I agree with um—Keith.
Ball:	You agree with Keith?
Mark:	Um hm, yeah.
Ball:	That it's 48 cookies, not 48 dozen?
Mark:	Yeah.
Ball:	Betsy?
Betsy:	I agree and I have a different way to show it.
Ball:	Okay, but could you talk toward the class? Can people hear?
Student:	Um hmm.
Ball:	Okay, Betsy, could you talk that way?
Student:	Yes.
Betsy:	Um, I—I agree with Keith and Mark, and I have diff—different way to show it.
Ball:	Okay.
Betsy:	Can I show it?
Ball:	Uh huh.

Mrs. Ball listens to every student, whether their answer is right or wrong. She takes them seriously. Harooun says the answer is 48 dozen when really it is 48 cookies. It is hard to tell if this is just a slip in language or he really doesn't understand, but Ball doesn't dismiss his answer, like many teachers would. She doesn't say, "Are you sure that's right?" or "Don't you mean cookies and not dozens?" Instead, she asks him to explain how he got his answer. All the students were listening because they still didn't know if their answer was correct or not. She later asks if there are any comments and when someone says no, she asks that student to explain what the answer should be. When Keith does, a different student is able to revise his answer. The students feel comfortable in discussing a problem because they know they will be taken seriously. The teacher listens and respects what the student has to say and lets the other members of the class make comments. She doesn't pass judgment by commenting herself. She merely guides the students' thoughts and lets them decide for themselves. Finally, another student says she has a different way to show the problem. Mrs. Ball says okay, but to direct her problem to the class, not to the teacher. Mrs. Ball asks if everyone can hear. She makes everyone feel like a serious part of the class. Everyone is a central member to what is going on. It gives them a sense of control and ownership in the class.

> Ball: Could you talk to the class, please?

Students are encouraged to engage their discussion with classmates, not look for approval from the teacher. Instead of one person in the position to give feedback (the teacher), a whole class is able to. This keeps students listening to each other for new ideas and involves the whole class, not just the teacher. Once again, Ball's language is important to note (a suggestion, not a demand) and the sense of how important "the class" is, not the teacher.

The next excerpt is from Dr. Lampert's class. She, too, takes comments seriously and doesn't pass judgment. She also asks questions that force the students to go more into depth about their thinking. They can't just answer yes or no. They have an investment made and Lampert takes it seriously enough to want to hear about it. She asks, "Why?" instead of just replying that someone is right or wrong. Many teachers are more concerned with the "right" answer and simply move on rather than checking for understanding underneath the number. She also offers students a chance to think on it more and revise their answers.

> Lampert: You think the whole clock is one-fourth.
> Donna Ruth: Yeah.
> Lampert: Why?
> Donna Ruth: Because, um, it's, the circle is one hour, right?
> Lampert: The circle is one hour, that's right. This circle is one hour. Do

	you want to hear some ideas, and think about it some more?
Donna Ruth:	Yeah.
Lampert:	Okay, Karim, you take a hand at . . .

Tyrone:	I think it's four-fourths.
Lampert:	Why?
Tyrone:	Because, like in fractions, if you shade a piece out, and it's four, it would be three-fourths, and there's nothing to shade it, like, and all of them are there and four, and then it's four out of all of them, so it's four-fourths.
Lampert:	Okay. What are you thinking about, right now, Donna Ruth?
Donna Ruth:	I'm thinking about four-fourths.
Lampert:	Why?
Donna Ruth:	Um, I think it's the answer but I don't know it's the answer, and I'm trying to think of a reason why.
Lampert:	Hm, that's, that's good.

Dorota:	. . . but you have to have a number to make this to work.
Lampert:	What do you mean?
Dorota:	Um, both of them should work, you have to have a number.
Lampert:	Okay, now, this is another uh example of the "it" problem. When you say "both of them can work," what does the— "Both of them" refer to?
Dorota:	Fifteen and 25 can work.
Lampert:	Okay, 15 and 25 can work. Can you explain your reasoning please?
Dorota:	Because 25 and 25 is 50, and another 25 and 25 is 50, and then you add them, and it equals to one hour. Fifteen and 15 is 30 and another 15 and 15 is 30 and it also goes up to one hour.
Lampert:	Okay, what does anybody else think about what Dorota said? Awad?

Lampert asks students to explain their reasoning. Students are not able to give a one syllable answer. They have to invest more time and energy into class and therefore they have more at stake in the discussion. Once again, their thoughts are being taken seriously and so they feel comfortable in discussing the problem. Being able to freely discuss their ideas and revise them if needed, students have some type of ownership in the class and want to be involved. Most American teachers (Polish teachers, too, from what I observed in my two years as a teacher in Poland) are more interested in the right answer and not the reasoning behind the solution. Dr. Lampert validates their ideas by asking them questions which require much more than a yes or no answer. She doesn't criticize anyone's argument, but takes comments from other students in the class and allows the class to form a solution.

This vid-bit is from Dr. Lampert's class. It is a good example of how language is used in creating and maintaining the classroom environment. The students listen to each other and change their answers. They discuss their problems and their reasoning... how they figured it out... why they changed it... exactly what they did. This involves a lot of thought processes instead of just a simple yes or no. Lampert doesn't stop the discourse by commenting on right or wrong answers, which is what most teachers would do. The students freely discuss their reasoning and are prepared to explain and prove it which enables them to have a clearer understanding of what they are doing instead of just memorizing a formula. This discussion involves the whole class as a community and relates a sense of "whole" to figure out what's going on. Knowing they will say "I agree" or "I disagree" forces them to understand their own thinking and how to verbalize it. They are putting their own ideas on the line and have to defend them. It isn't a simple matter of the teacher nodding his or her head and responding with a yes or no or good or bad answer. Students are responding to students and discussing their solutions by explaining their reasoning. The teacher guides the discourse, but the heart of the discourse is in the students' hands (and mouths!!!).

Lampert offers choice in her language. She asks a lot of "Could you" or "Would you" questions which allow students a choice of action. They are not being told to do something by an authority figure. It is a choice of what they want to do. Ultimately, they decide what they will or won't do.

Lampert: Do you think you could help her to understand? Maybe you could
            draw a diagram that would help her understand?

She encourages students to interact by suggesting they do so, not by telling
them. Then she guides how to interact by giving suggestions on what to do
and pronouncing it as if in question form. Students are then able to decide
for themselves what to do next and don't feel as if they are doing something because the teacher told them to do it. Once again, this helps them
feel like they are serious members in the group and their actions have an effect on the outcome. They are making their own decisions through the
teacher's guidance.

Mrs. Ball offers choice in her language, too. She suggests drawing a
line across students' notebooks in order to show a new day of work. She
doesn't tell the students to do this, she merely says if you want to.

Ball: When you open your notebook, you'll see that stuff that you
            worked on yesterday. Skip a little bit of space so you leave some
            space since yesterday. You can decide how much. Like in Latifa's
            notebook, I would skip about this much space. Okay? If you want
            to, you could draw a line across to show that it's a new day. And
            then do you remember, Chris, can you tell everybody what you
            write after you draw the line?

She guides the students by telling them what she would do, but she leaves
the ultimate decision in their hands.

Ball: The date and it's on the board. You could write that while I take
            attendance. I'll write the date over here, too. I forgot to do that.

Once, again, the teacher offers choice in her language. "You could . . . "
gives the students a direction without being told in a demanding way. It is
suggestive language, not authoritative. Choosing gives students a voice in
their own learning and I think they become more aware of the environment
around them. They have a part in the action and are not just doing something they are told to do.

Communication in the classroom is central to what the environment is
like. Since the teacher makes ultimate decisions, he or she is responsible for
creating this connection between everyone involved within the class. Dr.
Lampert and Mrs. Ball have created a communicative classroom through
their use of language and their treatment of the students. First, they make
students feel important. Students are serious working members of a group
and not just workers being told what to do and complying with it. Lampert

and Ball ask questions which require much more than a yes or no answer. Students have a lot invested in their work and want to justify their thinking. They have to engage in class in order to prove their ideas and agree or disagree with others. The word choice in a classroom is significant. Students in Ball's and Lampert's class use agree and disagree quite frequently. These word choices, instead of right and wrong, cause students to delve deeper into their thinking because they have to explain why they agree or disagree, as well as adding a feeling of respect and trust.

How a teacher interacts with the students sets the stage for the management and environment of a class. Dr. Lampert's class seems to be working well together. They have a good rapport. When they don't, Lampert recognizes and solves the problem immediately. My first example is when Lampert sees Ellie out of her seat and collaborating with another group.

Lampert:	. . .what are you doing over here?
Ellie:	My three members in my group won't help me.
Lampert:	Hmmm?
Ellie:	My team members won't help me.
Lampert:	Your team members won't help you? The solution to that problem is not to get up and join a new team, I'm sorry to say. Let's go see what I can do about it.

She returns, with Ellie in tow, to Ellie's group and tries to encourage them to interact more. She does this by reprimanding them and asking them to discuss the problem. She guides them into a discussion by asking someone to help Ellie understand the problem.

The next vid-bit is from Mrs. Ball's classroom. She calls on a student when she feels he isn't paying close enough attention. She asks him a question about the differences of what two other students are saying.

When he can't respond, she asks Jeannie to explain what she did again. Then, she tells Tembe to listen, but she poses her reprimand in question form. This gives him an option and he saves face. The teacher doesn't embarrass him in front of class, but she does recognize a problem and corrects it immediately.

This vid-bit is an example of a student-led discussion, too. The teacher interacts with the students by guiding them. They hold the discussion by answering the questions and explaining their answers. Mrs. Ball calls on students to explain differences in other people's answers. This keeps students focused on the objective, of how many two digit numbers can you make with a 9 and a 5. Mrs. Ball never answers her own questions, she just rephrases them. She waits for students to answer and even though there are long, uncomfortable, silent gaps, she patiently waits. This gives students thinking time and shows them how serious Mrs. Ball is in wanting them to have a solution. She wants them to lead the discussion, not her.

Lampert also acts as a guide in her interaction in the classroom. She poses questions and different students answer them. Lampert doesn't offer a "correct" answer, but she occasionally comments on something as interesting or important.

Lampert:	Dorota, what do you think?
Dorota:	They're both the same. Because 60 is one hour, but because your watch only goes up to 59, it only goes up, so when you put one more, it goes up to one—one hundred. So I think that it's 60, just 60.
Lampert:	Hmm. This is interesting. Connie, what do you think?
Connie:	Um, I don't think both of them would work because, um, one hour is only 60 minutes, so um if you add 15 and 15, that will be 30 and add 15 and 15 and that would be another 30 and add them both together, it's 60, and if you added 25 it would be 100, so it'd be 100 minutes, not 60.
Lampert:	Does anybody have a sense of what Dorota might be thinking when she says—the clock goes from 59 to 100?
Student:	Oh, yes!

Lampert:	So there's something about stopping at 60. There, that's important. Tyrone, what do you think?
Tyrone:	I agree with Ellie, 'cause 90 and 60 is one hour, one-zero-zero, and one hundred is one-zero-zero and so that would make it something like an hour, and I agree with Connie 'cause, you go to 50 and then it's 60, 60 minutes and it's an hour. So, both of them can be right.

Lampert: So again we're having this idea from the digital clock that an hour
             is one-zero-zero. And so this kind of seems like it should be right.
             Awad?
Awad: I think that Connie's right.
Lampert: Why?
Awad: An hour's only 60 minutes and —
Lampert: But how would you convince Dorota and Tyrone, because they
             think that is should be about to accommodate this idea that they
             can see on a digital clock where an hour is one-zero-zero?
Awad: Well.
Lampert: Think about what you might say to try to convince them to
             change their mind, okay? Giyoo?

Another mind-engaging tactic Lampert uses is asking other students to explain someone else's thoughts and reasoning. This keeps students focused
and forces them to think about ideas different than their own. Not only do
they have to think about the idea itself, but how the student reasoned it.
She asks them to look into a new thought and explain it. This requires some
serious thought. Students are helping each other by explaining work that
isn't their own. They have to understand not only their own thought
processes, but their peers as well. Then, they have to verbalize it. Most
teachers do not dig that deeply to check students' understanding. Dr.
Lampert's interaction with students in this way assures her of their level of
understanding and helps them stay focused on each other's conjectures.

    Now, I'd like to continue my analysis by looking through the teachers'
journals and what they were thinking before and after their lessons.

    It was great to be back!
    I feel very relaxed about having a sort
    of messy beginning of class—although it
    was far from being chaotic. So many
    routines are in place, the kids & I
    "understand" each other, there is a culture
    of sense making and mostly meaningful activity.
        I put the above problem up on the
    board and most kids dutifully came in, sat
    down and copied it into their notebooks.

This is from Dr. Lampert's journal. She had just returned from vacation and
due to the excitement of her return the beginning of class was a little messy.
One thing she mentions that is really important in classroom environment
is "routine." Kids like to feel secure and know what is going on. If a there is
an established routine in the class, if kids can come in and know what they

are supposed to do, they will do it. There was a written problem on the board, and Dr. Lampert's students "dutifully came in, sat down and copied it into their notebooks." The only question is, who sets the routines? From my experiences, ultimately, the teacher has the final vote. However, many teachers allow their students to make decisions about how they want their class structured. This is a wonderful idea!!! It gives kids choices in how they can best learn.

The next excerpt is also from Dr. Lampert's journal. She stops a conversation after she feels enough time has been spent on it.

> After what I judged (how?) to be
> "enough" talk about vacations and weekends...

It is interesting to me that she questions herself with the (how?). Teachers make judgment calls every day they teach. If they couldn't, they wouldn't be able to perform their jobs. Students would be on all sorts of tangents without any direction or guidance. This is why teachers are ultimately responsible for creating and maintaining the environment. A teacher's decision to end or begin a topic can be student led, or just an idea the teacher has, but the final call comes down to the teacher. Every day I'm in the classroom I'm aware of my time limits. It's so hard when all the kids want a chance to be recognized and speak, but if everyone has a turn, it would take all day. The fine art of making judgment calls is basically what separates one teacher from another.

In her journal, Dr. Lampert writes about the "collective" sense of the class and an "individual" sense of the class. She claims the classroom is both collective and individual "back and forth."

> I talked about how I asked the question
> about how long it would take to go two miles
> at ten knots because I wanted to do
> something like "survey" what people were
> understanding—there were interesting
> comments about how it was not a survey
> because kids listened to other kids &
> responded—not just everyone saying what
> they think as if no one else was there.
> Then there was also talk about a
> "collective" sense of the class & an
> "individual" sense of what a student does
> or doesn't understand and how one plans in
> response.

> It is both collective and individual
> back and forth.

This is an interesting point. She understands the need for students to have individuality, but also incorporate it into the whole group. This interaction goes back and forth...never staying the same for too long. It is also part of the environment because Dr. Lampert chooses to recognize it. How do you plan a response for a student who doesn't understand? Do you ask more questions? Do you answer it? Do you skip it and come back later? As a teacher, I know you will always get answers you are not prepared for and your reaction to your students' comments is essential to the environment.

This brings me to the fine point of "collaborative teaching." This is from Dr. Lampert's journal.

> While making the list, I was conscious of the
> issues listed above, conscious of this as
> "collaborative teaching," drawing heavily on what
> students were contributing but also shaping
> it to fit my own ideas about what
> they should be learning here. The real
> trick, it seems, is to do both, authentically,
> at the same time, so that students perceive
> their own thinking as legitimate, but also are
> disposed to listen and change their ideas.
> Lots of thought here about "language" in
> relation to "thought" —> how does what we
> say both express & affect our thinking?

What is collaborative teaching? Does it work? I think it is when the teacher lets the students take the class where they want it to go. The teacher creatively incorporates ideas and thoughts and student input together in forming a direction. In the end, the teacher is responsible for the guiding and the students are responsible for the learning. They will have decided what they want to learn and the teacher will guide them in the right direction. Yes, I think it works, but it is incredibly difficult. First, students should know the objective and it's a good idea if they can help the teacher formulate how they would like to organize their class in order to accomplish this objective. This is a prime example of collaborative teaching...the teacher and the students combine thoughts in order to form an objective and then brainstorm on how to organize the class to perform this task!!! There are many teachers who feel this is a waste of time. How many times have I been told in my 3 months of teaching in Detroit that this idea wouldn't work because it takes too much time? "It's so much easier if you just teach it and go on and then help the ones who need it," they say. "Some kids will just never understand." I disagree with this statement and collaborative teaching is well worth the time in my opinion. It keeps the students interested and the teacher on his or her toes. It gives everyone input into the focus and lets the teacher act as a guide instead of a controller. Students have choice and feel some kind of ownership in the class. The teacher becomes a link in the chain of knowledge instead of the only key!!!!

MY REFLECTION

Well, I have to thank you for making me work. I have never given a lot of thought to fractions and how to teach them or math in general, because math has always come quite easily to me. I've never thought about the different ways in understanding mathematical concepts. Now, I can honestly say that I've not only thought about how to teach fractions (all mathematical concepts really) but how I understand them as well. Your role in our class was to be a guide, not supply the answers, but to guide us in a direction to discover the treasure for ourselves. This has been incredibly frustrating at times, but rewarding overall. You have modeled well and I understand your point. The teacher's role in the discourse should be minimized to helping keep organization in the classroom (i.e., calling on students whose hands are raised) and asking questions which prompt their thinking (i.e., why? explain... instead of questions which require a simple yes or no). It is not to supply all the answers and problems and let the students take on a passive role. The students' role in the discourse is to listen to others and suggest / agree / disagree / persuade / and discuss the problems at hand and come to a logical conclusion about the answer.

I have tried your methods in my classroom and I'm amazed at the results. My five-year-olds use the words agree and disagree all the time. It is amazing to see. They love to talk with each other and discuss what their reasoning is. Of course, there are my students who always say, "Because my mamma told me." or "Because my daddy saiz so." It has taken a while for them to understand the conversation is among themselves and not directed to me. After a week or so, they felt comfortable in talking with one another and discussing issues. Now, when we count people in the room and we have established there are 15 girls and 14 boys, and someone suggests the total is 16, several students will raise their hands and respond with an "I agree" or "I disagree" and they'll be able to tell you why. Julius can add so he always says, "Because I know 15 plus 14 is 29 and I know 29 is more than 16." Now, several others are now catching on to this concept.

Other students will say they disagree because there are 15 girls in the room and a lot of boys and 16 is only one more than 15 so that doesn't sound right. Others will simply say they counted and it was 29 not 16. While still others say, "Because there's a whole lotta kids in here and it be more than 16."

What it means to know mathematical concepts and the ideal classroom environment go hand-in-hand. The environment should allow students to discuss problems openly without fear of rejection. It should be a place of interaction and communication and not a place where one person becomes "Simon" and tells everyone what to do. This ties into knowing concepts, because to "know" them, you should be able to explain your reasoning. Students should be able to answer the Why? and How? in their reasoning and the environment needs to be open enough to listen and provide constructive verbal feedback.

"How Asian Teachers Polish Each Lesson to Perfection" was an inspiring article. I thoroughly enjoyed the last class. What a great ending!!!! "With one carefully crafted problem, this Japanese teacher has guided her students to discover—and most likely to remember—several important concepts." This quote sums up the feelings I had in the last class. I am now starting to polish my own teaching skills and hope I can continue to carefully craft meaningful problems for my own students to discover the joy of learning.

HAPPY HOLIDAYS!!!!

Appendix B

PROJECT #1: AN INVESTIGATION OF MATHEMATICS TEACHING AND LEARNING IN HYPERMEDIA

We believe that learning how to ask and pursue questions is central to being a good teacher and to learning how to continue learning on your own—from your own practice as a teacher. This project is designed to help you learn to do that, as well as to give you an opportunity to define and pursue an issue of interest to you. For this project you will plan and carry out an inquiry related to some issue of teaching and learning mathematics, using the materials in the environment as the context and medium for your investigation. To do this, you will first frame and define a question and focus for your investigation. Then you will use the hypermedia environment to create a collection of evidence or information related to your question. You will analyze what you are finding, formulate a tentative conjecture about an answer to your question or about your topic, and support it with the evidence you have been able to uncover. Then you will organize your collection, arranging and annotating it to show your tentative analysis and findings. You will make a short presentation in class based on your investigation. Specifics about each part of the project are explained below.

Identify and articulate a starting point for your investigation.
Think about what you are curious about and interested in. Frame a question or focus for an investigation, making sure that what you are setting out to investigate can be pursued within the materials available in the environment. Write your question or focus in your notebook (your individual notebook or your group notebook). Explain why you are interested in pursuing this—what do you think you can learn by pursuing this and why is that important to your learning? When you think you have this formulated, please share your ideas with me and get some reaction to and advice about your plans.
Create a collection of items or evidence as you pursue your question.
Drawing from video, children's notebooks, and the teacher journals, collect items that are relevant to your question or focus. Our discussions

in class, the readings, and your investigations of the hypermedia environment can all help you to develop hunches of things you think are important to look at and to illustrate.

As your collection grows, keep taking stock of what you are finding. Analyze what you are finding—what sense do you make of what you are seeing and reading? What conjectures are you developing and what new questions are beginning to take shape?

Begin to make decisions about which items you want to include in your project, and how to best group the items you have collected. Begin to plan some kind of organization for your collection that helps to make clear what you are illustrating. It is up to you to design your own means of organizing and explaining your collection in your notebook wherever in your notebook you begin to organize the products of your inquiry.

Make a presentation of some of your examples, including commentary on what you think they show related to your question or focus (in class, November 12).

Select some items from your collection to present in class on November 12. If you are doing this in a group, you should design your presentation in such a way that each of you has some role in it. Your presentation should be approximately 15 minutes long, and should include a brief explanation of your project's focus and purpose, your current tentative findings, a selection of examples from your collection, and some commentary from you on what these examples show. This presentation should help you in finishing the organization and annotation of your investigation. Think of the presentation as a chance to try out some of your thinking for that analysis, and to get comments and questions from the rest of the class that can help you in completing your project.

Write an analysis of what your collection suggests about your original question (put in your notebook).

Formulate your tentative findings. What conclusions have you reached, at least for now, and why? Organize your collection to represent your inquiry, including what you did, what you found, and how you interpret the evidence you collected. You may decide to show conflicting sides of an issue, rather than to come up with a homogeneous "answer" to your question. You can use any format you like for this analysis, making sure that your presentation offers others a chance to understand what you were pursuing and why, what you found out, and what sense you make of it. We are interested in the depth of your reflections and your ability to connect your hunches and impressions with specific evidence from your investigations.

Appraise your work on this project (put in your notebook).

Finally, include a reflection on this project. What was it like to do this work? What was especially interesting about conducting this investigation? What was hard? What reflections do you have on your work and your group's work? This reflection should be in your individual notebook if you do a group project. If you do an individual project, you should just include it at the end of your project.

Evaluation.

Depth and thoughtfulness matter most for this project. We will look both at *what* you have collected and *how* you decide to organize and explain what you include, and how you interpret your data and back up your conclusions. For your presentation, we will focus on the clarity of what you present, and the thoughtfulness of the issues you raise in discussing your examples. Overall, we will be most interested in the extent to which your reflections probe deeply into the question you select and how you support your ideas with evidence.

The project is due on Wednesday, November 17. The entire project will be located in your notebook—your group notebook if you are working in a group and your individual notebook if you are not working in a group.

Appendix C

AN ANALYSIS OF CLASSROOM CULTURE IN MATH LESSONS: INVESTIGATIONS OF TEACHER'S ROLE IN DISCOURSE, STUDENTS' ROLE IN DISCOURSE, WORTHWHILE TASKS, TOOLS, AND LEARNING ENVIRONMENT

This project has five parts. In Part 1 you will use the hypermedia environment to *create an annotated collection of items* that you think exemplify key elements of the culture of the fifth-grade classroom. In Part 2 you will *make a short presentation to at least one other member of the class* of some of the examples you have collected, explaining what you think these examples illustrate about the culture of the class(es). For Part 3 you will *formulate a question* that focuses on a particular aspect of classroom culture that has become important through your investigation of the multimedia materials. For Part 4, you will *write an analysis* of what your collection reveals about this aspect of the classroom culture in this fifth grade. Specifics about each part of the project are explained below. For Part 5, you will reflect on what you have learned from all this about methods of teaching mathematics.

Part 1—Create an annotated collection of items that exemplify the culture of the fifth-grade classroom. (*Put in your personal electronic notebook. Annotated collections will be reviewed and commented on by Maggie and/or Angie on a weekly basis.*)

Drawing from videos of lessons, children's notebooks, and Lampert's journals, collect items that represent important elements of the classroom culture in the fifth-grade class. Our discussions in class, the readings, and your investigations of the hypermedia/multimedia environment can all help you to develop hunches of things you think are important to look at and to illustrate.

As your collection grows, make decisions about which items you want to include in your project, and how to best group the items you have collected. Develop some kind of organization for your collection that helps to make clear what you are illustrating. It is up to you to design your own means of organizing and explaining your collection in your electronic notebook or folder. (If you choose to do a folder, include transcripts of the pieces of video that you want to use. The videotapes themselves may not be copied.)

Part 2—During a mutually agreed-upon time in the Lab, make a presentation of some of your examples to one or more people in this class, including commentary on what you think they illustrate about the classroom culture. (*This is to be done before Thanksgiving break.*)

Select some items from your collection to present. Your presentation should be approximately 20 minutes long, and should include both a selection of examples from your collection, and some commentary from you on what these examples show about the classroom culture. This presentation should help you in refining what you write for Part 3. Think of it as a chance to try out some of your thinking for that analysis, and to get comments and questions from others in the class that can help you in completing your project. Lab time in the multimedia classroom can be used for these presentations on November 20, 21, or 22. PLEASE NOTE: You may add to your collection after your presentations and after receiving feedback from us.

Part 3—Formulate a question and make a conjecture about how you would answer this question based on the materials you have collected. (*This is also to be done before Thanksgiving break.*)

When you begin to collect materials about the classroom culture, you may have a particular question or focus to your investigation—you will have a "first draft" of some conjectures about how to answer those questions. As you collect and annotate materials, your conjectures should get revised and refined and your question, more focused. Identify a question around which to frame a written analysis/reflection drawing on your collection.

Part 4—Write an analysis of what your collection suggests about an underlying dimension of the classroom culture.

Whatever question you select, you should include both what you think and specific examples that back up what you think. You may decide to show conflicting sides of an issue, rather than to come up with a homogeneous "answer" to the question. You can use any format you like for this analysis.

For example, you could structure your written analysis as a dialogue between imaginary observers with different points of view. This analysis/reflection need not be *long*. We are interested in the depth of your reflections and your ability to connect your hunches and impressions with specific evidence from your investigations.

Part 5—Reflect on how your investigation of classroom culture might impact on what you would do or think about doing as an elementary mathematics teacher.

Return to the themes of Teacher's Role in Discourse, Students' Role in Discourse, Worthwhile Tasks, Tools, and Learning Environment. Comment on the connections between your thinking from the first part of the course about "what it means to know fractions" and your thinking in the second part of the course on "classroom culture." Write about your current thinking about what is entailed in learning "methods" for teaching elementary mathematics. Give your reasoning for any statements that you make.

Evaluation.

Depth and thoughtfulness matter more than quantity for this project. In your collection, we will look at both what you have collected and how you decide to organize and explain what you include. For your presentation, we will focus on the clarity of what you present, and the thoughtfulness of the issues you raise in discussing your examples. And in your analysis, we will be most interested in the extent to which your reflections probe deeply into the question you select and how you support your ideas with evidence.

Parts 1, 2, and 3 are due on Wednesday, November 23, by 5 p.m. Parts 4 and 5 are due on December 14 by 5 p.m. You may print out a paper copy of your electronic notebook for yourself, but you need not do so in order to turn it in. If you are not doing an electronic notebook, your annotated collection and your analysis must be turned in in hard copy to Maggie's secretary in room 4109. Hard copy written evaluations of all projects will be available in 4109 after the winter break.

Sample Questions for Investigation

- What does the teacher do or say to establish and maintain norms of classroom culture that are particularly conducive to students learning mathematics?

- How do students contribute to maintaining norms of classroom culture that enable them to learn mathematics?
- What does the classroom culture seem to reflect about what mathematics is and what matters in doing, using, and learning mathematics?
- What does the classroom culture seem to reflect about where mathematical knowledge comes from and how children can develop knowledge?
- What does the classroom culture seem to reflect about who can learn mathematics and who is "smart"?
- What does the classroom culture seem to reflect about what kinds of mathematical skill and thinking are valued and what kinds are *not* valued?

We will add to this list as we work on Classroom Culture in class in the second part of the semester.

Notes

PREFACE

1. See Ball & Rundquist (1993).

CHAPTER I

1. See Werner (1948, p. 228).

2. The beginnings of the school are documented in two progress reports (Prospect School 1968–9a, 1968–9b).

3. Jay Featherstone, in a pioneering series of articles in *The New Republic* (reprinted in Featherstone, 1971), and Lillian Weber (1971) brought these schools to the attention of American educational reformers in the late 1960s and early 1970s. See also Charles Silberman's penetrating analysis of why these kinds of reforms were needed and appealed to U.S. educators, *Crisis in the Classroom: The Remaking of American Education* (1970). It is interesting to note that this book was commissioned as "The Carnegie Study on the Education of Educators."

4. The program was a year-long preservice certification program and a series of summer and winter institutes for practicing teachers that began in 1968 and are still in operation.

5. See Silberman (1970), Chapter 7, for descriptions of these statewide efforts to reform schools and teacher education. The tenets of the Vermont Design for Education are included in *Open Education: A Sourcebook for Parents and Teachers,* edited by Ewald B. Nyquist and Gene B. Hawes (1972, pp. 55–62).

6. In his history of the Harvard Graduate School of Education, *The Uncertain Profession: Harvard and the Search for Educational Authority* (1978), Arthur Powell documents the assertiveness with which the school separated itself from the work of classroom teaching.

7. In his book *Lessons from privilege: The American prep school tradition* (1996), Arthur Powell examines the positive lessons that can be learned from such settings in the context of the questions raised by contemporary public school reform efforts.

8. The *Mimi* materials were developed by the Bank Street College Project in Science and Mathematics (1982).

9. See Lampert (1985).

10. See *Tomorrow's Teachers*, a report of the Holmes Group (1986), in draft form at the time I went to MSU, which called for major research universities to commit

"to make the education of teachers intellectually sound, . . . to connect schools of education with schools, and to make schools better places for practicing teachers to work and learn" (p. iii), *A Nation Prepared: Teachers for the 21st Century*, by the Carnegie Task Force on Teaching as a Profession (1986), which called for "clinical schools" to have an analogous role to teaching hospitals and a teacher education curriculum incorporating the use of the case method to illustrate teaching problems (p. 76).

11. See Lieberman and Miller (1992).

12. See Clifford and Guthrie (1988).

CHAPTER 2

1. The Elementary Intern Program (EIP)was a program at Michigan State University between 1967 and 1978. In addition to its extensive grounding in the field, in classrooms, the EIP was distinctive for its fifth-year internship in which beginning teachers taught full time, advised and supported by an experienced teacher who was released from local teaching responsibilities in order to function as the interns' "consultant." Financially, as well as educationally, EIP was a clever idea. Many teachers were prepared in this program and were in considerable demand by school districts.

2. See Berger (1974).

3. Ball and Cohen (1996) discuss how curriculum materials could be designed to provide opportunities for teachers' learning; see also Ben-Peretz (1990) and Russell (1997).

4. Bruner (1960).

5. What Shulman and his colleagues refer to as "pedagogical content knowledge" was what I was lacking (see Shulman, 1986; Wilson, Shulman, & Richert, 1987). I needed to know what the most powerful representations were for particular ideas and what to anticipate about children's thinking in these areas.

6. I am not sure what disposed me to take an experimental stance toward these classes. It seemed "natural" to me as a means to figure out what to do since there was so much I did not know.

7. See CSMP (1981).

8. See Heaton (1994) for a thorough analysis of what the CSMP curriculum presented as both guide and obstacle for her learning as a fourth-grade teacher. How curriculum materials serve as sources for or sites for teacher learning is something not well understood. See Ball and Cohen (1996) for a discussion of the role curriculum materials might be designed to play in teachers' learning.

9. See Wilson, Shulman, and Richert (1987).

10. See Heaton (1994).

11. Cuisenaire rods are colored wooden blocks used to model numbers and number relations.

12. My colleagues in this effort included Bill McDiarmid, Jim Mosenthal, Suzanne Wilson, Robert Floden, Mary Kennedy, Trish Stoddart, and Teresa Tatto.

CHAPTER 3

1. See Dewey (1933).

2. Although we describe our teaching of elementary mathematics only indirectly in this book, interested readers are referred to Lampert (1986, 1990, 1992) and Ball (1993a, 1993b, 1993c).

3. See, for example, Feiman-Nemser and Buchmann (1985); Zeichner (1981–82); Zeichner and Tabachnick (1982).

4. See, for example, Hoy and Rees (1977); Zeichner and Tabachnick (1982).

5. See Feiman-Nemser (1983).

6. See National Commission on Teaching and America's Future (1996).

7. J. Lanier and Little (1986) argue that students who enter teacher education may affect the curriculum through their resistance to analytic and intellectually rigorous approaches.

8. See Ball (1988a); Grossman (1990); Lortie (1975).

9. See Lortie (1975).

10. See Buchmann and Schwille (1987).

11. See Ball (1988b).

12. This section draws on the work of Buchmann (1984); Carter (1990); Feiman-Nemser and Buchmann (1985, 1986); Kennedy (1992); Lortie (1975); Zeichner and Liston (1996).

13. See, for example, Ball (1990), Grossman (1990); Grossman and Richert (1988); Hashweh (1987); Wilson and Wineburg (1988).

14. See Shulman (1986, 1987); Wilson, Shulman, and Richert (1987).

15. See Shulman, 1986.

16. This section draws on the helpful analyses of Darling-Hammond and Cobb (1996) and Lanier and Little (1986).

17. See Judge, Lemosse, Paine, and Sedlak (1994).

18. See, for example, Ball and McDiarmid (1990); Grossman (1990); Wilson and Wineburg (1988).

19. See Bolster (1983); Ball (1997); Buchmann (1987); Clark and Lampert (1986); Clark and Peterson (1986); Lampert and Clark (1990).

20. Connecting knowing and doing *in practice* has been called deliberate action by Kennedy (1992). Deliberate action, like the application of technical skills, the application of concepts and principles, and the capacity for critical analysis, is considered a mark of professional expertise.

21. See Harrington and Quinn-Leering (1996) and Harrington (1994, 1995) for both empirical and philosophical evidence about ways of knowing for teaching and what preservice teachers bring to their professional education.

22. For a fascinating analysis of action in the "real world" and why it is impossible to model on computers, see Agre and Chapman (1987) and Vera and Simon (1993).

23. Reviewed in Clark and Yinger (1997); Elbaz (1983); Clark and Peterson (1986).

24. We do not take sides in the debate between situated cognition and constructivist theories of cognition. We simply point out the parallels between some of the claims of those who attend to situativity and work on teacher cognition.

25. See Cole and Engeströmm (1993).
26. See Greeno, Smith, and Moore (1993).
27. See Greeno (1997).
28. See Resnick (1994).
29. See Spiro, Vispoel, Schmitz, Samarapungavan, and Boerger (1987).
30. See Spiro et al. (1987).
31. See Cohen (in preparation).
32. See Lortie (1975); Floden and Clark (1988).
33. See Cohen, McLaughlin, and Talbert (1993); Heaton (1994).
34. See Lortie (1975).
35. See Ball (1988a, 1988b, 1990).
36. Here our ideas are consonant with the current work in the field of "practice theory," which is organizing the way organizational psychologists and sociologists think about the relationship between education and the workplace.
37. Ball (1988a) compares knowledge for teaching with knowledge in other domains.
38. For sociological and methodological analyses of mathematical/scientific practice, see, for example, Lynch and Woolgar (1990) and Latour and Woolgar (1979).
39. See Rogoff (1990).
40. See NBPTS (1989).
41. See NBPTS (1989, p. 14).
42. See NCTAF (1996, p. 78).

CHAPTER 4

1. Lampert (in press) elaborates these ideas.
2. We saw this as connected to the idea of "pedagogical reasoning." In this view, learning to teach entails learning substantive knowledge—ideas and theories—and developing an epistemology of practice—methods of analysis and interpretation, of conjecture and justification, of pedagogical invention and appropriate adaptation. See Shulman (1987); Feiman-Nemser and Buchmann (1986); Ball (1988b).
3. In this regard, Schön (1983) has reported on studies of architects; Coulson, Feltovich, and Spiro (1989) on doctors; and Lindblom and Cohen (1979) on policy makers. For more general analyses of learning in apprenticeship situations, see Rogoff (1990); Lave (1988); and Lave and Wanger (1991).
4. Such a culture of investigating teaching exists, for example, in Japan and China. See Sato (1991); Shimahara (1997); Paine and Ma (1993).
5. This theory, characterized variously as "activity theory" or "situated cognition," derives from the work of Luria and Vygotsky in the former Soviet Union and the work of Mead and Dewey in the United States. For examples of this theory applied to the relationship between thought and language, see Scribner and Cole (1981); Newman, Griffin, and Cole (1989); and several of the essays in Hicks (1996).
6. See Feiman-Nemser and Beasley (1993).

7. Schön (1983) distinguishes between reflection *in* practice and reflection *on* practice. He argues that both thinking in doing and thinking about doing contribute to the learning of practice.

8. This term was derived from the term "hypertext" coined by computer engineer Theodor Nelson in the 1960s to describe the idea of nonlinear reading and writing on a computer system for annotating and collecting ideas. Nelson worked on beginning to design machines that would demonstrate an idea first used by Vannevar Bush in a 1945 article in *Atlantic Monthly* where he imagined a machine (which he called "memex") that would link information in multiple and flexible ways and allow users of that information to add comments and interpretations. Landow (1992) wrote: "Writing in the days before digital computing, Bush conceived of his device as a desk with translucent screens, levers, and motors for rapid searching of microfilm records" (p. 15). When designers began to imagine links among audio, video, graphics, and text, hypertext became "hypermedia."

9. See *The Apple Guide to Courseware Authoring* (1988). The first two chapters of the booklet are entitled: "Why Most Professors Have Never Tried to Write Courseware" and "Why Most Professors Now Can." We meet five professors who have tried and succeeded and we learn that "your courseware can be more than just software, incorporating videodiscs and CD-ROM to store and access multimedia images." See also Ambron and Hooper (1988) for several case studies of development projects in the educational sector.

10. See Yankelovich, Haan, Meyrowitz, and Drucker (1988).

11. See methodological essays by Goldman-Segall (1990); Granott Farber (1990); Harel (1990).

12. See Bransford, Sherwood, Vye, and Reiser (1986).

13. Levine, private communication (1990).

14. See Shulman (1986).

15. See Shulman (1986, p. 12).

16. See Shulman (1986, p. 13).

17. See Wittgenstein (1953/1968, p. v).

18. In this work, we were attending to the relationship between knowledge that is uncritically acquired from practice and so-called "scientific" knowledge that enables one to reflect on that knowledge and put it in perspective. Unlike most formal educational designs, however, we wanted what we did to value both kinds of knowledge and have them play off one another. Similar arguments about multiple literacies are made by Gee (1992).

19. We recognize that all records are in some sense interpretations, and that records and interpretations exist along a continuum in the documentation of experience.

20. Examples of this and the other records described here are included in Chapter 5.

21. We are indebted to Erickson and Wilson (1982) for guidelines, derived from the standards set in ethnographic fieldwork, for collecting multimedia records in classrooms.

22. See Feld and Williams (1975) for an argument supporting this approach.

23. Current technical development focuses on creating a flexibly cataloged

and dynamic set of all of the studies that have been done using the records collected in 1989–90.

24. Although we considered using "alias" creation as a method of cross-filing, we decided against it because of the lack of flexibility it imposed on workstation choices. As we write, changes are being made in the Macintosh Operating System that would make it possible to perform links and searches at the finder level.

25. A limited set of such links could be made in a Hypercard stack, but they would have to be scripted or constructed manually for each utterance on each transcript or for each small group working together in each lesson. We chose to take this approach for linking lines of transcript with frame numbers on the videodiscs, which could be read by available software. To write a script that would create the equivalent of a relational database within Hypercard would have required more time and programming expertise than we could afford.

26. For a description of how a large team of professional software developers worked to confront a similar set of problems, see Moody (1996).

27. The Intermedia Project at Brown University was one of the first "relational databases" using object-oriented programming to develop tools that could link files created by different applications (e.g., text and graphics). This project did not use personal computer hardware, but a Unix operating system on powerful machines, and although the programming was facilitated by using Object-Oriented Principles, it nonetheless required a large technical staff to complete each courseware package. See Yankelovich et al. (1988).

CHAPTER 5

1. At the same time, we were working on designing the electronic tools that teacher education *instructors* might need to teach in the ways we had imagined. We have continued developing a more general environment for investigation by different kinds of users, taking advantage of developments in the technology to come closer to the multiply linked and indexed system for all of the data and all of the annotations made on the data that we originally envisioned. Descriptions of these projects are, unfortunately, beyond the scope of this book.

2. In more current versions of the multimedia environment, we are making use of this technology since it has become more feasible.

3. Students can use Quicktime Movies in the most recent versions of the multimedia environment. Other versions are programmed entirely in Hypercard and allow users to create buttons that will play bits of video on discs.

4. Cohen (1990) describes a teacher who was convinced about the value of the tactile experience of manipulating materials to learn mathematics.

5. See Ball (1992) for examples of how students may interpret concrete materials.

6. See Ball (1992); Erlwanger (1975); and Mack (1995) for examples of how students construct nonstandard interpretations of mathematical ideas.

7. See, for example, related work by Palincsar, Anderson, and David (1993) in science; Grossman (1990) in literature; Wilson and Wineburg (1988) and Wineburg and Wilson (1991) in history.

8. Scheffler (1991).

9. This section draws on Dewey (1938) and also on Buchmann and Schwille (1987).

10. This problem is the same as that faced by teacher educators concerned with helping prospective teachers learn from their field placements.

11. We play a somewhat ambiguous role as we analyze these curriculum scenarios because we write both as teacher educators and as the constructors of a new pedagogy of teacher education. In the former position, our analysis reflects what we have learned by using the multimedia environment as a basis for curriculum development in our own teaching of prospective teachers. In the latter position, we speculate as designers of the components of a pedagogical system including multimedia records of practice as well as tasks and productive patterns of interaction between teacher educators and their students.

12. For this analysis, we draw heavily on the "revoicing" research conducted in mathematics classrooms by Mary Catherine O'Connor and Sarah Michaels (1996).

13. Edwards and Mercer (1989).

CHAPTER 6

1. Although the multimedia environment was used in courses other than mathematics methods, we chose to limit our scope in this chapter to students' work in the context of a single course.

2. Two more graduate students joined the work in 1994: Angie Sperfslage and Alice Horton-Merz.

3. Outside of this M.A.T.H. Project team, we have worked with teacher educators at our own and other institutions to adapt the records we collected to their own settings. We do not include in this book an analysis of the activities of teacher education students in those settings.

4. A discussion of this incident in the third grade can be found in Ball (1993a).

5. Ball's third graders referred to her as Mrs. Ball, and so the teacher education students tended to do so in their writing about the classroom.

6. Interesting to us was that this investigation was very close to one that Lampert herself was conducting as part of her own research. The student who did this investigation was enrolled in a section taught by Ball and had not met Lampert. For us this suggested that just as third and fifth graders at times become absorbed in mathematical questions that have occupied mathematicians over the centuries, so too can teacher education students sometimes pursue inquiries similar to ones pursued by education scholars. At the edges of the field, at times, can be found both novice and expert investigators.

7. NCTM (1989, 1991).

CHAPTER 7

1. Our thinking about the curriculum potential of these materials has been inspired by both Miriam Ben-Peretz (1990) and J. J. Schwab (1961/1974).

2. This task, entitled "An Analysis of the Teacher's Role in Establishing and Maintaining Classroom Culture in Math Lessons," can be found in Appendix C.

3. Names of teacher education students are pseudonyms.

4. Patricia's blue comments are in regular type, her *red* ones are in italics.

5. See Ball (1990); Post, Harel, Behr, and Lesh (1988); and Simon (1993) for examples of research on prospective teachers' understandings of fractions and rational numbers.

CHAPTER 8

1. Both of us have written elsewhere about this aspect of mathematics teaching. See, for example, Lampert (1985, 1991, 1992a, 1992b, 1994); Ball (1993a, 1993b, 1993c, 1995); Ball and Cohen (1996); and Ball and Wilson (1996).

2. See Wittgenstein (1953/1968, p. v).

AFTERWORD

1. See Herbst (1989).

2. See, for instance, Dewey's (1902) discussion of "psychologizing knowledge." Both Joseph Schwab and Lee Shulman pursued these ideas in subsequent work.

3. Some already have: See the growing body of scholarship that includes work by Magdalene Lampert, Deborah L. Ball, Paul Cobb, Suzanne Wilson, Sam Wineburg, and Pamela Grossman.

4. See Lanier and Little (1986).

5. See Lortie (1975).

6. For example, see Ball (1988a).

7. A related possibility would be to employ novices as fully integrated apprentices who worked with teachers and students within the classroom. As apprentices they would have something to contribute and would have some standing to inquire about the proceedings and take part in them. That would offer access to two sorts of experience—the teacher's and their own. But to be really useful apprentices, intending teachers would already need to know quite a lot. And to reorganize instruction to enable such work would dramatically change classroom life, organization, and purposes. Even if the reconstruction were accomplished, it still would require classroom teachers to manage the split-level curriculum and instruction sketched above, or that another teacher be assigned to do the teacher education.

8. Perhaps another reason for the inattention to fundamental issues is that until recently practice was available in schools only in its raw form. Hence those

who wanted better clinical teacher education had no alternative but to somehow use practice live.

9. The extent of supervision—in this case virtual supervision—would depend partly on at least two factors: how thoroughly multimedia records were reformatted and edited to become curricula; and how thoroughly they were permeated by instruction, questions, interpretation, and so on, authored either by the teachers whose practice had been recorded or by teacher educators who had composed and edited the records. A good deal of virtual supervision could be built into such records.

10. In many other nations, the elementary curriculum plays a central role in the curriculum of elementary teacher education. This stands in sharp contrast to current practice in US teacher education, in which intending teachers' studies are not coherently or directly related to what students learn in school. Connections between the two curricula has been a problem in the United States, because the political and organizational ties between teacher education and K–12 schooling are so indistinct.

11. The education psychology courses that intending teachers must take rarely focus on rich cases of students learning academic subjects; instead prospective teachers have been taught about research on learning, much of it not in classrooms, that has been done by psychologists. Such work can be illuminating, but the lack of opportunities to ground it in practice has been crippling; it is as though doctors were educated with only a few weeks' opportunity to actually practice medicine, after years of theoretical studies of anatomy and physiology.

12. Reading about practice is a version of such situated learning, but only a small portion of the literature on teaching is situated in practice.

References

Agre, P. E., & Chapman, D. (1987). Pengi: An implementation of a theory of activity. In *Proceedings of the Sixth National Conference on Artificial Intelligence* (pp. 268–272).

Ambron, S., & Hooper, K. (Eds.). (1988). *Interactive multimedia: Visions of multimedia for developers, educators, and information providers*. Redmond, WA: Microsoft Press.

The Apple guide to courseware authoring. (1988). Cupertino, CA: Apple Corporation.

Ball, D. L. (1988a). *Knowledge and reasoning in mathematical pedagogy: Examining what prospective teachers bring to teacher education.* Unpublished doctoral dissertation, Michigan State University, East Lansing.

Ball, D. L. (1988b). Unlearning to teach mathematics. *For the Learning of Mathematics, 8*(1), 40–48.

Ball, D. L. (1990). The mathematical understandings that prospective teachers bring to teacher education. *Elementary School Journal, 90,* 449–466.

Ball, D. L. (1992). Magical hopes: Manipulatives and the reform of mathematics education. *American Educator, 16*(2), 14–18, 46–47.

Ball, D. L. (1993a). Halves, pieces, and twoths: Constructing representational contexts in teaching fractions. In T. Carpenter, E. Fennema, & T. Romberg (Eds.), *Rational numbers: An integration of research* (pp. 157–196). Hillsdale, NJ: Erlbaum.

Ball, D. L. (1993b). Moral and intellectual, personal and professional: Restitching practice. In M. Buchmann & R. E. Floden (Eds.), *Detachment and concern: Topics in the philosophy of teaching and teacher education* (pp.193–204). New York: Teachers College Press.

Ball, D. L. (1993c). With an eye on the mathematical horizon: Dilemmas of teaching elementary school mathematics. *Elementary School Journal, 93*(4), 373–397.

Ball, D. L. (1995). Connecting to mathematics as part of learning to teach. In D. Schifter (Ed.), *What's happening in math class? Vol. 2. Reconstructing professional identities* (pp. 36–45). New York: Teachers College Press.

Ball, D. L. (1997). What do students know? Facing challenges of distance, context, and desire in trying to hear children. In B. Biddle, T. Good, & I. Goodson (Eds.), *International handbook on teachers and teaching (Vol. 2)* (pp. 769–817). Dordrecht, Netherlands: Kluwer Press.

Ball, D. L., & Cohen, D. K. (1996). Reform by the book: What is—or might be—the role of curriculum materials in teacher learning and instructional reform. *Educational Researcher, 25*(9), 6–8, 14.

Ball, D. L., & McDiarmid, G. W. (1990). The subject matter preparation of teachers. In W. R. Houston (Ed.), *Handbook of research on teacher education*
(pp. 437–449). New York: Macmillan.

Ball, D. L., & Rundquist, S. (1993). Collaboration as a context for joining teacher
learning with learning about teaching. In D. K. Cohen, M. W. McLaughlin, &
J. E. Talbert (Eds.), *Teaching for understanding: Challenges for practice, research,
and policy* (pp. 13–42). San Francisco: Jossey-Bass.

Ball, D. L., & Wilson, S. M. (1996). Integrity in teaching: Recognizing the fusion of
the moral and the intellectual. *American Educational Research Journal, 33*,
155–192.

Bank Street College Project in Science and Mathematics. (1982). *The Voyage of the
Mimi*. New York: Holt, Rinehart and Winston.

Ben-Peretz, M. (1990). *The teacher–curriculum encounter: Freeing teachers from the
tyranny of texts*. Albany: State University of New York Press.

Berger, C. (1974). *Science curriculum improvement study*.

Bolster, A. (1983). Toward a more effective model of research on teaching. *Harvard
Educational Review, 53*, 294–308.

Bransford, J., Sherwood, R., Vye, N., & Reiser, J. (1986). Teaching thinking and
problem solving. *American Psychologist*, pp. 1078–1089.

Bruner, J. (1960). *The process of education*. Cambridge, MA: Harvard University
Press.

Buchmann, M. (1984). The priority of knowledge and understanding in teaching.
In J. Raths & L. Katz (Eds.), *Advances in teacher education* (Vol. 1; pp. 29–48).
Norwood, NJ: Ablex.

Buchmann, M. (1987). Teaching knowledge: The lights that teachers live by. *Oxford Review of Education, 13*(2), 151–164.

Buchmann, M., & Schwille, J. (1987). Education: The overcoming of experience.
American Journal of Education, 92, 30–51.

Carnegie Task Force on Teaching as a Profession. (1986). *A nation prepared: Teachers for the 21st century*. Washington, DC: Carnegie Forum on Education and
the Economy.

Carter, K. (1990). Teachers' knowledge and learning to teach. In W. R. Houston
(Ed.), *Handbook of research on teacher education* (pp. 291–310). New York:
Macmillan.

Clark, C., & Lampert, M. (1986). The study of teacher thinking: Implications for
teacher education. *Journal of Teacher Education, 37*(5), 27–31.

Clark, C. M., & Peterson, P. L. (1986). Teachers' thought processes. In M. C.
Wittrock (Ed.), *Handbook of research on teaching* (3rd ed.) (pp. 255–296). New
York: Macmillan.

Clark, C., & Yinger, R. J. (1977). Research on teacher thinking. *Curriculum Inquiry,
7*(4), 279–394.

Clifford, G., & Guthrie, J. (1988). *Ed school: A brief for professional education*. Chicago: University of Chicago Press.

Cohen, D. K. (1990). A revolution in one classroom: The case of Mrs. Oublier.
Educational Evaluation and Policy Analysis, 12(3), 311–330.

Cohen, D. K. (in preparation). *Teaching practice and its predicaments*. Unpublished manuscript, University of Michigan, Ann Arbor.

Cohen, D. K., McLaughlin, M., & Talbert, J. (Eds.). (1993). *Teaching for understanding: Challenges for practice, research, and policy*. San Francisco: Jossey-Bass.

Cole, M., & Engeströmm, Y. (1993). A cultural-historical approach to distributed cognition. In G. Salomon (Ed.), *Distributed cognitions* (pp. 1–46). Cambridge: Cambridge University Press.

Comprehensive School Mathematics Program. (1981). St. Louis, MO: CEMREL.

Coulson, R. L., Feltovich, P. J., & Spiro, R. J. (1989). Foundations of a misunderstanding of the ultrastructural basis of myocardial failure: A reciprocating network of oversimplifications. *Journal of Medicine and Philosophy, 14*, 109–146.

Darling-Hammond, L., & Cobb, V. (1996). The changing context of teacher education. In F. Murray (Ed.), *The teacher educator's handbook* (pp. 14–62). San Francisco: Jossey-Bass.

Dewey, J. (1902). *The child and the curriculum*. Chicago: University of Chicago Press.

Dewey, J. (1933) *How we think*. Buffalo, NY: Prometheus Books.

Dewey, J. (1938) *Experience and education*. New York: Macmillan.

Edwards, D., & Mercer, N. (1989). Reconstructing context: The conventionalization of classroom knowledge. *Discourse Processes, 12*, 91–104.

Elbaz, F. (1983). *Teacher thinking: A study of practical knowledge*. New York: Nichols.

Erickson, F., & Wilson, J. (1982). *Sights and sounds of life in schools: A resource guide to film and videotape for research and education* (Research Series No. 125). East Lansing: Michigan State University, Institute for Research on Teaching.

Erlwanger, S. (1975). Benny's conceptions of rules and answers in IPI mathematics. *Journal of Children's Mathematical Behavior, 1*, 157–283.

Featherstone, J. (1971). *Schools where children learn*. New York: Liveright.

Feiman-Nemser, S. (1983). Learning to teach. In L. Shulman & G. Sykes (Eds.), *Handbook of teaching and policy* (pp. 150–170). New York: Longman.

Feiman-Nemser, S., & Beasley, K. (1993, June). *Discovering and sharing knowledge: Inventing a new role for cooperating teachers*. Paper prepared for the Workshop on Teachers' Cognition: Pedagogical Content Knowledge, Tel Aviv University, Tel Aviv, Israel.

Feiman-Nemser, S., & Buchmann, M. (1985). Pitfalls of experience in teacher preparation. *Teachers College Record, 87*(1), 53–65.

Feiman-Nemser, S., & Buchmann, M. (1986). The first year of teacher preparation: Transition to pedagogical thinking. *Journal of Curriculum Studies, 18*, 239–256.

Feld, S., & Williams, C. (1975). Toward researchable film language. *Studies in the Anthropology of Visual Communication, 2*(1), 25–32.

Floden, R. E., & Clark, C. M. (1988). Preparing teachers for uncertainty. *Teachers College Record, 89*, 505–524.

Gee, J. (1992). *The social mind: Language, literacy, and social practice*. New York: Bergin & Garvey.

Goldman-Segall, R. (1990, April). Learning constellations: A multimedia research environment for exploring children's theory making. In I. Harel (Ed.), *Constructionist learning* (pp. 295–318). Cambridge, MA: MIT Media Laboratory.

Granott Farber, N. (1990, April). Through the camera's lens: Video as a research tool. In I. Harel (Ed.), *Constructionist learning* (pp. 319–326). Cambridge, MA: MIT Media Laboratory.

Greeno, J. G. (1997). On claims that answer the wrong questions: A response to Anderson, Reder, and Simon. *Educational Researcher, 26,* 5–17.

Greeno, J. G., Smith, D. R., & Moore, J. L. (1993). Transfer of situated learning. In D. K. Detterman & R. J. Sternberg (Eds.), *Transfer on trial: Intelligence, cognition, and instruction* (pp. 99–167). Norwood, NJ: Ablex.

Grossman, P. L. (1990). *The making of a teacher: Teacher knowledge and teacher education.* New York: Teachers College Press.

Grossman, P., & Richert, A. (1988). Unacknowledged knowledge growth: A reexamination of the effects of teacher education. *Teacher and Teacher Education, 4,* 33–62.

Harel, I. (1990, April). The silent observer and holistic note-taker: Using video for documenting a research project. In I. Harel (Ed.), *Constructionist learning* (pp. 327–344). Cambridge, MA: MIT Media Laboratory.

Harrington, H. (1994). Teaching and knowing. *Journal of Teacher Education, 5*(3), 190–198.

Harrington, H. (1995). Fostering reasoned decisions: Case based pedagogy and the professional development of teachers. *Teaching and Teacher Education, 11*(3), 203–214.

Harrington, H., & Quinn-Leering, K. (1996). Considering teaching's consequences. *Teaching and Teacher Education, 12,* 591–607.

Hashweh, M. Z. (1987). Effects of subject matter knowledge in teaching biology and physics. *Teaching and Teacher Education, 3,* 109–120.

Heaton, R. (1994). *Creating and studying a practice of teaching elementary mathematics for understanding.* Unpublished doctoral dissertation, Michigan State University, East Lansing.

Herbst, J. (1989). Teacher preparation in the nineteenth century. In D. Warren (Ed.), *American teachers: Histories of a profession at work* (pp. 213–236). New York: Macmillan.

Hicks, D. (Ed.). (1996). *Discourse, learning, and schooling.* New York: Cambridge University Press.

Holmes Group. (1986). *Tomorrow's teachers.* East Lansing, MI: Author.

Hoy, W., & Rees, R. (1977). The bureaucratic socialization of student teachers. *Journal of Teacher Education, 28*(1), 23–26.

Judge, H., Lemosse, M., Paine, L., & Sedlak, M. (1994). The University and the teachers: France, the United States, and England. *Oxford Studies in Comparative Education, 4*(1/2).

Kennedy, M. (1992). Establishing professional schools for teachers. In M. Levine (Ed.), *Professional practice schools: Linking teacher education and school reform* (pp. 63–80). New York: Teachers College Press.

Lampert, M. (1985). Mathematics learning in context: "The Voyage of the Mimi." *The Journal of Mathematical Behavior, 4,* 157–168.

Lampert, M. (1986). Knowing, doing, and teaching multiplication. *Cognition and Instruction, 3,* 305–342.

Lampert, M. (1990). When the problem is not the question and the solution is not the answer: Mathematical knowing and teaching. *American Educational Research Journal, 27*(1), 29–64.

Lampert, M. (1991). Connecting mathematical teaching and learning. In E. Fennema, T. P. Carpenter, & S. J. Lamon (Eds.), *Integrating research on teaching and learning mathematics* (pp. 121–152). Albany: State University of New York Press.

Lampert, M. (1992a). Practices and problems in teaching authentic mathematics in school. In F. Oser, A. Dick, & J.-L. Patry (Eds.), *Effective and responsible teaching: The new synthesis* (pp. 295–314). San Francisco: Jossey-Bass.

Lampert, M. (1992b). Teaching and learning long division for understanding in school. In G. Leinhardt, R. Putnam, & R. Hattrup (Eds.), *Disseminating new knowledge about mathematics instruction* (pp. 221–282). Hillsdale, NJ: Erlbaum.

Lampert, M. (1994). Teaching that connects students' inquiry with curricular agendas in schools. In D. N. Perkins, J. L. Schwartz, M. M. West, & M. S. Wiske (Eds.), *Software goes to school searching for understanding with new technologies* (pp. 213–232). New York: Oxford University Press.

Lampert, M. (1998). Studying teaching as a thinking practice. In J. Greeno & S. G. Goldman (Eds.), *Thinking practices.* Hillsdale, NJ: Erlbaum.

Lampert, M., & Clark, C. M. (1990). Expert knowledge and expert thinking in teaching: A reply to Floden and Klinzig. *Educational Researcher, 19*(4), 21–23, 42.

Landow, G. P. (1992). *Hypertext: The convergence of contemporary critical theory and technology.* Baltimore: Johns Hopkins University Press.

Lanier, J., with Little, J. W. (1986). Research on teacher education. In M. C. Wittrock (Ed.), *Handbook of research on teaching* (3rd ed.) (pp. 527–569). New York: Macmillan.

Latour, B., & Woolgar, S. (1979). *Laboratory life: The social construction of scientific facts.* Beverly Hills, CA: Sage.

Lave, J. (1988). *Cognition in practice.* Cambridge: Cambridge University Press.

Lave, J., & Wenger, E. (1991). *Situated learning: Legitimate peripheral participation.* Cambridge: Cambridge University Press.

Lieberman, A., & Miller, L. (1992). Teacher development in professional practice schools. In M. Levine (Ed.), *Professional practice schools: Linking teacher education and school reform* (pp. 105–123). New York: Teachers College Press.

Lindblom, C., & Cohen, D. K. (1979). *Usable knowledge.* New Haven: Yale University Press.

Lortie, D. (1975). *Schoolteacher: A sociological study.* Chicago: University of Chicago Press.

Lynch, M., & Woolgar, S. (Eds.). (1990). *Representation in scientific practice.* Cambridge, MA: MIT Press.

Mack, N. (1995). Confounding whole-number and fraction concepts when building on informal knowledge. *Journal for Research in Mathematics Education, 26,* 422–441.

Moody, F. (1996). *I sing the body electronic: A year with Microsoft on the multimedia frontier.* New York: Penguin Books.

National Board for Professional Teaching Standards. (1989). *Toward high and rigorous standards for the teaching profession.* Detroit: Author.

National Commission on Teaching and America's Future. (1996). *What matters most: Teaching for America's future.* New York: Teachers College, Columbia University.

National Council of Teachers of Mathematics. (1989). *Curriculum and evaluation standards for school mathematics.* Reston, VA: Author.

National Council of Teachers of Mathematics. (1991). *Professional standards for teaching mathematics.* Reston, VA: Author.

Newman, D., Griffin, P., & Cole, M. (1989). *The construction zone.* New York: Cambridge University Press.

Nyquist, E. B., & Hawes, G. B. (Eds.). (1972). *Open education: A sourcebook for parents and teachers.* New York: Bantam Books.

O'Connor, M. C., & Michaels, S. (1996). Shifting participant frameworks: Orchestrating thinking practices in group discussion. In D. Hicks (Ed.), *Discourse, learning, and schooling* (pp. 63–103). New York: Cambridge University Press.

Paine, L., & Ma, L. (1993). Teachers working together: A dialogue on organizational and cultural perspectives of Chinese teachers. *International Journal of Educational Research, 19,* 675–697.

Palincsar, A., Anderson, C., & David, Y. (1993). Pursuing scientific literacy in the middle grades through collaborative problem solving. *Elementary School Journal, 93,* 643–658.

Post, T., Harel, G., Behr, M., & Lesh, R. (1988). Intermediate teachers' knowledge of rational number concepts. In E. Fennema, T. Carpenter, & S. Lamon (Eds.), *Integrating research on teaching and learning mathematics* (pp. 194–219). Madison: University of Wisconsin, Wisconsin Center for Educational Research.

Powell, A. (1978). *The uncertain profession: Harvard and the search for educational authority.* Cambridge, MA: Harvard University Press.

Powell, A. (1996). *Lessons from privilege: The American prep school tradition.* Cambridge, MA: Harvard University Press.

Prospect School. (1968–9a). *Progress report III: A methodology for evaluating innovative programs* (Title III Project 825). North Bennington, VT: Author.

Prospect School. (1968–9b). *Report II: A proposal for studying thinking in children* (Title III Project 825). North Bennington, VT: Author.

Resnick, L. B. (1994). Situated rationalism: Biological and social preparation for learning. In L. A. Hirschfield & S. Gelman (Eds.), *Mapping the mind: Domain specificity in cognition and culture* (pp. 474–493). Cambridge: Cambridge University Press.

Rogoff, B. (1990). *Apprenticeship in thinking: Cognitive development in social context.* New York: Oxford University Press.

Russell, S. J. (1997). The role of curriculum in teacher development. In S. N. Friel & G. W. Bright (Eds.), *Reflecting on our work* (pp. 247–254). New York: University Press of America.

Russell, S. J., & Rubin, A. (1994). Landmarks in the hundreds. In *Investigations in number, data, and space.* Palo Alto: Dale Seymour.

Sato, M. (1991, July). *Case method in Japanese teacher education: Traditions and our experiments*. Paper presented at the Japan/US Teacher Education Consortium, Stanford University, Stanford.

Scheffler, I. (1991). *In praise of the cognitive emotions and other essays in the philosophy of education.* New York: Routledge.

Schön, D. (1983). *The reflective practitioner: How professionals think in action.* New York: Basic Books.

Schwab, J. J. (1974). The practical: Translation into curriculum. In I. Westbury & N. Wilkof (Eds.), *Science, curriculum, and liberal education* (pp. 229–272). Chicago: University of Chicago Press. (Original work published 1961)

Scribner, S., & Cole, M. (1981). *The psychology of literacy.* Cambridge, MA: Harvard University Press.

Shimahara, N. K. (1997, May). *The Japanese model of professional development: Teaching as craft.* Paper presented at the Norwegian Conference in Educational Research.

Shulman, L. (1986). Those who understand: Knowledge growth in teaching. *Educational Researcher, 15*(2), 4–14.

Shulman, L. (1987). Knowledge and teaching: Foundations of the new reform. *Harvard Educational Review, 57*, 1–22.

Silberman, C. (1970). *Crisis in the classroom: The remaking of American education.* New York: Random House.

Simon, M. A. (1993). Prospective elementary teachers' knowledge of division. *Journal for Research in Mathematics Education, 24*(3), 233–254.

Spiro, R. J., Vispoel, W. P., Schmitz, J. G., Samarapungavan, A., & Boerger, A. E. (1987). *Knowledge acquisition for application: Cognitive flexibility and transfer in complex context domains* (Tech. Rep. No. 409). Champaign-Urbana: University of Illinois, Center for the Study of Reading.

Vera, A. H., & Simon, H. A. (1993). Situated action: A symbolic interpretation. *Cognitive Science, 17*(1), 7–48.

Weber, L. (1971). *The English infant school and informal education.* Englewood Cliffs, NJ: Prentice-Hall.

Werner, H. (1948). *Comparative psychology of mental development.* New York: International Universities Press.

Wilson, S., Shulman, L., & Richert, A. (1987). 150 different ways of knowing: Representations of knowledge in teaching. In J. Calderhead (Ed.), *Exploring teachers' thinking* (pp. 104–124). London: Cassell.

Wilson, S. M., & Wineburg, S. (1988). Peering at American history through different lenses: The role of disciplinary knowledge in teaching. *Teachers College Record, 89*, 525–539.

Wineburg, S., & Wilson, S. M. (1991). The subject matter knowledge of history teachers. In J. Brophy (Ed.), *Advances in research on teaching* (Vol. 2; pp. 305–345). Greenwich CT: JAI Press.

Wittgenstein, L. (1968). *Philosophical investigations: The English text of the third edition* (G. E. M. Anscombe, Trans.). New York: Macmillan. (Original work published 1953)

Yankelovich, N., Haan, B. J., Meyrowitz, N. K., & Drucker, S. (1988). Intermedia:

The concept and the construction of a seamless information environment. *IEEE Computer, 21*, 81–96.

Zeichner, K. (1981–1982). Reflective teaching and field-based experience in teacher education. *Interchange, 12*, 1–22.

Zeichner, K., & Liston, D. (1996). *Reflective teaching: An introduction*. Mahwah, NJ: Erlbaum.

Zeichner, K., & Tabachnick, B. (1982). The belief systems of university supervisors in an elementary student teaching program. *Journal of Education for Teaching, 8*, 34–54.

Index

About the Authors

Magdalene Lampert received her doctorate in Education from Harvard University in 1981. After nearly 20 years of teaching at every level from preschool through graduate school, Lampert joined the faculty of the University of Michigan in 1994. She has published widely in the fields of research on teaching, teacher education, and mathematics education.

Deborah Loewenberg Ball received her doctorate in curriculum, teaching, and educational policy from Michigan State University in 1988. Currently Professor of Educational Studies at the University of Michigan, Ball draws on her many years of experience as a classroom teacher for her work. Ball's publications include articles on teacher learning and teacher education; the role of subject matter knowledge in teaching and learning to teach; endemic challenges of teaching; and the relations of policy and practice in instructional reform.